Researching Life Stories

Researching Life Stories reflects critically and pragmatically upon the use of life stories in social and educational research. Using four life stories as examples, the authors apply four different, practical approaches to demonstrate effective research and analysis.

As well as examining in detail the four life stories around which the book is written, areas covered include:

- Method and methodology in life story research
- Analysis
- Reflections on analyses
- Craft and ethics in researching life
- Policy, practice and theory in life story research.

Throughout the book the authors demystify the issues surrounding life story research and demonstrate the significance of this approach to understanding individual and social worlds.

This unique approach to life story research will be a valuable resource for all social science and education researchers at undergraduate and postgraduate level.

Dan Goodley is Reader in the School of Education, University of Sheffield. **Rebecca Lawthom** is Principal Lecturer in the Department of Psychology and Speech Pathology, Manchester Metropolitan University. **Peter Clough** is Professor of Education at Queens University, Belfast. **Michele Moore** is Director of the Inclusive Education and Equality Research Centre at the University of Sheffield.

Researching Life Stories

Method, theory and analyses
in a biographical age

Dan Goodley, Rebecca Lawthom,
Peter Clough & Michele Moore

RoutledgeFalmer
Taylor & Francis Group

LONDON AND NEW YORK

First published 2004
by RoutledgeFalmer
11 New Fetter Lane, London EC4P 4EE

Simultaneously published in the USA and Canada
by RoutledgeFalmer
29 West 35th Street, New York, NY 10001

RoutledgeFalmer is an imprint of the Taylor & Francis Group

© 2004 Dan Goodley, Rebecca Lawthom, Peter Clough and
Michele Moore

Typeset in Sabon by
Florence Production Ltd, Stoodleigh, Devon
Printed and bound in Great Britain by
MPG Books Ltd, Bodmin, Cornwall

British Library Cataloguing in Publication Data
A catalogue record for this book is available
from the British Library

Library of Congress Cataloging in Publication Data
Researching life stories : method, theory, and analyses in a
biographical age / Dan Goodley ... [et al.].
     p. cm.
   Includes bibliographical references and index.
   1. Social sciences–Biographical methods. I. Goodley, Dan, 1972–
H61.29.R47 2004
300'.72'2–dc22   2003020014

ISBN 0–415–30688–4 (hbk)
ISBN 0–415–30689–2 (pbk)

Contents

Acknowledgements

We would like to thank the following people for comments and insights on the drafts of this book – Grant Cossey, Bill Hughes, Marie McGuran, Griet Roets and her Violent Femmes, Kevin Paterson, Jane Tobbell, Nick Watson, Open University summer school students Durham 12–18 July 2003, R&J.

For inspiration thanks to Christine Abbott, Simone Aspis, Lisa Capps, Jackie Downer, Jeremy Hoy, Khadam Hussain, the Libertines, Kevin O'Sullivan, Elinor Ochs, Joyce Kershaw, the Manic Street Preachers, Underbank Working Men's Club, Jeannie Wilson and 'Kevin' and 'Karen' from Stockport.

And finally, thanks to some of the storytellers who continue to make our efforts seem so cheap: Kevin Fehin, Tony Parker, Ken Plummer, JD Salinger and Nicky Wire. Libraries gave us power . . .

Dedication

This book is dedicated to our children – Ruby and Rosa, David, Eve and Charley.

Preface

Researching Life Stories picks at some of the tangled weaves of narrative research. Our belief is that life stories – our chosen form of narrative – tell us much about individual and collective, private and public, structural and agentic and real and fictional worlds. Stories occupy a central place in the knowledge generated by societies. Expert discourses are being challenged by exposing their narrative construction. Notions of identity are linked into projects by which people write their own lives in varying conditions of alienation and empowerment. Taken-for-granted 'truths' are understood as stories to be told and, often, replaced by stories of a seemingly more plausible nature. Grand political and cultural narratives are under attack by personalised and localised narratives, though simultaneously these 'mini narratives' are part of a wider movement of global storytelling made available through advances in technology. Bowker (1993) and Booth and Booth (1994) observe that we now find ourselves in an age of biography. We consume stories of celebrity, plug into stories of reality TV, blur child and adult fiction in our search for escapism, creepily marvel at the 24-hour nature of wartime storytelling. The individual and collective victims of dominating knowledges counter such subjugation by celebrating their localised, indigenous and personal tales. Maybe this is the truly emancipatory position – when a story *by* challenges a story *of*. Perhaps Marx was right: all that is solid melts into air. Medicine, socialism, science and religion fold under the weight of their narrative construction. (Other) Stories are there for the taking and the telling. Contemporary societies and cultures are increasingly being understood as fragmented, uncertain, risky postmodern spaces. Stories fundamentally capture the diverse and changing nature of individual and social lives at the start of the twenty-first century. But this is far too much relativism for our palettes to take. The nasty taste in our mouths left by anarchic postmodernism suggests that there is more to life than simply stories. Narratives are always politicised, structured, culturised and socalised. Questions remain about the political, structural, cultural and social artefacts within life stories and their telling. Narratives may be our best hope of capturing structures that continue to shape, divide and separate human beings.

Researching Life Stories is a *very* modest attempt to immerse oneself in the minutiae of the biographical age. But it also endeavours to step back and look again at what can (and should) be done with stories, where they come from, how they are told and for what purposes.

Hitherto, a number of texts have promoted narrative and life story research (Bertaux, 1981; Plummer, 1983; Parker, 1990; Riessman, 1993; Smith *et al.*, 1995; Atkinson, 1998; Booth and Booth, 1998; Denzin and Lincoln, 1994, 1998; Erben, 1998; Goodley, 2000; Chamberlayne *et al.*, 2000; Miller, 2000; Clough, 2002). We believe that while these volumes have made a clear case for the narrative turn in the social sciences, and have resonated with contemporary social theory, they have focused less on the actual doing of life story research. Furthermore, we have often felt that previous work fails to explicitly account for the relationship between different epistemologies, method/ologies and analyses. This book aims to provide a coherent narrative of ways in which we may approach the project of *Researching Life Stories*.

The book is organised around four life stories (Part 1), four approaches to method/ology (Part 2), four analytical frameworks and analyses (Part 3) and four specific takes on craft/ethics, audience and theory/policy/ practice (Part 4). We embrace four different disciplines (sociology, psychology, disability studies and education), four different epistemologies (poststructuralism, feminism, social model of disability and literary theory) and four different research areas ('learning difficulties' aka 'mental retardation' and self-advocacy, women and work, disability and human rights and educational policy). We have written an interdisciplinary text that will be relevant to a host of students, writers, researchers and practitioners. In the process of unpacking life story research we may end up deconstructing the life stories that we initially present. Never mind, we hope we have done some justice to our narrators/narrative subjects and encouraged others to consider stories as the very stuff of research. We start the book by presenting four original life stories – the beginning of our journey into *Researching Life Stories*.

Part I

Four life stories

The four stories presented in the first part of this book will form the focus of subsequent discussions. For now, we invite you to put this book by the side of your bed for some late night reading. Alternatively, take this book away for a holiday read or a long train journey. Or, you might just want to dip in and out of these stories at odd times, here and there. Whichever way you read this book, we hope you read the stories before any of the other chapters.

Chapter 1

Gerry O'Toole
A design for life

Dan Goodley

Here are some of my precious stories. Events that shaped me. *You* won't have heard of them. It's time to start listening to what *we* have to say. Sooner or later, you'll listen. *You* will have to.

It's difficult to explain to you about places you may have never experienced. You have seen people like me, though. In shopping malls, in fast food restaurants, in minibuses with steamed-up windows. In small groups, shadowed by senior, more competent adults; middle-aged women or young trendy blokes with goatee beards. Our cultures sometimes cross swords. You have words for people like me. Retard, Joey, defective, idiot, spaz, mong. You might not use these words now but if pressed you would shamefully recall a childhood vocabulary that flourished with such insults.

> *'Frog', Paul shouted, 'Frog'. The gang fell about, giggling. ('Frog' was all Paul said, that and 'I love Jonny Vickers', much to Jonny's embarrassment. Paul once spent the day spray painting 'I love Vickers' on lampposts around the town. He was one of only two lads in our secondary school who had support workers with them at all times including bus trips as well as class time. He was a minor celebrity in this sense but a celebrity for people to laugh at. We kidded ourselves we were laughing with him.)*
>
> *Then Paul pulled down his pants and asked us, 'Do you want to see it wee?' 'Yeah – ha, yeah – I want to see it wee!' shouted Tez. And so Tez did – Paul neatly peeing into the drain. And we all laughed, all eight of us in Litton Close, a cul de sac near our primary school – recalling a place where our prejudices weren't so vicious.*

Now, I guess, things are more subtle. You will feel it inappropriate to catch my eye, to smile or to acknowledge me. And if you do clock me, you'll probably wonder afterwards if it was the right thing to do. You can't win and neither can I. We are – how do they put it? – always batting for different sides.

I am a resident. You reside.
I am admitted. You move in.
I am aggressive. You are assertive.
I have behaviour problems. You are rude.
I am noncompliant. You don't like being told what to do.
When I ask you out for dinner, it is an outing. When you ask
*   someone out, it is a date.*
I don't know how many people have read the progress notes
*   people write about me. I don't even know what is in there.*
*   You didn't speak to your best friend for a month after they*
*   read your journal.*
I make mistakes during my cheque-writing program. Someday I
*   might get a bank account. You forgot to record some*
*   withdrawals from your account. The bank called to remind*
*   you.*
I wanted to talk with the nice-looking person behind us at the
*   grocery store. I was told it was inappropriate to talk to*
*   strangers. You met your spouse in the produce department.*
*   They couldn't find the bean sprouts.*
I celebrated my birthday yesterday with five other residents and
*   two staff members. I hope my family sends a card. Your*
*   family threw a surprise party. Your brother couldn't make it*
*   from out of state. It sounded wonderful.*
My case manager sends a report every month to my guardian. Its
*   says everything I did wrong and some things I did right. You*
*   are still mad at your sister for calling your mom after you got*
*   the speeding ticket.*
After I do my budget program tonight, I might get to go to
*   McDonalds if I have enough money. You were glad the new*
*   French resturant took your charge card.*
My case manager, psychologist, occupational therapist, nutritionist
*   and house staff set goals for me for the next year. You haven't*
*   decided what you want out of life.*
Someday I will be discharged . . . maybe.
*You will move onward and upward.**

What do you feel when you see us? When you saw that 'mongey guy'
in the street? Is it pity, sadness, a sense of fortune? Well, you might be
right in having those feelings of concern. But the reason you feel like you

---

* This anonymous poem entitled 'You and I' was given to a member of Values into Action
(a British campaigning organisation for people with learning difficulties) while on a visit
to the USA (no date).

do is less to do with my 'condition' and more down to the world that creates me in its own vision. In spite of or because of these difficulties we have in relating to one another, people like me – my comrades and I – we have been quietly getting on with changing things. You just never knew anything about my story and all the others that have come from this new burgeoning, exciting, radical movement called People First. But our successes are never easily achieved. Some difficult terrain has been tread.

> *It was freezing. As usual I hadn't worn a coat. As a boy, my mother often told me that I had a strange little body. I became sweaty after the lightest of walks on the coldest of days. But today it was sub zero. As I entered the outdoor market, Gerry was, as always, conspicuous. Red, white and black bobble hat that just hid his long, straggly thinning hair. A greying stubble made him look 10 years older than the 39 that he actually was, though warm, piercing green Irish eyes ensured that you were charmed. A beige canvas bag full to bursting with papers and documents weighed down Gerry's left shoulder to the point that he walked with an uneven gait. Scruffy green combat jacket, brown waistcoat, cream shirt, brown trousers and new white trainers completed the 'vision'.*
> *'How are you, Gerry?'*
> *'Fine. There is this chap who wants to come to the People First meetings.'*
> *'Who is he?'*
> *'I don't know.'*
> *'Is he a member of staff from the centre?'*
> *'I don't know.'*
> *'Is he a researcher wanting to find out about self-advocacy?'*
> *'I dunno.'*
> *'Is he a person with learning difficulties?'*
> *'Dunno – didn't ask him.'*

My background? What? Oh ... family. Ha! You've opened a can of worms there! I come from a large Irish Catholic family. Three brothers, two sisters. My father moved over from Galway on the West coast of Ireland in the 1950s. He met my mother at a ceilidh in Manchester. She was born in Blackburn. They were only together for a while before my mother got pregnant with my brother Jack. A quick wedding was organised and they managed to get themselves a small terraced house in Rusholme in Manchester. My mother and I, my brother Kevin and his wife Julie, we still live in that very house. My auntie lives next door. My Dad passed away six years ago. I remember his funeral as if it were yesterday. The coffin was laid open in the front room and neighbours, friends and folk from the church paid their respects. I stood by my Dad throughout the day. His skin was waxy and his hair looked thicker than it was when he was alive. He would have liked that – the hair bit, I mean. Only my mother, Jack, Michele and I could bear to look at Dad. Colleen, Kevin and Callum never went near Dad's coffin. They wanted to remember him as he was.

My father was a tall, strong, vocal man. He smoked Woodbines and loved a pint in the local working men's club. He was funny and imposing. When I was 18 he took me and my older brothers to the club to celebrate. I am now a paid-up, card-carrying member. The Friday after my Dad died I went in. At the bar, Clive the secretary tells me that I need to pay for my membership. 'You're a member in your own right now Gerry. Now your Dad has gone, God rest his soul, you can't be his guest, you need to be a proper member.' I asked him how much it was. '85 to you.' 85 quid, I thought, 'can I pay in instalments like me Mam does with the washing machine?' '85 pence, you daft bugger!' laughed Clive. They often get me like that.

Somehow, there was always someone around. If my Mam and Dad were at work then there was an older sister there to make my tea, run my bath, tickle me until I burst with frustration. Every morning when I was young my Dad walked me to school. We would stop at the dual carriageway across from the special school and watch as my schoolmates were ferried past in ambulances. When they finally arrived at school they were travel sick from the rough journey. Jeremy would make me laugh, telling me how they'd hang onto the stretcher that was kept between the rows of seats. Of course, when they went round a corner the stretcher would move and they'd be pulled to the back of the bus, scattering those who stood up, kids flying into one another. Once in school, things were never so bad for me. I have friends now who never had a family, a safe haven. Sophie's mother couldn't cope. Sophie was ordered off to hospital when she was young. She never said much about her time there but I know from others that she was made to wear weighted boots in institutions and they used to drug and hit her.

A zillion dormitory keys held menacingly by his side. My brave face as Mogadon kicks in. On to avant-garde dance troupes and loud meetings of comrades. But always one of them, at the day centre or at Main House, my new 'home'. Waiting for failure, ready to punish.

I was in and out of special school and eventually left at 15. They were strange places, funny buildings, you were *labelled* as soon as you got there. Lessons were boring, colouring-in books that were already covered with the crayon scribbles of previous years' students. Class after class with the headmaster playing piano. Asking us which piece of classical music he was murdering. Keen, lively, young teachers joining us straight from teacher training college only to promptly leave by the end of their first or second term. Broken people. Students sound asleep in class, drooling onto the desks where they rested their heads. My mother would complain, 'Why can't Gerry be taught proper mathematics and English,' she would tell the teachers. They told her I was struggling so much that I wouldn't be able to do the things my brothers and sisters were doing. Daft really, because when I worked with my Dad on the markets I was really good at counting up the change people needed. One teacher said to my mother that I would never be able to read and write. I did, though. At home. It wasn't the best of places. One day, I broke into the caretaker's office. I nicked a spade. Some time later, the teachers caught me trying to dig myself out of the school – I was trying to escape under the fence. I got into trouble a lot at school for talking or having a laugh in class. The school was eventually burnt down by some big lads off the estate.

After I had left, some of my mates managed to get themselves into the 'normal schools'. They told me that they had loads of parties, drinking with the other kids in the pubs in town.

The sixth form had some new members – 12 people with learning difficulties from the Day Centre. Kevin – Down's syndrome lad – was the only one who was school age. Kevin followed Bant around, much to the amusement of Bant's fellow sixth-formers. Bant was popular – stupid but popular. And then when Bant got bored he would play to the crowd.

'Whose your favourite, Kev?'
'Bant.'
'Who do you love?'
'Bant.'
'Course yer do.'
And then Bant would run out of the classroom for a ciggie. Too quick for Kevin, who would bury his face in the seat – sobbing his heart out.

Others joined the special needs group at the tech. I was never going to be packed off to some 'life skills class'. As a teenager, school meant little to me. Well, I was on the market stalls at the time, so it wasn't really interesting. I really started to get into the market stall work. Some of my mates either went to the day centre full time or, if they were lucky, got a job (if that's what you can call not being paid to work) farming, T-shirt printing or decorating old people's houses. My brother jokes that we are part of the Irish Catholic mafia. A job was always going to be there for me.

The boys' toilets. Lunchtime. Brid [18 years, small in stature, long hair, eyes too small for his face], Jano [20 years, large frame, short-haired, piercing brown eyes] and David [short, overweight, mouse-like, scared, thick-rimmed glasses].

Brid: *So, twatter – is it true? Is it true, then? 12 toes, 'ave ya? Ya freak.*

[Brid pushes David into the cubicle, David covers his face with his lower arms.]

David: *No . . .*

Brid: *Jano shut door, man.*

[Jano firmly closes the door and rests against the door. He is laughing.

Brid punches David hard in the stomach, and struggles with David's shoes, eventually prising them off, as he forces David to sit on the toilet seat. David is howling. Awful screams echo.]

Brid: *Fucking hell (laughs) look at this Jano, look – it's the elephant man! Jesus, that's horrible [laughs].*

[Jano moves into the cubicle and squeals with delight. Brid and Jano catch each other and run out of the toilet, their laughter echoing in the toilet while ringing out over the factory floor.

David pulls himself up from the seat by the door and stoops down to collect his shoes and socks. As he moves out of the toilet we catch a reflection of him in the mirror. We can make out the mirror image of chalk marks scrawled on the back of his long grey coat 'I am a knobhead. Kick me!'

David was bullied for two years. He had a meeting with his mother, his keyworker, an occupational therapist and the work supervisor. The occupational therapist asked him if he wanted to take a holiday. He said yes. He hasn't worked since, that was 12 years ago. I heard that David has spent the last three years at home. He never leaves the house, even though his Mum and sister want him to get out, to make friends. He stays in bed, all day, every day.

For me work has always been a laugh with my cousins, my brothers, our pals. Five a.m. start, breakfast in the market café at eight and back in time for the punters. Lots of *craic*. Weekends we get off somewhere different – York, Newcastle, Glasgow, Rotherham, all the different markets. I am well known, always asked if I need more work. From time to time I collect glasses in Mulligans which is a really cool Irish pub. A trio play rebel songs every Friday night and it is packed with regulars as well as students nursing a pint or two. One Saturday night, Trevor the landlord asks if anyone knows of a right wing-back who could play for the pub football team. I overheard him. So did my brother Callum. 'Our Gerry's got a sweet right foot, you want to ask him.' I am now a regular. Scored two last match. Somewhere in all of this I got drawn into People First.

'Dear Editor

I am writing on behalf of Partington People First group, as we were shocked to see in your magazine that someone showed us on 1ˢᵗ September 1988, with four people who you called mentally handicapped people. Those people were at the International Conference in London where they and others from all over the world were fighting to get rid of labels like 'mental handicap'. We feel very upset because you have done the opposite to what you want. You do not seem to understand that we want to be called People First and not what you put in your magazine. I have heard that these magazines go all over the country and people will read it and they will still think of us like that. We might as well have stopped at home and not gone to the conference if people like you do not listen to us. So next time can you say 'people with learning difficulties'. IT DOES NOT COST ANYTHING MORE. Thank you and I hope your next magazine will be more interesting.

Yours faithfully Maddie Harrison (Secretary)'

Maddie Harrison – the founder of our group. Without her, well, maybe we wouldn't have got things together. Most of the group were in a rut. Day Centre. Bed. Maybe the Gateway club on Thursdays if they were lucky. I used to pop into the day centre on Fridays, still do actually, to have a coffee with some of my oldest friends. Well there I was, 15 years ago now, and Maddie waltzes into the canteen. Her long red curly hair flows all around her as she unbuttons her jacket and throws it onto the back of her chair. She has been chatting with Shirley, her keyworker. She has heard about this new thing: self-advocacy. She corners me and Bob. Resting her arms on the table – all DI Regan off 'The Sweeney' – she puts her face in mine. 'You could do this with me,' she instructs.

'You stick up for yourself, Gerry, don't you?'
'Yeah.' [I wasn't sure what she meant.]
'And you, Bob. You have your own flat now, don't you?' [Bob smiles smugly, making patterns with his spoon in the coffee froth.]
'And we could get others to join. What about Denise? She could do with speaking up for herself more and more. Have you heard that Doreen [Denise's carer] won't let Denise out to bingo anymore? Says that she's not behaving herself.'
'And what about Sophie?' Bob asks.
'Well, she can be trouble, but she does let them know what she wants, that's for sure.'

> *'I agree, Maddie. Shall we get some others together?'*
> *'Yeah, but we'll need some leaflets, telling folk about the group, do it properly – work can make us free.'*

Before long, there were 14 of us with Shirley from the centre. We would meet every second Saturday of the month at the steps of the local Co-op. The shoppers hurrying past with bags of rubbish would look up to us on the steps. We were out of the centre, out of group homes and institutions. Only the Co-op, but the first real taste of community life for some of us. Not a keyworker in sight, well, apart from Shirley. After a while, Maddie sweet-talked the manager to give us a regular room in which to meet. I would work a few hours at the market and then rush over to the meetings. Eventually, the Co-op gave us our own key to the building. I looked after it for years.

> *'We don't want to be called mentally handicapped. We're just as good as anyone – maybe a little bit better.' (Maddie Palfreeman, 4th International People First Conference report)*

Maddie was everywhere. She travelled to Canada, London, Scotland and Wales. Sometimes I went with her. Other times someone else. We spoke at conferences with other People First groups. We made pen pals with people with learning difficulties in Ontario, Canada. We told students at the local college about sticking up for yourself and about them having to treat us with respect. We recalled the starting up of our group at conferences to rooms full of suited men and women. And always Maddie. It meant everything to her. She would complain in meetings if people were talking too loudly. Jon was always chastised. He had awful sinus problems. 'Stop snorting,' Maddie demanded. And she was quick to ensure that trivial matters did not dominate the meeting. 'Well, it's alright you talking about *Coronation Street*, Asif, but what are we going to do about people calling us mentally retarded?' In many ways she ruled the group. But people were not put off. We quietly admired her, I think. Asif, Jon and the rest of us continued to come along. She was sticking up for us – as well as herself. Anyway, many of the group had enough to worry about.

> *The meeting started and members of the People First Group took turns to tell of their news. While there was much talk of holiday plans and nights out, a number of vignettes had a more distressing feel. Rachel has finally moved out of her group home. She was the only woman resident. One of the other residents had been 'touching me up. That's how my sister's friend Julia explained it.' Maureen hates it at her house. The staff insist on her leaving the door open when she is having a bath. Matthew, too, he 'was fiddled with' by a guy from the end of his street. They were friends. Matthew's social*

worker reported it to the police. No actions were taken. Meanwhile, there is still no sign of Katy. Where is she? She never misses a meeting.

As the years passed we became stronger. And we took no prisoners. After a couple of years, we asked our supporter Shirley to leave. Maddie and I had spoken about how Shirley wanted to make it her group. She told us what we should do. What we should and shouldn't say. She often stuck up for the members of staff we criticised. Then *that* meeting. I was in awe of Maddie. She had spoken to other members as well, got the go-ahead, but was still nervous.

'We want to thank you for all the help you've given the group, Shirley. But, we want to run our group our way now. We would like it if you didn't come anymore. This is our group and we want to run it.'

It was a lie. We still needed a supporter – but someone outside of the day centre, away from services. Someone who could help us with our problems, with the new service plans, with bullying staff. Not folk only interested in bettering their own careers. Someone with access to a computer to type up our minutes and agendas. Luckily, Shirley left and Rebecca joined. We needed people who believed in us.

Imran found an old lighter in the supporter's car. He asked if he could have it. The supporter, Dan, gave it to him with a patronising warning, 'Now don't go burning down your mother's house, will you?!' He looked at Dan with despair and retorted, 'I'm not fucking stupid, you know.'

As our membership grew, we soon changed our venue for meetings, so Peter, Michele and their sticks could get in. Whatever happened to Peter? I must ask his support worker, he often pops in the market. Meetings are often a rehearsal for what we do outside. For some, being in the group has allowed them to become confident enough to struggle with more powerful others. Meetings are the bedrock of our being there.

Five years ago, I travelled with Sophie, Maddie, Lucy, Barbara and Michele to a conference in Scotland. We went by train. Took the adviser Rebecca with us. It was quite a journey. Sophie wasn't happy with the sandwich Rebecca had bought from the buffet car. She threw the carton and her coffee at the window, covering this businessman's papers in the opposite seat. As he was swearing at Sophie, we realised we had lost Barbara. It wasn't until Newcastle that we found her sat in first class, much to the annoyance of this suit whose pleas to have his seat back were being ignored! At last, we turn up at the conference and make our way to these student flats that we're staying in. Rebecca hands us our keys, points us to our rooms. I unlock my door, collapse on my bed and get my head down for an hour. When I open up to see what everyone else is up to, Sophie, Lucy, Barbara are still stood outside in the corridor. They'd never had their own door key. We laughed it off. That first night we were in the bar until 3 a.m. Support workers' earlier demands for Lucy, Babs and Sophie to take their drugs were by the by. It was our night, some starting off on an unknown journey towards independence.

Yet, our struggles continued. They never seem to subside. Matthew was telling me today that he'd finally moved into his own home: 'On my own, my own space, my own place at my own time: just 11 years too bloody late.' He'd been asking different key workers for years and years to get him out of the group home. Finally, he nagged just long enough with the current worker who helped to set up the move.

The group has had enough. Maddie and an adviser Lucy traipse down to Cunningham Lodge, Katy's institution/home. Maddie demands to see the manager, Dick. The duo wait. After an appropriate amount of time, in the opinion of the manager, the two are called in. Dick offers tea. No, replies Maddie. Coffee?

'Why aren't you letting Katy come to meetings?'

'Well it's not that simple, I me . . .'

'WHY aren't you letting Katy come to meetings?'

'Look, Maddie, I don't want to fall out with you or with you eh . . .'

Lucy looks left out of the window. This is Maddie's moment. Dick continues;

'. . . If she doesn't behave then she will not be allowed to come.'

'What has she done?'

'She is exhibiting . . . eh . . . often very challenging in her behaviour, without reason.'

'Well, if you didn't stop her from coming to our meetings then perhaps she wouldn't be so annoyed.'

'I reserve that right as the person who is paid to look after her.'

'She has a right to come.'

The exchanges continue for another 10 or so minutes. Dick offers an olive branch.

'Shall we agree to disagree?'

Maddie takes the branch, snaps it off and swipes him firmly across the face.

'We shall agree that I am right.'

Katy came to the next meeting. Maddie had been ringing Cunningham Lodge every night before reminding them of the meeting. A success.

The next meeting, Katy wasn't there. Maddie phoned. Ill in bed, we were told. Katy missed the next meeting. Maddie popped around, Katy told her she was not interested any more.

Charlotte missed the January meeting. And then, the next. Very unusual
for her. Charlotte and her housemate Christine always attend meetings and
have done for over 10 years. Rebecca rings up Charlotte's house. The senior
house officer answers. Charlotte has been moved to a new group home six
miles away. It was decided that it was in her best interests. They will see
how she gets on and if the assessment is positive it is likely that she will
remain in the new home. Christine didn't attend these meetings either.
Somehow, breaking the two up had wrecked long-fought plans. That was
because it was overlooked, the staff told us. I get Charlotte's new home
number and ring. They didn't know about People First, it wasn't mentioned
in her file. I ask the house manager if they can let her know about the dates
of the meetings. They ask me to post the dates. Rebecca seeks assurance
that Charlotte will be brought down to the meeting. 'If that is what
Charlotte wants then we shall bring her – but only if she wants to come.'
Well, at least they were asking her opinion, maybe they should have before.

*Ricky – four days of the week, for seven years – 'therapeutic earn-
ings' of £15. Unpicking balls of string in the centre. His friend Muriel
lies with her head flat to the table top, snoring loudly. And then there
was Ricky on the stage. Pretending to juggle, like a circus clown.
Concentration etched in the furrows on his brow. And around him
the other performers played out the background of a street party. He
shone. He moved to the front of the stage. He was electric. Ricky –
one night of his life: the centre of attention: attention that he had
sanctioned. What price now for a shot at peace and dignity?*

Last Wednesday I rushed down to the Day Centre. Quick coffee. Then, we
spent ages helping each other with our aprons – Steve's difficult to dress in
his wheelchair. Then June, who's staff, bakes a cake. Mixing up the ingredients, adding dried fruit, whisking away, talking us through her handi-
work. She does it all. Always has done. We are her willing audience. We
wait in relative silence watching the cake rise through the glass of the oven
door. Rebecca asked me why I even bother – 'Can't cook, won't ever be
allowed to bloody cook' she mocks. I tell her – I come to see my mates.
Questions? Anyway, that day I get home for about 6-ish after stopping off
for a chat with the lads in the bus station. And my Mum is in the kitchen.
It's Friday night fry-up, the full works, with chips. As she places the bacon
rashers in the frying pan, she turns to face me. Solemn.
'Rebecca rang, from People First.'
'Oh, right, what did you say.'
'She asked if you knew that Maddie Harrison has died. Tuesday last.'
No one had said anything in the Centre. No one had rang to tell me.
Rebecca had heard only by chance. She lived next door to Ravi who is
staff in the Centre. He had been to the funeral. It was yesterday. It had

been a lovely service. But not one member of People First was there. We spoke about it at the following meeting. No one had been told. Not even the ones who go to the Centre every day. Maddie hadn't been to the meetings for years. When they retired her from the Day Centre, I suppose she retired from the group. We used to ring. Tell her about a conference we had been to. About the local day centre having a 'consultation' day which was crap, but the sandwiches were nice. About the age-old problem of a member of staff not letting one of our members out of the group home for the meeting. She had lost that wicked sense of humour and her anger. 'Oh ... I'm sorry', she would say. Distant. Removed. Defeated? And on the day of resting her body in the ground next to her mother, we weren't there. I would have been there. I would have stood by Maddie throughout the day.

> *I'm pretty bothered by his absence. No sign of him for over three months now. Tried leaving messages. His mother says she will let him know, but there is a dismissive air to her promises – like she's not quite clear what this People First business is – and still no Gerry. So, I leave the meeting of the group early. The group has decided: find Gerry. I walk into the market, the strong stench of fried onions from the hotdog stall always fills me with nausea. Past the bootleg CDs and jeans stalls, over to the shoe stall owned by Gerry's uncle Francis.*
> *'Hiya Francis, how are you, sir?'*
> *'Very well. Myyyy, Rebecca, looking good, girl!'*
> *'Thank you.' [He eyes me up and down: blush.] 'Have you seen anything of Gerry? The word from People First is he's too busy to come down to our meetings on Saturday.'*
> *[Francis emits a dirty laugh, putting his arm around me.]*
> *'Noooo, he can have all the time off he needs, he knows that, B'Jesus he's been knocking off early on a Saturday for yeeeears to come to that group of yours.'*
> *'I know, that's why we miss him. So where is he going instead?'*
> *'Gerry's in Rochdale, my love, the outdoor market. Goes every weekend now with me brother Ken. He's in love – one of the stall-holders there – Janine.'*

I have left People First for the love of a good woman. Watch this space.

Chapter 2

'I'd never met a vegetarian, never mind a lesbian'

Colleen's life story

Rebecca Lawthom with Colleen Stamford

Nowadays people can do whatever they like at whatever age they want whether retraining or going to uni., this is a good thing. I sound like an old crock but times have changed and my life has gone full circle in some ways. I guess some of my life and my values are part of my growing up and what was considered tidy and proper. . . . My Dad, I know he's really proud and my Mum has been dead now for seven years but he always, always says 'Your Mum would be so proud,' and she certainly would because definitely I would never have gone to do nursing training. It would never have entered my head to do it because I would have thought that was far above me anyway.

When I was younger, growing up, my family were hard workers, you know they had a work ethic which was very strong. And I can remember then you were almost ashamed to say where you lived. Where I lived, it had a very bad reputation whereas now it is quite trendy to be working class, isn't it? When I was young it definitely wasn't so accepted. Where I lived, people did work but had poorly paid jobs, either poorly paid manual jobs or they didn't work. My family was considered to be quite well off – well, relative to where we were living. Both my parents worked and that was unusual – as women tended to stay at home. My Mum had two jobs at the same time. She had a string of part-time jobs and was a qualified seamstress. She used to do afternoons in a tailoring factory, a large mill in town, but this wasn't paid well. It was piecework so you got paid for each item. The women who worked there used to have sandwiches at the machines, knee-deep in material, all sat in rows. The conditions were terrible as well, a proper sweatshop it was. Nowadays, it would never pass Health and Safety guidelines. When she finished there in the late afternoon she would do evenings at a fish and chip shop round the corner. It meant we often got free fish and chips.

Unusually, because my Mum worked, the childcare was done by the male side of the family. The family was me, my younger brother, my Mum, Dad and my retired granddad. My Dad was a postman and did 'earlies' all the time so was home for lunchtime. My mother disliked housework (which I am sure she passed on to me) and I can't really remember her doing any. My Dad used to do the cleaning and the cooking and my Mum would manage her part-time jobs around school and stuff. I can remember running after her not wanting her to go but she had to. There just wasn't any formal childcare really – you were either cared for by your family or left. People would look out for each other's kids, and everybody would be out playing in the street. It was safe and nothing traumatic happened – you know, accidents, abduction, knocked down, etc. So, my Dad would clean and 'do' in the afternoon but he wouldn't have wanted anyone to know that. I remember him once saying he would do anything but he wouldn't hang washing out in case somebody saw him (laughter). He did it all because I remember my Mum, she used to get poorly, she used to suffer with depression and so my Dad not only did he work, he carried on working through all that. I remember him doing a lot of childcare, the cooking, everything. So you know he probably was a New Man a bit too soon. In those days, they probably thought he was off his rocker doing that, a man doing all the housework. He was very quiet about it, I think he just loved me mam and would have done anything for her. It didn't bother him that she didn't like doing housework.

Because both my parents worked, we had a bit more money to do things with. It was unusual to go on holiday but we used to go in a caravan every year to Great Yarmouth. For our holiday, my Dad had a very old Austin A25 which he had hand-painted bright green. It was dead embarrassing and when we went off, he got this trunk to put on the top and my mother was so embarrassed because we had to drive past the chip shop where she worked. I think the fact that everyone in my family worked and had a good work ethic, it probably was really unusual. I knew *I* didn't want to work in a shop, which is what everyone ended up doing. No, and I didn't want to do tailoring – two things for a young woman to do. Those were the expectations and I wasn't particularly bright at school. I was in the O level class* but I left before I took them because I daren't do them. I didn't pass my eleven-plus so I went to a secondary modern school. I coped alright and was put in for O levels but was dreading it. One of the girls in the class was going to go to secretarial college – I had no desire to do it but I saw she could leave and not do O levels so that's what I decided to do. It brought the entire family a lot of pride because you know I was going to Greenlands College and I was really posh, you know. I'd opted out, not staying on to do O levels but

---

* O-Levels – school qualifications taken in England and Wales usually at the age of 16. A-levels, typically taken between 16–18 years of age, are qualifications often required for university entry.

I remember for my Mum and Dad it was the only time they ever went to school. Because I went to a convent school and the headmistress, who was a known tyrant, wouldn't take my word for it that it was okay to leave, and my parents had to go down.

But I started secretarial college at 16. I was there for a year and I absolutely loved it. I learnt shorthand, typing, English, office practice. I can only remember this NCR he used to talk about – no carbon required, it was the first time you got them forms where you didn't have to have a piece of carbon paper. I feel like an old codger – 36 years ago. But I did enjoy it because I'd gone to a convent school and being at this place where you didn't have to stand up when teachers came in or open a door, or carry their bag or carry their books. It took me months, I kept standing up all the time (laughter)! Every time somebody in authority came, up I shot.

We were all young women, no boys. In fact, in all my school career there were no boys, except junior school, because that was mixed, but secondary school was an all-girls convent school, and all-girls college and in fact, when I did get my first job I was horrified at the thought of having to work with men. I was easily shocked and totally embarrassed. Every time they spoke to me, I just blushed to my roots. I finished secretarial college in about a year and then got a job easily. In those days, you could pick and choose, it was easy enough to get a job. I got a job in an accountants' office but doing this one-year course filled me with confidence and because of where I lived I was quite proud of myself really, because I felt like I'd done alright. So I'd be catching the bus to town to work and you know my girlfriends would be getting off at Burtons or the market, they'd go and work in the market. I felt quite posh because I'd stay on the bus. And I had to dress differently, I had to dress smart and I suppose because I had done this course and I was going for interviews for jobs I was really choosy, I mean I can't imagine what they must have thought. But anyway I chose this job and I remember . . . you know you had a good choice and I got £5 a week and I got paid monthly. Very posh – salaried.

I don't know why I liked the job. I guess it was just having some money, you know a bit of pocket money of my own, I had to pay board at home but I just felt like I'd loads of money and I just loved it. I made friends that I'd never . . . you know, where I lived it was rough and ready I guess really and everyone did the same thing, had the same background and here I was mixing with people who lived in posh parts of the city.

I think I spent a lot of time feeling not quite up to the mark and always feeling like I had to make an effort and probably because of that I went a bit over the top with it all, I think. I can remember feeling over-dressed a lot of the time. You know, new things and that's when the obsession with shoes came in and, you know, because when I was little I only ever had one pair of shoes, I had just a pair for school which had to be kept tidy. So working where I was working we had a bit of kudos 'cos I had a proper job, a tidy job. I stayed there and continued going to college then. I went to nightschool for shorthand and typing for two or three years, just getting more qualifications. In those days you used to move around just to get a bit more money, you know work further up. I went to be a secretary to someone as opposed to just junior, like, yes, so I just moved up the ladder a bit and got a secretarial post at the hospital which I liked and I stayed there for about three or four years and got married while I was there.

I was quite late getting married, though – when I was 18 people were already getting married. I met him in a pub and it was my best friend's birthday and his birthday and we were all sort of celebrating together so I met him then and sort of fell into it. I had never had a long-term boyfriend at all and already you were beginning to think maybe it wasn't going to happen and then what would you do. I have to say when I got the job, I always thought in the back of my mind that it didn't really matter what I did because it wouldn't be for long, I would get married and have a baby. Because that was the expectation. Once I got married I went on to pay a smaller insurance stamp then because you were going to be like with your husband's. Before marriage, I just had kind of odd dates with ones, I guess, that I came into contact with. Mostly I wasn't really that bothered. I had a very, very best friend and we just used to do everything together and the only times I ever went out with anyone else were if we all went out together in a group. At 17 they were dating, courting seriously and a lot of my friends got married at 18 or 19, got pregnant even. Most of my friends were Roman Catholic. There was no way they could have sex either and not be married never mind get pregnant, and so my choice of friends were getting less and less as I got older.

I knew one or two lads who we used to hang around with and would ask me out and I always used to say 'no' because I used to have more fun with me mates ... and then I thought, 'Sod it, needs must' and then my friend had yellow jaundice and I remember saying 'Oh go on then,' and I went out with him while she had yellow jaundice and then the minute she were better I ditched him. Nothing swept me off my feet and I got the feeling from my family and where I lived and stuff that everybody got married and eventually I would have children, you know that was the plan? Certainly if you hadn't got married by the time you were 20 you were definitely thinking you were going to be left on the shelf, and I remember when I got pregnant at 25 I was old. My mother definitely thought there was something going on ... I got married at 20 and I didn't have Julia until I was 25 so I had been married all that time and, I mean, my mother thought there was something wrong, you know, thought we couldn't have children and also you weren't meant to use birth control because we were both Catholics.

I think she had either been lucky or unlucky because she'd never used birth control and only got pregnant three times. So, yes, there was a lot of pressure on from church and it is surprising what you take on board yourself without anyone actually saying anything. You just like mini clock what you see. I have to say my Mum and Dad seemed really happy and although some of the families we lived near must have been completely dysfunctional they were still what ... a man and woman living at home with often a lot of children. So you never thought about whether you'd be happy doing that or what would happen if you didn't.

Yes, and the thoughts of not being married were worse than any thoughts about having some plonker, you know. I probably wasn't going to have me pick of the crop, I used to have this feeling that I wouldn't meet anyone, so I don't know. I didn't brim with confidence, I was more confident than when I was at school but not anywhere near like I am now. When you have been brought up to, like, do certain things in a certain way it is just easier if you haven't got to reinvent the wheel. So I started having children at 25 which was quite late at that time and then I stopped working for about nine years. I had one at 25 and then two years later and then two years later and it was when the youngest went to infant school (at 5) that work was an option. Because there was just no child-care ... I mean they were just beginning to get child minders then but they were very few and far between and my mother, although retired, made it perfectly clear that she wasn't interested in providing childcare. As far as she was concerned she liked the nice bits, you know of seeing them, but she didn't want to do the day-to-day stuff. I had had the children and they were my responsibility. And to be honest I was happy staying at home, I think that I liked doing it and I did it well and I felt confident with that and I think the thought of getting a job frightened me really. I had been away from the workplace then for so long and I always thought that's what would happen.

I really enjoyed it though. I just got involved in their lives then, at school and nursery and playgroups and fund-raising and voluntary work, anything I could have done that fitted in with them and school and stuff like that and I liked it, I made lots of friends so I had quite a nice life with the children. I think once I got married I was sort of semi looking forward to having a baby because I had gotten to the point then where I didn't like what I did, it was boring, it was the same thing and I realised then that I was never going to be able to do anything else. I had gone as far as I could go with those qualifications. Still people when you applied for jobs were asking did you have O and A levels and I regret, not now though, but up until, say, 10 years ago, I still really regret that I didn't really have anything to put down on an application form. Oh, I had loads of office type-things but when I was going back to work they weren't as relevant then because computers had come in and it didn't matter that you could do shorthand and typing stuff . . . words per minute etc. So I remember going back to college again then. I decided I was going to maybe try and get a part-time job. I enrolled at college then, in Reinsford to do computer studies. There were all sorts of schemes to get women back off into the workplace – return to learn? The courses were free because I wasn't working and that was good and a confidence thing really. You needed to know your way around a computer so that if you were going to go back to work you could just develop some skills. I think I would never have thought about having a career change. There were certain things and to this day I would never, ever, want to work in a shop. I don't know, that would have been the end of my life if I had had to work there. I think I was shy and any type of interaction in a shop, behind a bar, I would have hated anything like that. I was quite happy with a machine and I felt confident with that, so I would never have wanted to work in a shop.

When I was at home with the children, I did lots of things. With the confidence thing maybe I did make a subconscious decision to work with people who I felt not better than but I felt more confident with that so I maybe was a bit choosy where I worked. The people I were involved in fund-raising with or for were always either elderly or learning disabilities (18 years ago, I mean, it weren't 'learning disabilities') or doing voluntary work. I suppose I had a fear of always feeling not quite up to scratch or maybe people might make a judgement of you. Maybe it was because of being brought up where I was, I don't know. If you had no expectations of yourself you could easily have been left out and done nothing. Very hard to break.

I think even my mother once said to me I was too big for my boots. She would have been happy, I think, if I had worked in a shop because that's what she always wanted to do. She got that job in the fish shop and she was made up because she felt it was a bit flashier than the tailoring. And the fact that we got fish and chips free I suppose was another bonus so it is funny, isn't it, what you think is a good job. Once or twice I thought . . . I did used to think I was a bit of a cut above. I hope I wasn't a snob but I guess I wanted to think I was better than some. I also did some fostering, before I went back to work . . . it was when the youngest of my kids was three, I did that for two years. I remember I were in a panic about what was I going to do when they went to school, so I got involved with the Catholic Welfare Society through church – they needed homes for these babies to go to while they were waiting to be adopted, so I got involved with that and did that for two or three years and I loved it, absolutely loved it. It just got a bit painful giving them back and the other thing was my own children used to get upset because they liked them, they got attached to them. I had one very traumatic time of having to give a baby to its adoptive parents, having convinced myself they wouldn't be able to place her because she was poorly. I think I decided then that that were enough and I think I realised I were just trying to fulfil a need in me or even to stay at home, you know. I didn't want any more babies myself so I just felt confident with doing that . . . it was just the fear of training, I think.

I think it was when the youngest went to school that I decided I should really get proper employment. It was the School of Dentistry in Middletown University and I saw a job advertised, term time only, so I got a job there so I didn't have to start while I dropped the kids off at school and I could leave in time to pick them up. It was perfect in school holidays. My mother thought I was mad. She couldn't understand why . . . I didn't really have to go back for the money, which was a good thing because my ex-husband worked hard so we were alright really. It were just for myself, I needed to do something for myself, but that concept was lost on my Mum because you didn't do that sort of thing. What more could you possibly want, you know, so I think it was just a thing of being Danny's mum, Rosa's mum, was sick of being someone's mum or someone's wife, I just needed to see if I could do something away from there where no one knew you. You could be a new person.

I wasn't bothered about talking about family or what I did at home so I just had like another little life. I enjoyed it, I enjoyed it too much apparently because I split up with my husband and I think it was going back to work that really did it, I think, realising what a big mistake it all was, really scary. Me working didn't interfere with him at all because he didn't have to do anything and it wasn't equal. I got upset then because although it was my choice to do it, obviously I wasn't at home as much, and at that point I used to do a lot of running, and I was still trying to fit that in. Sometimes, I would be maybe getting into work a bit later so that I could go for a run, so I would expect him to pick the kids up from school, so he would have to finish early which he could because he had his own business. But he didn't want to, he couldn't understand why I now wanted to run as well as work. But then I saw the light and I am thinking, 'Oh hang on a minute, why should I work and do the house-work, and do the shopping and do the ironing and do everything?' and all he had to do was go out to work.

He did absolutely nothing and never did even when the children were young. Typical sort of old-fashioned relationship where the women did . . . you know he never bathed them and sometimes would get upset because they would never want him to take them to bed. You just drop into these ways by accident. It is only when you see a different alterna-tive lifestyle, when you hear other people talking, you think it were wrong and I felt dissatisfied.

It brought about a lot of changes really, it felt like it were a good thing but it threw my ex-husband into complete confusion as well because I'd changed. I'd gone from being this quiet, you know, fall in with anyone, do anything for anyone, always like putting myself out to the detriment of myself because I didn't like to say no and all of a sudden, I was questioning things and actually having an opinion about things. That is when things started on the downward spiral. I realised then that in all the time we'd been married, we had never really spoken about anything, we had just got on with our separate jobs if you like. I'd look after the kids and the house and he'd gone out to work and I'd been happy with that, I didn't know anything else. If I had never have got that little job I would have probably been there until the children left home I think, because I remember even when Rosa went to school feeling completely panic struck because I just didn't know what I was going to do any more. Yes, the husband wasn't enough because I realised then that I didn't love him like that, not enough to want to be there. You just sort of got on with it and hoped it were going to be a long way off. We had everything – our own house which me mam and dad had never done (you know council houses were the norm really) so I had made it in their eyes. Yes and that were it, your life stopped then, you'd no need to bother doing anything else. The new job that I took on made me feel so confident, I think just meeting other people made a difference. Where I worked before I suppose I always just thought like I was mediocre, everything I did, I wasn't a sparkling personality, I wasn't particularly attractive. There was nothing about me that would have stood out from anyone else, but when I started this little job they had an older woman working and she was retiring. She used to use a typewriter for everything so I came along, could use a computer and they all thought I was absolutely wonderful. They were getting work back within half an hour whereas she had like a work basket full of stuff. People were so complimentary, they were so nice, a very alternative group of people that I'd ever met, they were all very different. And just to be told that you were good at something was really nice, I don't think I had ever been told that before. People didn't give feedback … it's different now than it was then, but I don't think we do that very well, do we? We are very good at telling somebody when they are doing things wrong.

But I think that is the first time I remember anyone ever saying, you know, being pleased with something I'd done. I used to seek that out and I used to do things so that people would like me. Some sort of sad person, but I did. Children, they grow like flowers if we give them lots and lots of praise as opposed to being knocked down. I had never met such a nice group of people, and I started going out for meals and things and the conversation, I used to think they were all so clever, I daren't speak for a long time. I had been at home, and they were talking about all different sorts of things and where they had been on holiday and it was the first time I had met a vegetarian (laughter). I wasn't quite sure what it was.

It was lovely when I was at work but hard at home. So I really liked going to work and often went in times when I didn't need, just to be there because I liked it. I felt confident there and it was different from being at home. After four years, I went full-time then and that was a bit of a nightmare with childcare. He didn't say a right lot, he just had to do it, but you know things weren't good then at home, things were beginning to break down already and he could notice it by then as well.

But, I didn't tell anyone. We never talked, my ex-husband and I didn't talk about it either. I never said I wasn't happy, he never said he wasn't happy. And I guess it just got worse and worse. I kept hoping that he'd leave or find somebody else. But sadly he didn't do that. When the children were around it was okay and I guess they were still only young, Rosa was only 9 and I can remember feeling really panicky all the time and having panic attacks. Just thinking all the time what would I do. The fact that they were still young, I felt that imminent that they were all going to leave and leave me there, leave me behind, those sorts of feeling, it was awful but I don't remember saying anything to anyone.

And so eventually I took the bull by the horns and decided to do something. You know it just wasn't the thing to do, but I had met someone else as well which added all to it, I guess, and I panicked then. What should I do? Should I let the opportunity go and hope that it would go away? It was complicated by the fact that it was a woman and not a man and I felt because of that, I couldn't take the children with me because I thought that would be too much for them.

And I didn't know what was going on myself, I'd only just met a vegetarian, I'd never met a lesbian (laughter). I just thought it would be better if they could stay where they were happy. Even now it is really painful to think about. I think I must have just had some sort of, lost like track and blocked it all out, I don't know, I spent days, I lost weight, I couldn't eat anything. It wasn't the done thing to leave. I did try to tell my mother at that point that I was really unhappy and say that I didn't know what I was going to do. I had said that I was going to move out into the spare room or share with one of the kids and I remember her saying 'Well, he's not going to stand for that' as I was breaking my heart and I thought, well, whatever I do, I am just going to have to just do it.

I suppose it made me stronger and I realised that maybe I could do things and I suppose the way I've rationalised it now is I think at the time I did the best I could in the circumstances. I've stopped feeling guilty. I went and lived with the person who is now my partner in Middletown and fortunately because she had a really different background from me, although her family are working class. Well, she thinks her family are working class – I suspect that if she was working class I must have been the under class (laughter) or she must have been upper working class. She had had a really good education and was really encouraging. I had a really nice job in Middletown where I met lots of nice people and again met people from different places. It just made me feel unfulfilled in a way, when you see people getting all these nice things, and really angry almost for not doing it, probably angry with myself. Prepared to settle for so little or that women were, you know, when I was younger.

I went through a period when I was unhappy then at work, felt like I needed a change but didn't think there was any point in changing because I would have just done another office job. I had gone to college to do an A level to see if I could do it because I had never done O levels or A levels and while I was there everyone there was doing it to gain access into higher education. Somebody just said they were going to do nursing or midwifery. We got chatting and I ended up going on an open day with them for nursing. I just sat there and thought 'Oh, I could do that' and decided to. So I chatted it over with my partner who was really, really supportive and really pleased that I had made the decision to do that. I was 46 at the time and chose to do learning disabilities because when the children were young I did voluntary work. So I chose to do that because I felt confident again in that area. I daren't be too daring so I still felt like I needed to choose something that would be safe. I was glad I had and I just loved it, I absolutely loved the course. The whole student thing was brilliant, I really, really enjoyed it and was really pleased that I could actually do it, with a lot of support but, you know, complete the academic side. I knew I'd have no problem with the practical side of it. With the academic side I was pleasantly surprised. I used to enjoy it, not the handing in bit and waiting for the marks, I didn't like that, but I do remember being over-confident.

You know, up until I was about 39 even, I had lived in a really closed world, although it was slightly different from when we moved out and were married, it was just the same, but in a different house, with a bit more money, but still women were doing that sort of thing. And being held back in a way from ever reaching the potential and expecting so little of themselves as well. I think because a lot of women stay at home, no importance is placed on that role at all. You know, it is a job basically, a 24-hour, 7-day-a-week job and very little importance is placed on that. If you had to pay someone to stay at home to look after children it would cost a fortune. Whatever you do is on top of, anything extra I did was on top of everything else I had to do, never in place of anything. It is still like that to some extent, still women do exactly the same thing, they are just under a different guise now. If the husband manages to pick them up a couple of times from the childminder or something. I work with women who do it, who do a job, arranging the childcare and the shopping. I am sure a lot of women think they have come a long way. The childcare has improved and that is about it, I think. I think we still do as much. Whether that will ever change, whether ever anyone will ever think it is a really wonderful job that women do I don't know. Whereas when men stay at home to look after the children as a house-husband permanently or whatever, everyone thinks that is absolutely wonderful and will talk about it and how they made a cake and he baked and a woman will do that day in and day out and it is just not even referred to.

My job has come full circle back now. Having worked for a couple of years with adults with a challenging need, having qualified, I then got a job working with children in a respite centre and I just absolutely love it, you are dealing with family dynamics. Having come from the back-ground I have come from, it is almost like you don't have to go to the North Pole to know it is cold, but I think as a mature student and now working I think I feel I have got a lot more to offer than someone straight out of school. Because when you are dealing with families you just need to be so aware of what is going on other than what you can see, you know, that it is not always visible, is it?

I am so happy now though. I got an advanced diploma and then last year I did the higher degree and I got 2.1 which I was very pleased with. I couldn't have done it without a lot of support though. I think the easy side of it is actually looking after the children. I think the difficult side of it is dealing with the family dynamics and what is going on in the family and you know ... I don't know, communication with everyone and information sharing. It is interesting, isn't it, that one of the things I said was that I didn't feel good at interaction so earlier I picked jobs purposefully to avoid that contact. I have ended up now in a job which has huge amounts of that and more of that than anything else. Actually I am finding out that I like it. I think that just came about with training, I mean, I used to be petrified going on placements. It is surprising how it has come full circle and I hadn't realised until talking about it that the thing I like doing the most, like being around children and babies ... I've ended up working with that. Yes, whether it is an unconscious or a conscious choice I have ended up doing it.

Chapter 3

The death story of David Hope

Michele Moore

November

I sat in the car waiting for a personal assistant to leave before it would be convenient to be admitted to meet David. A mutual acquaintance had asked me to get in touch with him, explaining 'he broke his neck in a diving accident. He's depressed. He hates being paralysed and wants to die. Do you think you could help him or help his mum? Just find out if there's anything you could do? He talks about suicide all the time. No one knows what's wrong with him.'

There had been a time when I had come to know a great deal about the lives of men with spinal cord injury. I had been part of a team interviewing one in four patients discharged from the National Spinal Injuries Unit at Stoke Mandeville Hospital (Oliver *et al.*, 1988). When the project began it was taken for granted that survival after spinal cord injury depended on the personality of the injured person. Extrovert sportsmen, who break their necks in heroic feats, it was assumed would overcome the practicalities of living with paralysis better than quiet types who tripped over their own carpets. The research had shown there could be no mistake about it: survival after spinal cord injury depended very little on the injured person. Outcomes are, in fact, determined almost entirely by what happens to the person following injury. I was sure I needed to know not *what was wrong with David*, but what was wrong with his circumstances and what could be done to change these for the better.

I think I made up my mind what was wrong before I was even out of the car. I knew him to be about my own age, yet he was living with his Mum and Dad in the three-bedroom semi of his childhood. He didn't have his own accessible front door and his Mum, Sheila, let me in. She showed me through to an extension that took up most of what had once been the back garden and I knew that if I was confined to living in a one-room extension on the back of my Mum and Dad's house without even the facility to let my own guests in and out, then I'd be wanting to commit suicide too. His room was large and airy and dominated by a hospital bed. He shared it with a blue budgerigar, some posters of half-naked girls, various hoists and an assortment of medical equipment. It was there that David spent most of his days since he'd broken his neck nine years earlier and it was there that he had fixed on the idea of committing suicide.

He was sitting in a wheelchair between the bed and the wall. He didn't look at me, said 'It's nice of you to come', but reminded me he hadn't wanted to meet. He'd gone along with the idea because it might help his Mum. He said he probably wouldn't say anything. He had no reason to trust me and people he'd trusted in the past always let him down. I told him I wasn't sure why I was there. I had no professional brief and had come along only because various mutual acquaintances were intent on getting us together. I did tell him I had talked to a lot of men with spinal injury, enough to know it wasn't inevitable that he should lead a life that got him down as much as his apparently did.

He stayed unapproachable. I couldn't face getting straight back in the car and played for time. 'Let me sit here a while. You don't have to talk.' The only reason he let me stay was because he noticed I was wearing a short skirt. I knew, because he lifted his eyes from the carpet to my knees. I was acutely self-conscious but had to hope it was a fair enough exchange. Eventually he said, 'I'm pathetic. People haunt me. I think all the time that I can't see a way out. There's not much point you being here.' I asked him what had happened.

Gradually he started to talk. He said he thought all the time of suicide, planning ways to do away with himself given the problem of his high level of physical incapacity. Starving was his preferred option but he could not bear the thought of being force-fed. Throwing himself under a car or freezing to death would also be possible but implicated other people too much. Twenty minutes later I thought 'God, he really *is* talking. I should be taping', but he wouldn't let me. 'I don't trust anyone,' he said. 'I don't trust you.'

But he carried on. He told about the accident in a holiday hotspot where he broke his neck showing off, diving drunk into a swimming pool. His insurance company flew him to a specialist unit back in England. Ten months later he was discharged to a local residential hospital for war pensioners while an extension was built so that he could be sent to live behind his mother's kitchen.

He said he was quite cheerful for the first couple of years. He thought he might get back the use of his arms. But slowly the enormity of what had happened began to sink in. A few months after leaving the place he called 'the old people's home', 'trouble began'. His relationship with his girlfriend came to an end he'd long seen coming. A spinal injured friend he had met in hospital committed suicide. He began to comprehend the undoubted permanence of paralysis 'from the chin down'. He developed a nauseating impression of the weight of his head. He was disturbed by a sensation that his head hovered around in the ether. Confusion swamped his mind, making him incoherent and giving him a blinding headache. His thoughts were 'speeding, saying words round in my head'. He was muddled, powerless, growing terrified and not able to discuss his anguish with anyone at all. Everyone around him was thinking 'The worst is over, he's home now.' He had realised that worse was yet to come.

He didn't want to complain so sat in the garden where people left him alone, thinking he was enjoying peace and sun. But he was in turmoil. He said he was lonely, miserable and in immense pain. He sat in the sun hour after hour, day after day, until his face and neck were so badly burned that the skin blistered, oozed and smelled of sulphur. He said he was trying to burn his face away. He thought if he could change his face then maybe he could summon the strength to change his mind.

He realised he was losing a grip on things and was panic-stricken. He dreaded visits from his mates who he said lost respect for him. He avoided conversation and felt unspeakably tired. He demanded sleeping tablets, mixed with alcopops and super-strength lager, always shocking, intensely shocked and petrified. He was admitted to a psychiatric hospital. 'But not with the spinal injury, mate,' he said. 'It wasn't breaking my neck that made me break down.'

He described admission to hospital as a brutal and terrifying experience. He had been drunk, protesting, shouting and thrashing through spasms, convinced the ambulance men were carrying only his head on their stretcher. He thought his parents would refuse to have him back home and insisted on staying only long enough to have his sleeping medication stabilised. People told him he was selfish 'for not staying long enough to get properly cured'. He'd spent the years since then trying not to let people have reason to think he should be sectioned. Ever since, he was threatened with sectioning whenever his behaviour pushed the limits of other people's tolerance – which, admittedly, was often.

He alternated between periods of deep, silent depression and uncontrollable, aggressive, often drunken, outbursts. He was ashamed of showing no gratitude towards those who provided his physical care, and humiliated by total dependence on his mother. He said that every night, about an hour after his medication kicked in, he found himself apologising to her whether or not she was in the room. Profusely apologising, over and over, promising to try not to shout at her tomorrow. He wanted to give and receive affection but said 'I can only be nice when I'm relaxed and out of pain.'

After the shock of the disclosure I grasped two things: first, his situation was a socially constructed disaster being played out again and again in the lives of young spinal injured men, and second he had just called me 'mate'.

I ploughed on, asking him to tell me the things he most wanted to be different. He was barely audible. 'I want to be sound in the head. I want to be relaxed, able to make eye contact with people. I want the pain in my eye to stop. I want to be able to make relationships with people and to have visitors. I want a girlfriend. I can't see that any of it is possible.' He stopped and stared at the floor. There was heavy silence. I said something inadequate about his decision to talk being a brave one. He never once went near 'wanting a mended neck'.

He was choked and couldn't talk, so then I talked. I told him about people I knew with similar impairments who had independent lives and fulfilling relationships. I tried to say, 'There is another way of looking at what's happening to you – it's not about your spinal injury and what you can't do, it's about everyone else and what they can do to make a difference.' 'I can't see it,' he said. 'I can't see there could ever be any change.' Somehow we drifted into a conversation about personal power and avoiding self-defeating beliefs and gradually he began to articulate changes he longed for. He'd been talking for a long time when we realised he had focused on three specific things he was saying might help him start to get his life back:

1. to get rid of a pain in his eye
2. to get his printer fixed
3. to have a better relationship with his Mum.

Once David noticed these difficulties were all surmountable he couldn't think of anything else. To get rid of the pain in his eye he decided he would ask his GP for a second opinion. He wanted the printer fixed because he wanted to write about the way he was feeling and he had hundreds of things he wanted to say. He struggled on ways of improving his relationship with his mother and finally settled on trying to say one nice thing to her over the coming week when he was not in a drug-induced state. That was my idea. He'd kept on and on asking 'Can you help me think of something?' It was the only do-able thing I could come up with.

Before I left, he asked if we could keep talking. He was worried that meeting meant a 500-mile round trip for me. He kept checking whether I wanted to bother with him. I mistrusted my courage, but I had incurred an inescapable compulsion to somehow support him. We agreed to stay in touch by letter and phone and to meet again in a few months' time. He expressly said, 'If I don't ring, you will ring me, won't you?' So I did.

I wrote, and we spoke many times on the phone after that. He said he was thinking so much he was becoming less able to speak. He was thinking constantly about change and this plunged him further into the depths of despair than ever before. He was worried about causing me too much trouble. I was very afraid. I had known when I first agreed to meet him that a dangerous cocktail of uncertain personal, professional and ethical boundaries would be shaken. Now I was gravely implicated in his life and desolation because I had pursued, and then become part of, his story.

January

The next time we met he was naked and lying in bed on a rubber cushion. His body brace was bruising his back and ribs and without it he had to lie flat on his back. He had a raw, draining bedsore and redness around the sore causing serious concern. He could not get pressure off the sore without using the brace. He was cold but having copious, drenching sweats for which no explanation was apparently forthcoming. His eye pain was intermittent, often excruciating, but the GP found nothing amiss. His face showed exhaustion, resignation and agony. 'It's impossible, mate,' he said. But we managed to talk again, and later on he said getting a new body brace could help things improve. He decided to insist on his Mum calling the GP in to get the ball rolling. She was hesitant, afraid of taking up too much of the doctor's time.

He asked about independent living. 'Do people in this state really manage? Are there ways of trying it out, perhaps short-term, on a trial basis?' I resolved to find out. We agreed his top priority would have to be to sort the body brace because his skin would break down without it. And then he mentioned that the printer still wasn't fixed. He didn't want to hassle his brother but agreed he would have to ask him again.

Lying prostrate, looking ill and in obvious discomfort, he said he had been thinking about trying a week of living on his own. His parents were due to go on holiday and he wondered if he could try staying at home without them. Otherwise he would be admitted back to the old people's hospital while they were away and the thought of it gave him nightmares. He wondered whether it would be possible to bring in a support team that would make it possible for him to live independently of his parents in his own home for a week or two. He said he was obsessed with the idea of spending a week on his own at home. His immense personal strength, which meant he was willing to try to forge change in the face of so much adversity, bound me to try to help him to make this happen.

February

It turned out that a specialist agency would provide live-in personal assistants to cover the support gaps that would arise when David's Mum and Dad went away. He had warned his parents that he wanted me to find out what was possible. I offered to talk with them, to avoid getting wires crossed or doing anything they were unhappy about, but they didn't take this up. A couple of weeks after booking the support, David rang me to say his Mum and Dad wouldn't agree to having assistants in the house after all. They wanted him to be readmitted to the old people's hospital because they couldn't face the thought of strangers staying in their house. He said he couldn't do anything without his parents on side. They were afraid that trying out new support arrangements could jeopardise their existing provision. He was disappointed and angry.

His mother had dialled the call for him and I heard him force her to pick up the extension and talk to me herself while he listened in. I didn't particularly want to get into a confrontation with his mother but he implored me to speak to her. I was unnerved, saying: 'David, make sure I'm saying what you think I should be saying. Stop me if I've got something wrong . . .' At first his mother didn't say anything. Then she asked in a clipped, quiet but infuriated tone what I thought I was doing stirring up ideas about change in David's mind, intruding in their lives and making everything worse than before he'd met me.

There was hardly a single moment during the time of my relationship with David when I had clear insight into what I thought I was doing. Once again now I was wading in, out of my depth, hoping for the best outcome for both of them. My only certainty was that the responses forming in my mind stemmed from the unshakeable belief that this man's life should not be miserable because other people were making their support difficulties a reason for his oppression. I had nothing exact in mind, but was desperate to keep open some level of productive dialogue about the impact of restrictions in David's life.

I heard myself say that David was very, very unhappy. He wanted to change things and had told me he wanted to live an independent life. I told his Mum he felt he was ruining her life and wanted her to be free of him. He didn't say a word so I carried on. Staying at home while his parents were away would give him a small space in which to see what he could cope with and try out living with different kinds of support in place. 'Yes,' she said, 'I know the old people's home is not great but it doesn't do him any *actual harm* [her emphasis]. He only lies in a bed anyway.'

He was listening. His sense of hurt and condemnation was acute. I ventured to say he should have a better life than that. A better two weeks if possible. She said he wouldn't cope. David was audibly upset and swearing at her. I told her I thought he could try. 'He has got what it takes to live his own life. He's warm and funny and strong and opinionated, he could do it.' 'We've said it all before,' she replied. 'At the last minute he won't go through with it. Like the time when he went into the mental hospital. He only let them sort out his drugs and then he wouldn't stay any more.' By now David was irate. I had nothing dependable to say.

I tried to put across a gut belief that he now wanted things to change and that he trusted me. I was absolutely certain I trusted him. All the time I was asking David to back me up or put me straight, saying, 'David, listen to what I'm saying to your Mum, you *must* tell us if I'm getting it wrong,' and he kept saying 'Just tell her, mate, please tell her.' I tried to explain it takes a good ten years to come to terms with living with spinal cord injury. I thought he was having a very tough time and living an extraordinary life.

She was outraged: 'What do you mean an *extraordinary* life?' 'Well, it's not a life like many other blokes of his age lead. It's not like his brothers live. He never was the sort of person who would have chosen to live at home with his parents. He has attitude and audacity in his eyes. That's why he always has a number one haircut. That's why home care attendants fall head over heels for him. He's defiant and stroppy. He never was going to be a mummy's boy. He should have his own life and you should have yours. He knows what he puts you through. He wants to give you and Michael your lives back. Sometimes he's cross and loud-mouthed and cruel, people are tired, they don't always find ways of saying things, but he knows how much you do for him ... he can't tell you ...' and then I heard David's tremulous breathing and thought 'Crikey I have really gone too far here.'

There was unforgettable, empty silence. After a while I tried vaguely to fill it, attempting to articulate a notion of advocacy and to explain it as being different from professional intervention. I acknowledged feeling myself to be completely on David's side but argued this didn't mean I was not on Sheila's side too. That was why I had wanted to talk to her much earlier on. She conceded – reluctantly – that David had no other advocate. But she insisted she had to protect her 30 days a year when she could absolutely rely on David being in the old people's home. She repeated the point about 'He stays in bed and does nothing anyway. At least we know he's looked after there,' and said she didn't want to talk about it any-more. She put down her phone and David said, 'I'd better go, mate. Ring me again.' His Mum disconnected the call. I burst into tears at my desk, realising that when David was in a fight like that there wasn't a thing he could himself do to get out of the way. If I phoned back he couldn't answer.

A week later he had another call put through. He said the row had gone on and his Mum and Dad were adamant they would not have strangers staying in the house. He asked for information about a Trust I was involved in that enables disabled people to live independently with direct payments and 24-hour personal assistance. He said: 'If you could manage to send that then I can at least try to believe that an independent future might be possible.'

But a real block remained. His parents steadfastly refused to let him try living independently at home for the two weeks when they would be away on holiday. We talked about different ways of trying out independent living. Sheila came on to the phone and told me not to sort anything out. 'Better not then, mate,' said David. Sheila disconnected the call.

March

In due course David was sent to the old people's hospital while his parents went on holiday. I went to see him there. It was a small Victorian community hospital. A couple of bewildered old men sat nodding on benches in the entrance hall. The silent, tiled corridors were empty. It was without doubt an institution specialising in the business of certain social death (Miller and Gwynne, 1972).

David was in a sunny, single room looking at the ceiling. He had been in bed all week and would stay there for the entire fortnight. His body was covered with a white sheet. There was no one around. I could not believe this clinical and isolated care for elderly and bewildered people was the best respite arrangement that could be provided for such a young and vibrant person. I pulled a chair close to his bed, picked up his fingers and held tightly on to his hand. I was shocked, exhausted from the journey and trying not cave in to an overwhelming sense of his personal tragedy. I was trying hard not to let him see me cry. A disembodied voice from the far end of the bed said: 'The only way I'll know that you're there, mate, is if you touch my face.' And so I touched his face and it was for us both a fatal act of human contact because the boundaries of our connection were then intimately and radically changed.

I remember the long, hot afternoon. David talked almost without stopping. At 6 o'clock visitors were turned out. I returned at an appointed hour for a strange and humid night of listening on into the very small hours. In the darkness, David wanted me to fix my hand on his face and then, for the first time since I had known him, he completely relaxed. He closed his eyes and started to breathe more slowly, talking, quietly talking and asking questions.

He made me tell him over and over again about the lives of other disabled people I know who live independently. He wanted to know about their houses, their jobs, their children, their gardens, their everyday journeys, how did they get their shopping, who chose the meals, the television programmes they watch, the time they have a bath, what about the sleeping arrangements? He said that more than anything he wanted to live on his own and to create a life of his own. He said he wanted a partner who wasn't responsible for his physical care. He wanted children. He said he longed to hold his nieces and nephews but his brothers and their wives could never trust him in case their children fell off his lap. He was taken aback by the idea that the children would find their own ways of cuddling whoever they wanted to cuddle. He asked whether he could have children. He asked whether he could adopt.

He refused his night-time sleeping draught. He insisted on darkness. He asked so many questions, in which I recognised myself and my friends. If he had asked these questions before, they had been interpreted as signs that he wasn't adjusting, wasn't facing up to his injury. The questions that I recognised as the authentic concerns of people our age were denied an existence in the life of a person with a C4 spinal cord injury. He fell asleep in a kind of happiness, having conjured up a picture of an independent future with the girl of his dreams and an adopted Chinese baby girl. I crept out, drained and disoriented.

The next morning he was pitched back into black and certain despair. He wanted too much. He couldn't wait. Until I began to tell him about other disabled people's lives he hadn't realised what he was missing. I might be giving him false hope. Did I realise the magnitude of his humiliation and shame? Did I comprehend the despair he felt over the enforced bodily intimacy his personal care needs imposed upon his mother? He needed an erection for his catheter to fit properly but nurses laughed at him and said they weren't there to have sex with every Tom, Dick and Harry. If it didn't fit properly then there would be piss everywhere and nurses shouting at him about having to change sheets, and more often than not he would be *put to bed* for the rest of the day if that happened.

Did I think his father knew what his mother went through every day? Of course not. She was silent. She couldn't bear to tell anyone the reality of their mutual wretchedness. David would be sectioned if he talked of this shared degradation because his mother would deny it. Did I know this sort of collusion went on? Did I? Did anybody know? Could social services departments comprehend the real reason why he so wanted his own place and independent personal assistance?

'She does it out of love,' he said. 'But if that's how she's got to go on I would rather be dead.' Above all, he wanted to protect the dignity and reputation of his mother. His injury was permanently transformed there and then in my mind and had nothing further to do with spinal lesion.

He was passionate and angry and upset. He felt himself vindicated in his belief that things had gone too far for adequate change to be possible. He understood that lack of attention to the social origins of his despair had nailed him permanently to a future characterised by humiliation and indignity, not only for himself but also for his mother. Could change be effected? It was intensely necessary, but he doubted it. I had brought him some meaningless blue irises. I put them in a jar, left him a tape that wouldn't be played unless someone called by, drove home shaking. He stayed exactly where he was for the next two weeks, looking at the ceiling, tears streaked across his ears, head on a sodden pillow.

April

According to David, over the next week or so, nurses convinced him he could not be force-fed if he refused food while in hospital. His GP confirmed this and told him to engage a solicitor if he was serious about suicide. David said if he hadn't been assured he couldn't be force-fed then he would be pursuing his own place, but if force-feeding could be avoided then suicide was the more palatable and achievable option. 'In a way,' he said, 'I am still planning my own place mate.'

We were suddenly at an unexpected and critical crossroads. He phoned to say the long-awaited appointment to re-fit his body brace had come through. He was trying to decide between going for the appointment and the chance of getting back out of bed and hopefully starting to live again, or cancelling the appointment, opting to stay in bed and starve to death. A major factor against going for the appointment was the prospect of the gruelling, slow ambulance journey intensifying his already unbearable pain. Besides, he had discovered it might take only take three weeks to die, which was less time than he had thought. He became very anxious to speak to the mother of a friend who went through with starvation some years ago but was conscious of the distress this could cause her. Basically he wanted to know the appalling details of the death by starvation process. Will I go blind? Will my bones split my skin? Will my flesh rot and stink? Will I cry out in pain or terror? Will I have lurid dreams? He asked me to find out.

We agreed to speak again in a few days. He decided to continue eating until then. He said having information about the possibility of living independently would make him think about life rather than death. He said his Mum and Dad now agreed he should have his own place. '*You might have saved my life, mate*,' he said '*or you might not.*'

May – and maybe

There followed a period of frantically trying to mobilise independent living options. Over the next few weeks I called every housing department that could be tracked down, rang every relevant housing officer with a phone number and spoke to numerous housing association advisers. I met with the local social services, talked to the district nursing team, rang specialist medical centres, faxed expert professors in the UK and abroad. Representative organisations of disabled people were contacted, euthanasia societies, information services, disability agencies and networks across the country, the Independent Living Fund, local authority needs assessment hotlines, centres for integrated or inclusive living, in short anyone and everyone I could possibly think of.

Those who responded were helpful but said a home of one's own would take a long time to organise for David. Several pointed out the fine line to tread between highlighting the urgency of his situation and the risk of sectioning under the Mental Health Act. Some offered to add David to waiting lists or to new build development lists. Others never rang back. There was no immediately available emergency option.

June

Colleagues told me Social Services would have to do an assessment of David's situation within 28 days of his asking, and I sought advice from trustees of independent living agencies on the best way to support him in this. 'It's very important to be agreeable,' the various trustees said. 'Don't appear to be challenging the local providers. Be conciliatory, say, "We have a breakdown of what we think a person needs to survive. Can you do one for David and then we could get together and see what kind of agreement we can reach?" Be helpful. Smile a lot. Record everything in writing, including phone calls. Present the exercise as to identify the ideal service for David and then he can reluctantly let them beat him down . . . you will have to keep saying "We appreciate you've budgeted for X but what about Y? What is your view? In your view is Y critical for David to be able to live independently?" If they propose residential living, call their bluff and ask for the costs – even better ring someone up to have costs of local residential ready in hand.'

I was hundreds of miles away and reeling. I was prepared to put David's case, but he was preparing to die and my job seemed to be about placating those who should prevent this. David's senior social care worker refuted the emphasis on urgency, saying David was probably attention-seeking and wouldn't go through with his threat of starvation. She said she was just as worried about her own son, who had bought himself out of the army and was at a loss for what to do next. Twenty-eight days later it was too late for David to be assessed.

In the middle of June he left a voice message: 'It's David. Ring as soon as you can. It's quite important. It's about sorting out my own place. Help me. Please help me, mate. It's vital. I've got to get my own house. Come down here. Ring as soon as you can. I'm in deep shit. I've got to leave here and I'm really for it. Please, please ring. . . . Please, please ring.'

I rang and then went straight to see him. I never found out exactly what had gone on but he was desperate to fill out a form for new housing. His Mum and Dad were supporting him. He dictated his application:

> As reported in Section 21 I have a complete spinal cord injury at level C4 which means I am completely paralysed from the neck down and need 24-hour personal assistance for all aspects of daily living. I am currently residing in an annexe attached to the home of my parents and my mother provides personal support with some back-up from

home care workers. Over the years this situation has become less and
less satisfactory until now an irretrievable breakdown in family relationships has materialised. ~~My mother is no longer able or willing~~
We are no longer willing or able to continue this arrangement. I have
experienced prolonged episodes of depression.

I now wish to pursue an independent living situation and am
therefore applying to the Council for necessary ground floor accommodation. I need 24-hour personal assistance which necessitates my
application for two-bedroomed accommodation.

The situation of living in my parents' home makes me feel more,
not less, vulnerable, not least because of their age. It's their household, with their rules. With the best will in the world I lack personal
choice. My previous crisis (depression) stemmed from this situation
and I was admitted to psychiatric hospital where I needed high levels
of medication for sleep deprivation and mental stress and distress.
I have spent the best part of three years in hospital most of which
comes from the serious difficulties surrounding my housing situation
rather than from medical complications my spinal injury throws up.
The lack of social experience which my living situation allows brings
intolerable psychological pressure. The stress and distress I experience
ruins my parents' lives too.

His mother quickly sent me details of David's savings, benefits and
allowances. She did everything she could to help complete the housing
application and we sent it off. The senior social care worker undertook to
convene relevant purchasers and providers but telephoned the family to say
that confirmation would be needed at a forthcoming case conference that
this is what David wanted and that he would have to convince the committee of his capacity to cope with an independent living situation.

The end of June came around and it was finally arranged that to
convince the committee of his aptitude, David would try staying at home
with live in personal assistance while his parents went on holiday. I phoned
him several times during this period and he seemed to be upbeat. The
personal assistance was working well. He was particularly positive about
having seen a solicitor and made a will to formalise his request that he
should not be force-fed if he opted for starvation at any point during his
life. This made him feel calm and he said he was enjoying his time home
alone. At the end of the fortnight the senior social care worker left me
a message saying the last two weeks had shown it would not be possible
for David to live independently.

I tried and tried to call him to find out what had happened but could
not get a reply. When I finally reached him he hadn't eaten for three
weeks and was tired and forgetful. 'He's been hiding so much', the senior
social care worker said. 'We have to respect his wishes.'

July

David hadn't told me of his decision to begin starvation. He was deeply concerned that I shouldn't be upset because I was pregnant. 'I didn't want you to hear bad news. You did everything you could.'

I called my most respected disabled friends and colleagues, seeking to share liability for knowing what was going on. Their responses varied from those who advised pleading with David, saying to him, 'Having looked over the edge you owe it to all of us to look over again, spend some time, take longer,' and those who urged me to find out more about the status of his living will so that if I was satisfied that his decision was the right one for him I could support him from a position of knowledge. But they all said, 'Whatever you do you've got to live with it.'

August

In the end I went once more to see him. His Mum showed me in. He was in bed, thinner, struggling to concentrate, his face sallow and washed in cold sweat. The curtains were drawn. He fixed my gaze and said 'Sorry, mate.' I asked if he was sure he wanted to die. He said he was sure. He asked me to touch his face. Slowly he asked me to support him in his decision. He asked me not to come to see him again because he would worry about the baby and because there was nothing I could do. He spoke with great difficulty but kept saying 'Thanks, mate.' He asked me to look after his Mum when he was dead. He asked me to tell his story so that others didn't come to this same deathbed. I sat with him, tracing his face with my fingers. He was in and out of consciousness. After a while I had to go.

September

An emergency case conference was convened, after which the senior social care worker confirmed they were not looking to section David. Their main concerns related to withdrawing home support staff who felt compromised by his actions. Social Services reserved the right to decide whether David should be moved to a nursing home or if they would allow his mother to care for him at home. The importance of respecting David's rights and also the rights and wishes of his family was continually stressed but sounded ironic to me.

The senior social care worker seemed reassured by her judgement that David was 'sane'. She said in her view David made his decision to commit suicide because he was shocked by the cost of independent living. I never found out what figures he had been shown but it seems he was persuaded that the price for his life was too high. She also attributed his desire for suicide to what, according to my notes, she referred to as 'a bizarre relationship with his mother'. I sat at my desk incredulous at the lack of insight into how social care policies and practices were shamed by David's relationship with his mother, not knowing what to say. 'If David dies', she went on, 'back-up support may be offered to his parents but this would be informal' – *I'll be around if you need me* style. She rang off.

Later that month, David died.

Sheila said there was a big turnout for his funeral.

David's story was told differently in the newspaper. It was stated that 'he felt there was no point in living' and that this was because 'he had been unable to come to terms with his enormous handicap'. He was described as 'making immense demands'. An inquest concluded that David died from starvation after electing not to be fed after severe injuries suffered following a swimming accident.

Chapter 4

Frank

Peter Clough

'You could call it "Being Frank", couldn't you?'

'Frank' burned out spectacularly in the late 1990s: left his wife of twenty-six years, rehearsed the febrile cliché of late-found middle-aged freedom – a motorbike, a boat even, a leather jacket, a tawdry (and, as it turned out, dyed) blonde – and came out of the spin only when his racing blood dramatically sought to avoid an infarction and he all but died.

I had known him at college thirty years before, kept fitful touch over those years and was aware of his local success: turning his back on his professional training as a teacher, he had worked for some years as an auxiliary in a mental hospital – this was the early seventies – then teaching part time in a borstal before joining a school for 'maladjusted' boys as a houseparent. By thirty-one he was deputy headteacher, and got his own school – one of the largest residential places in the country for what were now emotionally and behaviourally disturbed boys – at thirty-four. At forty-eight he tore it all up, and at fifty-one he phoned me to ask: would I write his story?

I always thought he was a prick – pompous and quite undented by doubt. Perhaps there was some envy there: women seemed to like him. But his ideas – unremarkable enough in themselves – were sufficient for his preferment, and indeed his school became something of a showcase for his county's policies. (My wife was fond of saying he had 'a station above his ideas'.)

Quite what happened is not entirely clear to me. Certainly he got bored with and left his school – presumably it was the same with his wife.

We met just the once in a pub near St Pancras. He brought his diaries and said that he'd read 'Rob' (a story I'd written earlier about a deputy head, see Clough, 2002) and said – quite unabashed – that he wanted me to write – and publish – his story. He said he wanted to be called 'Frank' in the story. Guided by him – 'that's a powerful piece, isn't it?' – I flicked through the diaries and he bought us each another pint.

* * *

16th April

He was there again this morning, my father. When he is there he is usually naked which is the strangest thing, for I never during all his life saw him without clothes; now he is – bare. This is the better word for an old man without clothes and without passion.

Of course he is not really there, nor is he dead though it sounds like it. But on the mornings when he is waiting for me – always bare – as I am waking, he is with me for the rest of the day.

17th April

For the second morning he was there.

I feel that I know why my father needs to be naked

17th April 11.30

There is no full stop to that sentence and I cannot remember now why I stopped nor what the feeling of that knowledge was.

But he was always very clothed. When we were little he would cover himself up quickly – a leg, I mean, or a loosed shirt button – if we went into his bedroom; actually he would curse us for going into the room. He had white and quite hairless legs I think; we had glimpses of his shins if his trousers rode up as he sat. But of course we must have seen more than this; there were visits to the beach or the baths, remembered just because they were not common. These memories are unwholesome so I feel the muscles of my face reaching for a sneer of disgust. My brother says: he was seven or eight and taken – again remembered for its uniqueness – to the baths by him; my brother looked at him changing and he hit my brother, hit him and pushed him into another cubicle and said You dirty little bugger

And now he goes weekly to a Naturist Club which holds its winter meetings in Gresham Baths! Yes, a nudist! I don't know whether this is hilarious or disgusting; certainly it makes me angry.

2nd November

I am seven, eight and on this light summer's night I can't sleep; maybe I have been down two or three times already but I am not prepared for what happens. My father is there; he is dirty from work; in a rage he seizes me – this is the word I always use – he seizes me and all of one action pulls my pyjama trousers to the ground / has his belt off from his waist / pushes me face down onto the table / lashes my bottom with his leather belt.

My brother says my father put him to bed one night as my mother worked and Colin remembers this: violation, my father tearing off Colin's clothes and Colin's shame at standing naked before him; the impropriety of it all; rough hands pushing...

My other brother – my older brother – says he has no memories like these.

When I met my father a few years ago after a silence of many – when he told me he was a nudist! – he was so changed physically that I was shocked. In my childhood he was big, loud, vigorous even. When I saw him last he was shrunk, his eyes milky, his hair like grey wool and his face florid; he had a pencil-line moustache which makes me say seedy and he went to piss four or five times in the two hours I was there. Most of all he was deaf; we have all soft voices – my mother, my brothers and I – and I had to speak uncomfortably loudly and say things several times. I had planned to tell him he was a fucking cunt but could not imagine having to repeat myself.

23rd February

There are times when I become my father; in fact the truth of the last few years is that I have not known how to keep him out of my selves. There are times when – in a certain posture of the nerves – I am him. The worst of all – the most exhausting of all – is when I am also my own son. This is not mystical or pathological; it happens like this: say I am so cross with my son that I begin to loose the control that normally contains my anger and then – at a certain point – I hear and feel myself saying things that have a terrifying familiarity – of tone, if not of words themselves. I am moved by the demons that drove my father, and at one with the terror which the son feels. After this I am depressed, exhausted, wrung out.

13th March

Whatever it meant then, he must have been bright; he went to P— Grammar School in Burnley, but was taken out at fourteen and apprenticed as a painter. It's hard to tell what his childhood was like. When I saw him a few years ago he talked fondly of his 'Mum and Dad', words I think never to have heard from him; but in the time he lived with us I never saw anything but bitter, bitter resentment towards them. When I saw him a few years ago he said 'she was a grand old woman' and 'she was marvellously brave' and 'he was a lovely man...

lovely, mind. When I was twenty I described a friend of mine – Martin – as a lovely man and my father said don't come that bloody malarkey

But he was born in 1921; which means that war broke out when he was eighteen, and he then spent nearly four years in the desert. And it was here, at last, that he took his clothes off; before putting them on again for forty-odd years.

I can only think – from the photos and from bits gleaned here and there – that it was a mean childhood in Blackburn; and then, after the promise of translation through the Grammar School, the bitter chains of a hard apprenticeship. And then: life began in Libya. He spent four years – from 18 to 22; from 1939 to 1943 – in Libya.

13th December

When he told me a few years ago that he was a nudist, what he said was: 'I've a private yard here at the back I can strip off in summer' and later: 'o yes we used to strip off in the desert' and 'I spent the best part of four years bollock-naked in the desert' and later: 'I go to Gresham you know, a sun-club in the baths there'. He was sixty-eight when he told me this.

Four years naked in the desert? No no no; not this so-clothed man with his smells closed in around him; not this man whose emotions yet stood out like gnarls beneath those clothes; I refuse to let the sun find him out open and innocent, this prickly man.

But look, there is an explanation: the sun snaps off at six and beneath that fearfully starry sky it is cold, very cold; supper done, tired of endless cards, there is nothing but an early bed. This is a six-man tent but he shares it only with Bill; or Trevor. And to lie warm next to another body and – often gently, tenderly – to hold each other's penis, to pull gently; this frail eighteen year old sleeps open-mouthed and open-limbed like a child, a million million miles away from home

And the next day and the next day and all the nights are the same: Trevor, Ralph, Harry. O this is life. And if there is jealousy; and if a sergeant demands, and is rough and hurts, then this too is life, life far from all things mean.

It must have come to an end all that sun and sexuality; and what a cautery the order to strike camp and so home; and no blood in this campaign but so much seed spilled in the sand; and so much shame to bury later in cold little wives and homes. So much desperate, obliviating fucking to catch up on; so much rutting and up-ending for this is what it's really for; stick it here, in here, here

The desert love left no mark on him that we could see: Kenneth Williams was a bloody pooftah; we should beware the man in the corner shop who was a bloody bender; even, when I was seventeen, Jeremy Thorpe a bloody brown-knob; and of Martin: don't come that bloody malarkey

Or maybe there just simply was no desert-love; maybe he was simply horribly buggered by the sergeant and left to hate; or maybe not that, even: maybe just unloved.

7th May

St. Annes-on-Sea is nowhere to live a life. A man should rage and be foul there; a man should spoil it and foul it. It has no future and no past.

It is a perfect machine driven on a fuel of greed, smugness and deep ignorance.

I only ever heard it ask one question, as if trying on a dress: will this look alright?

There is of course no history to it. On sand, it was founded on money, idle money; it made nothing, it was built on sand to play in, a monster play-pen for the old rehearsing their achievements and their wealth.

It has no roots, and how could it, built as it is on sand? The sand blows away; they plant star-grass on the sand-dunes to stop the erosion. This is not generally viewed as an ironic act. And without irony some – clutching at the star-grass in the face of the north wind which blows all away – some 'locals' call themselves sand-grown 'uns . . .

Can you blame a town? Yes, you can; you can say you are lying, little town . . .

It was invented to be apart from history. It was just laid down on the top of that windy coast; it was settled with deliberation there to be what it is. Men were not pulled there by the attractions of metals; or drawn to harness or simply fish great waters. They went there to do what they did: to make piles of red brick on sand in which to sit and celebrate themselves.

Can you blame a town for this? Yes. I do.

The town was not there to do anything; it had nothing to overcome and nothing to become. The people who settled it had done with becoming; they had no use for history; this was just the point of coming here; here you could be away from all the meanness. This is the point: they were here, and with history elsewhere – in the backstreets of Bolton and Bury – there was nothing to transform.

There was a special need to do it like this with rude Blackpool only four miles up the road; and just fourteen miles behind, Preston like a gate with all of industrial Lancashire pressed up against it.

So here I was born into a town with no future and no past. It was birth into the day-care room of an old people's home; an affluent day-care room maybe, but beneath the deodorant spray and the daffodils the smells are the same: old flesh, old gums. (Or: birth into a perpetual January on one of those retirement coasts of Spain; or – this is worse – born on a perpetual cruise.)

There are worse births? Yes, but this was mine.

12th May

My family should never have strayed into this place; they were the decent poor, and in neither respect should they have been housed here. St Annes should have been better policed at the boundaries, and they should have turned him back up the road to Blackpool or Preston.

So here is this man returned from his war in Libya; married – of course – to a warm woman; and he takes on with his parents this huge joint mortgage in St Annes; it's a small house but it is improvement for them all, away from the terraces of Blackpool and Preston and Wakefield. In these places they teased us that we lived in Saint Arns. How is life in Saint (not snt) Arns then lads. And the old folk live upstairs, and the young – with their two small boys – are downstairs; and the old man dies, and there is all the mortgage to pay. Why not then go back to Blackpool, or Dewsbury?

Because it is going back.

14th May

I never heard my cousins or other relatives referred to but they were bloody this or they were bloody that bloody weedy Earnest – my mother's loved brother – that bloody oily Jimmy; your mother's bloody lot in Wakefield or my mother's bloody lot in Blackpool; Ernest-bloody-know-all; what's-her-name, that do-bloody-gooder in Clayton?

The point is: so how could he go back up the road to Blackpool? Or back over the hill to Dewsbury?

And something in the very air must have started to corrode my father. He was slowly eaten away – hollowed out – by the place.

But of course he was: there was no history to eat on; there was no nourishment in that place, and he had left forever the other places . . .

3rd September

He must have been – must be – the loneliest man I ever came across. I can only think of one man who might have been a friend as I would think of it, and this man – Ken – he beat up one night in a back street because he thought his girlfriend – his girlfriend – had slept with Ken.

He set a ladder – a decorator's ladder from an adjoining yard – against the back wall of Kath's yard. This was late, after throwing-out time. He watched and Ken came and sat drinking (coffee?) in the back room. He waited and when Ken left – Ken did leave – he somehow talked him into the back street and beat him; he punched him and then he held Ken's head by the ears and bashed it against the wall and then bashed it against his own van.

My father told me this quite carefully when I was eighteen and he showed me a dent in the wing of the van. He was then forty-three and I am now forty-three.

But he laid waste around him; already cut off, he cut off and cut off. The neighbours were bloody know-all bloody Jenkins, Harry bloody Rowlay; that smart bugger Sanderson, that bloody weed De Freitas. The

men he worked with were Buckethead or Little Zem; or, at best, bloody
Ken or plain Barker. And they were too clever by bloody half; or else
bloody idle or messy buggers ...

But there's a particular sound which goes with these epithets: it is something like tur – slightly softer than the breath spat out by air-brakes – so
it would be tur/that bloody weed Earnest or tur/Harry-bloody-Owen? tur/a
wet if ever there was ...

It comes through the teeth but it is bile come through the heart.

This tur was part of a complex and routine sneer, but a sneer so deep
you might – in the unlikely event that you'd been visiting us – you might
not even have seen it on the surface; you might even have thought that
it was: banter. We in the family knew what it was and – like those who
live by the volcano hear as a privilege its harmonic tremor – we knew
what depths it came from and we mostly knew how to – leave our homes?
go under tables? – read its power. (Actually I never did, really, learn to
read the signal; or, rather, never learned to resist it. I used to walk up
the cinder track even when the geysers were hissing and spitting.)

This tur is standard to us: I have it, my brothers have it and even my
mother – though clearly by a different process – has it, though none,
I think, can use it as I do. I can all but kill at twenty paces with it.

We're mostly good around each other; but a single, unguarded tur is
bane.

19th October

My mother?

Many years later my therapist said to me: you want to bury an axe in
your mother's cunt. This was shocking – I mean he shouldn't have said
it – but it was also untrue. Let's get this straight once and for all.

I think my therapist had a problem with his own mother; I think
that he wanted to bury his axe so. But these were different axes and
different cunts. I wanted to bury an axe in a cunt, but the cunt was my
father.

My mother: is about seventy-eight as she reads this. She was born in
Dewsbury in 1920. Her father – my grandfather – was strapping although
bantam; he lifted a half-hundredweight of potatoes on each shoulder
though he was no more than five feet six. He pushed tunes – 'Bread of
heaven' and the like – with a barrelled tongue through his teeth like a
hissing kettle; he sang songs like 'Mockingbird Hill' with only a doy-doy-
doy and a dee thus: dee-dee-doy-doy-doy-doy-doy-doy-doy-dee-dee-doy.
He lifted a cheek to fart very fruitily, (though in no way sought to witness
it). He smelled of mustard and wintergreen and pigs.

He kept pigs, my grandad. His father and then he ran a horse and cart
with vegetable produce; they prospered and bought land, many acres

including a small early eighteenth-century farmhouse which they turned to work with horses, cows, pigs and chickens. My grandad – Ewart was his name – Ewart kept on with the pigs till I was about twelve, though the buildings were falling about them.

He owned at one time: eighty-nine acres (of which forty-six were to become building plots); a whole terrace of eight stone houses; fourteen cows, three horses, sixty pigs, countless chickens. You see, this was a man of substance.

Also, he stopped only months before he died at ninety-one going to the wholesale market at Dewsbury twice a week at five-thirty in the morning to buy a bag or two of carrots or peas, potatoes; and then taking the stuff round marked up for small pence to the old regulars.

He hated through his life the Co-operative Society. He was a Whig. He talked of the 'Pakis' who came in numbers to staff the wool industry in the fifties and sixties but I think – I think – it was a fairly unloaded abbreviation. I think so.

The point is: here was a real freemason, one of nature if not society's masons.

At the time of the disclosures about nudism, I asked my father did he think my mother could have been abused – sexually abused – by her father. I was in therapy at the time. He didn't answer, perhaps didn't hear my question.

15th October

Ewart's greatest excitement was homosexuality: 'ah'd geld 'em; an o-ffence before the good Lord; lahk she-ep wi' two hee'ads'.

'My God my Father while I stray' Whatever did that mean?

The point is this: I have the feeling that this old man was the last whole man – man of mirth and industry – in our family. Yes, yes: he was an old sod, a tory, a powerful patrician; a Churchillian, a petty bourgeois; a sort of bully; an intolerant, ignorant man; an old fart even. But the point is: here was a natural freemason

My father hated the history which met in Ewart: industry, capital, chapel; and the confidence this gave him to be beholden to no man. And his popularity: in the leafy peninsular suburb that Drayton then was to Dewsbury they called him – with fond irony which he well liked – the squire. My father hated his strong views which were all but cathedral.

But most of all – it comes to me now – my father must have hated the normalness of that family; its harmony, the love there was, the terrible exclusiveness of that sort of family tur/they're bloody medieval! Squire bloody Ewart and his poor bloody yokels And that bloody wet Earnest! Earnest! bloody Earnest! Tur!

30th June

I was looking at the old photos the other day. My favourite picture of the old man is the favourite one still on my mother's wall: an old man of seventy-six or so with a round old face riven with mirth, eyes a merry fury; his head just atilt back and a worsted cap tilted on the back of that. His mouth is slightly open – an oval on the point of saying something – in the middle of a chin rough with two days' white stubble. Just before the photo disappears at the bottom there is a glimpse of collarless shirt.

When you look at the photos you see at a glance what excited my father's hatred: at the centre of this family are Earnest and Annie clearly loved. Oh, they are loved in the quality of the stitch that binds their collars, their knickers; they are for that matter loved in the ninety-year-old buff cardboard picture frames on which persists in gilt: 'Harold Yewdall, Family Photographer, 4 Royal Parade, Harrogate.' (I mean only that love is sometimes swelled by money); but mostly: I swear you can tell they were loved in the eyes and the turn of the mouth. Even in the grim Sunday School group photographs, the brylcreem and plaits and severe collars and all: these only just stop the loved ones breaking through. It is this: these photographs quote from – these photographs intend – a whole world of relationships around these children.

Oh but look at the few pictures of my father's childhood: they are not organised by the relationship of their subject to anything living: he is merely there, leaning against a wall, all but of the wall. He is dead already; the only points are the small dead carbons of his eyes. The rest – with his body in it – is an undifferentiated field of greys. And to be sure, the stuff of the scene is poor: the socks, the jumper, the wall, the quality of the photograph. Do you see?

Or: this picture of him in his uniform in Libya in 1942 standing with three others (Trevor? Harry? Ken?): here is a man whom love has never touched.

I can see why he set about my mother's family in the way he did. It was – like a good Victorian family – a conservative little society in itself. So he set about my mother's family because it was good and whole; it was – like all families that work – a conservative little society; it regulated . . .

Thinking about my family makes me think about 'class'. I don't understand the gradations of class well enough – nor the method of history needed – to know how my mother's family were located socially. They had some money – all the acres and so on – but their position is better seen in the sombre light falls through the chapel window: they had the assumption goes with high Wesleyan Methodism.

5th August

There was a life to this chapel continuous with the Hebrons. At ten –
10! – my mother played the piano for Sunday School and Earnest, two
years her elder, was (the) Chapel organist! There was Men's Fellowship,
Wives meeting, Missionary Society, Bible Study Circle, Prayer meeting,
Christian Endeavour … Youth Fellowship: so on and so on, a dense grid
of lodges in the heavy masonry of the chapel.

When we visited there as children in the 1950s and early 60s, there
would always be – on what my grandfather had sold to the chapel – a
cricket-match: Drayton Meths, redoubtable whether 'A' or 'B', watched
on Saturday afternoon (despite Dewsbury Athletic and Leeds United) by
thirty, maybe sometimes fifty people. And: served plated teas from C.C.C.'s
own pavilion, a shed of sorts but a dedicated pavilion for all that.

I don't know where God figured in all that.

But the point is this: my mother and my mother's family were deeply
involved in Drayton, in the chapel. So: the house was untidy, dirty even;
so was my grandfather and my grandmother. Actually very untidy and
really quite dirty. Of 'high culture' they had none. But the chapel bestowed
on them an authority and a role which they claimed as rightly due status.

And there were four or five old aunts – sisters to my grandfather. They
and their houses smelled of the stale propriety of life in the shadow of
the chapel. Their antimacassars, their carriage-clocks and whiskers; their
dark front-rooms and their [do-we-have-to-eat-this-mum-yes-you-do-and-
don't-let-me-hear-another-word-out-of-you] potted-meat sandwiches: these
seemed of the provenance of the chapel.

These are impressions; but I see as I assemble them now in this haphazard
way – I feel the thrill of – my father's hostility to it all. It was like some
rural idyll in a way; all in its place and all of a piece; and all vulnerable.

Now do you begin to see?

It is beginning to come clear, isn't it, the tattoo to which my father
marched in this particular war of the roses? In the streets of East
Lancashire, my father's family measured its days in bobbins, its nights in
ales and its earnings in rent. Now only – what? Twenty-five? Thirty-five?
– miles away in the West Riding of Yorkshire, my mother's family was
known in swine, in hymns and in acres.

These are similar folk, mind.

What did my father make of – think of – marriage?

Returned from Lybia to Marston Moor where my mother had been
drafted as a cook, how could he not see in this woman – this beautiful,
innocent woman serving the cabbage on Marston Moor! – how could he fail
to see his very escape from life to date? He is no fool, this man: here is
a woman of transparent but quiet breeding such that she cares to be embarrassed – though she serves 3600 meals every day – when he teases her.

15th February

What he did not see – how could he know it in himself? – was that the cost of getting her was – eventually – her destruction. The simple goodness would have to be smashed.

What structure of experience is at work here? I mean when I wrote that?

I only know its reality because I have done it myself; do it myself, again and again. I destroy good things. 'You want something until you get it', said Sarah.

From the position of your fracture; from your fracture, how can you see beauty, wholeness and not want to see it as perverse? Deviant? Contrived? Privileged?

So I am at war with myself, with the father in me.

But what is the point in all this display? It's this: I'm not interested in evoking a particular stratum of life in suburban Dewsbury in the 20s/30s/40s/50s and so on as a historical project; I'm resolutely not interested in it as history as such. I am interested only in understanding the psychological history of my parents; my father in particular. And this so that I can understand something of my history. This is wank of course.

20th October

'History is what hurts . . .'. Who wrote that?

Of course, I understand that I can only get to my history through these histories, through events constructed – made accessible – through historical moments and the colours with which historians paint them. But my intention here is not historical, if to be historical is to seek to catch a character rather than to live for a moment in an evocation of it.

6th August

It occurs to me that after a certain age I would lie to my father as a matter of biological reflex; I lied in many ways to save my life.

There must have been, early on, some mechanism for encouraging truthfulness; but after a certain point it must have failed. I even wonder whether I ever had a truth of fact: how many apples are there in the bowl? seven, or three or seventy-three but – certainly – not the number You see dad.

So now my truth is falling apart . . . when did that begin?

28th November

'Looking back my relationship with the truth was always. . . .'

. . . accounts stitched together for survival

But when I start to talk of truth falling apart I realise that I started telling 'untruths' not long after my first breath. . . . . . .

This may be true ... This loose, this casual relationship with the truth.

In Golding's The Spire, there is a moment when the Archbishop realises with a full – as it were a complete horror – that his bishop had never learned to pray; he never learned to do what the church calls prayer. And I have been thinking recently that I never learned what a fact was; I never learned what is the truth. Anyway lying is much more fun, is creative.

I would lie to my father as a matter of biological reflex. I could not not lie.

19th October

I could never buy Tim's explanation of me; all that mother's cunt and father's prick stuff: you'd like to take a cleaver, a big meat-cleaver to your mother's cunt you would well, no, I wouldn't.

I have no interest in facts. I can't do with explanations of any sort; never could. I've always had to re-invent knowledge, cos I won't believe other people's narratives ... unless they're really good narratives; which is why I have to burn myself before I know that fire burns ...?

18th September

I was bound by so many rules; it seemed it was all rules. There were the rules of my damaged family, which of course were not so visible; the rules of the neighbours which my mother feared and whispered about; the rules of the fucking methodist church, and of school. The whole thing, the central principle, was containment, no growth, conservatism ...

I've thought hard about this, and I think the whole thing

I know I say you must understand that my father was so damaged too but you must excuse me if I don't understand it. I can't hold my pain and his pain together in the same account; my pain hurts me, not him.

16th February

Paint on his overalls was always the splash of someone else's brush.

18th September

Without history there can be no future: the very meaning of conservatism.

It is not that there is too much money in St Annes. Of course, there is too much idle money there

It is held together by a coalition of deep greed, smugness and ...

There are mile after mile of neat houses ...

And there are, of course, two sides to the tracks; but literally, the railway roughly divides an affluent from a less affluent. On the coastal side of the railway the houses are bigger, many of them very big, but hardly a one touched by thoughtful design. The older ones were built mostly . . .

A town erected with a high wall and admission fee far away from the rudeness of Blackburn and Manchester and Bury; and Blackpool.

But you have to understand that my father was so damaged too. His father – the story goes – was a ne'er do well; and gassed in the war; and seldom worked, maybe even drank. And his mother worked severely. I suppose you have to understand that, to understand anything of the rest.

3rd January

I don't know why I never – really – loved other men.

* * *

We were on our third pint – Frank seemed to down the first two with some speed, and I had the feeling that he kept my glass full so that I would continue to read. Much of his diary was turgid. I could do nothing with it.

– I must go soon.

– You'll write it? Do something with it? Interview me? Let me see a draft?

I was disgusted by his enthusiasm.

He insisted that I took the diaries with me when I refused the fourth pint. Inside the cover of the first he wrote his phone number.

I phoned him a few weeks later, said I couldn't make the diaries into a story; I was a researcher – albeit a life-historian – not a writer.

I told him they might speak for themselves – but that they needed ruthless editing.

– Do it, he said.

So how d'you like this, 'Frank'?

Part 2

Doing life story research

Part 1 of this book has presented you with four life stories. These narratives capture specific narrative styles and forms; position the narrator and writer in various ways; draw upon contrasting philosophical, theoretical and methodological concerns; and engage with four overlapping but discrete areas of social scientific enquiry. In Part 2 of this book, we identify some methodological considerations of researching life stories. Chapter 5 examines four *methodological persuasions* that gave rise to the four stories presented in this text. The focus here is on how we approach our subject matter, our stories and our narrators, participants or narrative subjects. In Chapter 6, we consider some general concerns associated with method or the *doing of life story research*. Each of the writers of the four life stories considers issues of method including access, ethics, how we each wrote our life stories and our relationship with our informants. This is a substantial chapter and aims to demystify the doings of researching life stories. Chapter 7 completes our engagement with method/ology by exploring the ways in which methods are always directed by the assumptions of knowledge held by researchers. Here we expose some of the ways in which the four life stories are the products of particular *epistemological locations*.

Chapter 5

Approaching
Methodology in life story research

Introduction

In writing the life stories of this book, the positions we have adopted –
in this case, in relation to methodology – are somewhat contrived (in the
best pedagogical sense). We are aware that the methodological landscape
that we paint below, as well as our appearance on this scene, is somewhat too clear and transparent to be true. We know that researchers
adopt a whole host of overlapping and mutually inclusive methodological positions when they enact life story research. However, for the
sake of clarity, we have each deliberately assumed a distinct – perhaps
exclusive – methodological position in the writing of our stories in order
to demystify method/ology in researching life stories:

- Chapter 1 – *Gerry O'Toole: A design for life* – reflects a non-participatory ethnographic approach undertaken by Dan Goodley;
- Chapter 2 – *'I'd never met a vegetarian, never mind a lesbian':
  Colleen's story* – is the product of an emancipatory interview approach
  adopted by Rebecca Lawthom;
- Chapter 3 – *The death story of David Hope* – reflects a participatory ethnographic approach utilised by Michele Moore;
- Chapter 4 – *Frank* – is Peter Clough's piece of non-participatory
  fiction.

This chapter allows us to explore our chosen methodologies. A number
of shared concerns emerge. First, we are discussing methodology, not
method. The former refers to the persuasions from which our stories
emerge, the latter to the doings of research (considered in the next chapter).
Second, methodologies denote different levels of participation on the
part of the participant/informant/narrator or narrative subject in the doing
of life story research. Third, the authority of the researcher will change
according to the methodology. Fourth, methodology enacts an approach

to research that combines a commitment to our participants and the generation of theory, alongside an attention to narrative qualities of plot, characterisation and readability.

A non-participatory ethnographic approach –
Dan Goodley

Gerry O'Toole's story is the product of a particular methodological approach (ethnography) and mode of research production (non-participatory). My voice, as the writer of the story, dominates. Events and occasions from a number of characters enter the fray. Gerry's 'first-hand account' permeates the story, shaping its structure and offering narration. More than this, there should be a sense of a particular viewpoint being made by the story. But from what position in terms of methodology does this story emerge? In this section, we turn to the role of non-participatory uses of the ethnography in the bringing together of material and the writing of life stories.

Introducing ethnography

Ethnography is an approach to research that involves immersion within, and investigation of, a culture or social world. Broadly speaking, researchers enter a given culture and draw upon a variety of methods in order to make sense of public and private, overt and elusive cultural meanings. Hence, ethnography can be conceived as a methodological persuasion: a guiding approach to research, in which the researcher attends to the rich generation of meanings by social actors, as a consequence of various structures and decisions made by individuals. As Vidich and Lyman (2000) point out – *ethnos* is a Greek term denoting a people, a race or cultural group that is described (*graphic*). However, this approach involves moving far beyond description to explanation.

Historically, ethnography is rooted in descriptive anthropology (Tedlock, 2001; Vidich and Lyman, 2000). The renowned modern anthropologist Malinowski (1922) argued that the role of the ethnographer was 'to attempt to grasp the native's point of view, their relation to life and to realise their vision of their world' (cited in Edgerton, 1984b, p. 498). Consequently, there are clearly the remnants of a colonialist past in this view of ethnography, with the omnipotent Western visionary attempting to make sense of the unknown, dark, hidden culture of the 'native'. However, what remains in a hopefully more egalitarian postmodern research landscape is the conceptualisation of ethnographic research as *making the strange familiar*. This involves getting to know people by being there, alongside them, during ordinary days, to try to capture their experiences at first hand. Corbett (1998) describes ethnography as an immersion within the deep culture of a social group that attempts to find hidden treasures and submerged dangers. In principle, ethnography is committed to representing the actions of the relatively unknown, perhaps oppressed and ignored, insiders of a given social group. Ethnography has been used in studies that have tried to ground their analyses in everyday realities of a variety of social groupings whose agendas and meanings have been under-represented in theoretical, practical and policy debates (see Lincoln and Guba 1985; Erlandson *et al.*, 1993).

While there is a clear vision of ethnography as making sense of the culture of the 'other', the use of ethnography in practical and policy-making contexts *by practitioners* – particularly in educational, health and social care settings – has given rise to a different conceptualisation of ethnography. Here, the aims are *to render the familiar strange*. Many readers of this book may well be interested in using ethnography and life story to make sense of the professional and personal contexts that they inhabit on a daily basis. Indeed, for many practitioner-researchers, classic ethnographic texts fail to resonate with their aims to understand further (and change for the better) the very cultures that they are, and perhaps for a while have been, immersed within. Ethnographic research can be embraced as a methodology that aims *to look again at the cultures we may feel we already know so well*. In this sense, ethnography is about turning a critical eye onto practices, dynamics, policies and meaning-making within familiar cultures. It means turning social contexts into research contexts: the latter associated inevitably with the participant-turned-researcher examining the social context anew through the perspective of a critical enquirer. While you might well want to take on the ethnographic challenge of examining some context of which you know little, you may also take on an ethnographic stance in relation to a well-known context.

Both of these takes on the aims of ethnography highlight one over-arching concern. When researchers become part of the cultures that they describe, then researcher and participants interact together to produce the data (Charmaz, 1995). Even when a covert approach to participation is adopted – and there are clearly ethical issues that we need to explore – the researcher's perspective on the actions of participants forms a dialogue from which understandings emerge. Meanwhile, overt participant observation in a field of enquiry – where the researcher clearly states their reasons for involvement in the field and their research aims – will, of course, alert participants to the possibilities that their conduct is being watched. Turning social contexts into research contexts raises more general considerations about the nature of 'truth' in research and brings with it a variety of troubling but often rewarding debates.

The ethnographic study of people with learning difficulties

Perhaps the first issue to consider when we are looking at how ethnographers go about doing their research is to recognise that this approach digresses markedly from the classic view of the dispassionate, distanced, objective scientific observer. In many ways, ethnography is about immersing oneself within a culture of investigation, drawing upon a variety of methods and analyses in order to tap into that culture:

> Wherever it has been adopted, a key assumption has been that by entering into a close and relatively prolonged interaction with people (one's own or other) in their everyday lives, ethnographers can better understand the beliefs, motivations, and behaviours of their subjects than they can be using any other approach.
>
> (Tedlock, 2001, p. 456)

According to Spradley (1979), ethnographic study aims to observe behaviour, but goes beyond it to enquire about the meaning of behaviour. The artefacts and natural objects of a culture are described, but also considered in terms of the meanings that people assign to these objects. Moreover, emotional states are observed and recorded, but the ethnographer goes beyond these states to discover the meaning of fear, anxiety, anger and other feelings to cultural members. This all sounds rather grand and abstract, wouldn't you say? If we return to Gerry O'Toole's story, the writer of this life story had one key ethnographic research question that he wanted to answer:

> *What can one life story tell us about the social and cultural worlds inhabited by people with learning difficulties?*

The term 'learning difficulties' is used in this chapter to describe people who have been labelled at some point in their lives as requiring specialist 'mental handicap services' (Walmsley, 1993, p. 46). This term is chosen instead of other synonyms such as 'mental handicap', 'mental impairment' or 'learning disabilities', because it is the term preferred by many in the self-advocacy movement. As one self-advocate puts it: 'If you put "people with learning difficulties" then they know that people want to learn and to be taught how to do things' (quoted in Sutcliffe and Simons 1993, p. 23). Moreover, as we shall see later in Part 3 of this book, it is suggested that the very phenomenon of 'learning difficulties' is constructed by institutional practices:

> What should concern us is the mystifying fact that so many social scientists ... do not regard mental retardation [*sic*] as a social and

cultural phenomenon. I say mystifying, because nothing in the prob-
abilistic world of social scientific reality is more certain than the
assertion that mental retardation [*sic*] is a socio-cultural problem
through and through.

(Dingham, 1968, p. 76)

Ethnography has a long history in the field of learning difficulties (e.g.
Braginsky and Braginsky, 1971; Edgerton, 1967, 1976, 1984a, 1984b;
Edgerton and Bercovici, 1976; Mercer, 1973; Angrosino, 1994; Goodley,
2000). Crucially, following Whitemore *et al.* (1986), ethnographic studies
of the cultures of people with learning difficulties have illuminated the
socio-political, professionalised and policy-led discourses which have
disabled people so labelled. The narrative in Chapter 1 aims to add in a
very modest way to this tradition: to demonstrate how disability discourses
and practices of exclusion are experienced by people with learning difficulties. In particular, the life story reflects upon my (Dan) involvement
(for the past seven years) with people with the label of learning difficulties and their aims to promote alternative disability cultures to the ones
that they are often forced into (see also Goodley, 2000).

Non-participatory approaches to research

While Chapter 1 is a reflection of ethnography as methodology, the mode
of research production is inherently non-participatory. In contrast to the
stories in Chapters 2 and 3, the emphasis in Gerry O'Toole's narrative is
on the researcher's ownership of the data collection and narrative construction. As we shall see in the next chapter, the stories, anecdotes, conver-
sational exchanges and events that form O'Toole's life story are the product
of my intensive involvement with/in specific cultures of a small number
of people with learning difficulties.

  This raises a number of methodological debates, particularly when
research aims to capture the voices and experiences of people whose
agendas are often ignored by researchers. The stance here is to make use
of a collection of narratives that allow some insight into the specific and
localised life worlds or discursive spaces and material conditions of a small
number of people. While the mode is non-participatory – the researcher
works from the position of final and perhaps constant ownership of raw
material – the use of life story aims to emphasise the significance of a
number of experiences of people with learning difficulties. In this sense,
while our characters have no hand in the writing of their own stories, an
ethnographic stance encourages the writer/researcher to try to authentically capture their stories in meaningful and accountable ways. Gerry's
story is an attempt to authentically demonstrate not only the oppression
but also resistance of people with the label of learning difficulties. We

return to these issues in the next chapter but for now it would make sense to unpick some key elements of this approach in relation to Gerry O'Toole's narrative:

- The ethnographer/researcher/writer owns the writing of the story.
- Data collected by the ethnographer are used to inform the story.
- No member of the culture under investigation is permitted decision-making in the putting together of the story.
- With ownership of the story come issues of accountability and intention – which the writer would do well to address.
- In being non-participatory, the writer's own engagement with knowledge generation and the applications of research often dictate the writing process.
- The writer's own subjectivity must be interrogated in order to tease out some of the reasoning behind the writing of the story.

An emancipatory interview approach – Rebecca Lawthom

Colleen's story is a collaborative project between the interviewer and interviewee. The emancipatory framework from which this account is produced allows the interviewee – or co-researcher – to shape the story, have full editorial control and present a first-person narrative. Clearly, in all interview techniques, there is an element of participation, namely, the interviewee is exhorted to tell/account for or explain how s/he feels or acts or behaves. In emancipatory research, the focus is not only on full participation but ownership of the narrative. A key element of this approach is the idea of emancipation, doing research ethically so the interviewee might usefully gain something from the production. In all forms of research, the researcher always gains from the collection of data, while the researched generally stands to gain far less from the research interaction. Emancipatory research in its purest form has roots in action research paradigms (Duffy and Wong, 1996; Heller *et al.*, 1984; Reason, 1988, 1994; Kagan, 2002) and alliances with feminist research methodologies and disability studies.

An emancipatory framework

What kind of paradigmatic understanding do we need to undertake emancipatory research? Many forms of research undertaken are conceptualised, designed, executed and analysed with participants playing a role primarily in the execution of the design. Within an emancipatory framework, the researched may have a voice within all stages of the research process. This results in greater involvement and interest and can result in useful outcomes for the participant. The voice of the researched is given a much more equal weighting in the research process.

In order to locate emancipatory understandings, we should explore the feminist influence. Feminist theory has played a huge role in contextualising research with and for women. Feminist methodology has placed much emphasis upon the role of the researcher at all stages in the research and suggests a transparent approach to positioning the researcher in relation to the research frame.

> Scientists firmly believe that as long as they are not conscious of any bias or political agenda, they are neutral and objective, when in fact they are only unconscious.
>
> (Namenwirth, 1989, p. 29)

Whilst feminism can be a standpoint, it is rather difficult to define succinctly. Russell (1996, p. 248) suggests that feminism is a perspective, based on a set of values, which are used to inform all aspects of practice. As she says:

> (feminism is) a way of construing the world, our experiences and the possibilities which we see for the future. It is a perspective which defies rigidity, while genuinely affording value to women's experience as of central importance and worth. ... Feminism is a way of seeing the world which works towards helping women take an equal place in society ...

Humm (1992) sums up the core of feminism slightly differently, stressing the political dimension:

> Feminism is a social force ... (which) depends on the understanding that, in all societies which divide the sexes in differing cultural, economic or political spheres, women are less valued than men. Feminism also depends on the premise that women can consciously and collectively change their social place. ... (It is) a belief in sexual equality combined with a commitment to eradicate sexist domination and to transform society.
>
> (Humm, 1992, p. 1)

Feminist definitions and critiques are far from uniform. Harding (1986) makes a now classic distinction between three different kinds of approaches: feminist empiricist, feminist standpoint and feminist postmodernist. However, whichever approach one takes, a fundamental link is the relationship between the personal and the political. We will return to this in Chapter 7.

Emancipation and voice

Within the feminist arena, there have been critiques around representation and voice concerning authority. Whose voice is being heard and who is talking or speaking for whom? (Wilkinson and Kitzinger, 1995). It is possible to engage in feminist research methods both without being a feminist (the toolbox approach to methods rather than methodology), and without being emancipatory. To address this latter point, we can explore paradigms which have actively explored emancipatory approaches such as disability studies (Oliver, 1996) and community psychology (Duffy and Wong, 1996). Whilst the paradigm Colleen's narrative emerges from is emancipatory, this process was not labelled as such for Colleen. Being transparent about the process, I talked in terms of dialogue and interpretation. As Larson (1997, p. 459) notes,

> When researchers share their ways of seeing, understanding and interpreting life events with story-givers, they surface the fissures between their own life worlds and those of the people they portray.

Dialogue allows the meanings of self in relation to others and community to be negotiated (Witherell and Noddings, 1991). So the narrative involves not only the story being told but the active engagement with the audience. This audience design occurred both within the actual storytelling episode as Colleen becomes aware of herself in relation to the co-researcher, 'I sound like a right old crock', and beyond the immediate episode to the wider audience. In terms of the latter, Collen invokes an audience 'when will people realise that women are doing a good job etc.?' At these key times, the design of the audience is undoubtedly considered as a coherent story is being told. Emancipatory approaches to life story research can be analysed using Ochs and Capps's (2001) narrative dimensions. The dimension 'tellership' is important when exploring the nature of the relationship and the control/power exercised by the co-teller/interviewee. Goffman's (1959) 'animators' are tellers who range from recounting stories to active telling in conjunction with others. Ochs and Jacoby (1997) note that the role of the teller is distinct from that of the author. It is possible for the author (while contributing little content to the story) to shape the story with non-verbal behaviour and verbal cues of interests. Moreover, 'the authorial shaping of a storyline is not the same as physically telling a story' (Ochs and Capps, 2001, p. 24). The shaping of the tale, the editing of the story and the analysis of the narration were done with Colleen. We shall return to many of the issues during analysis and interpretation, but let us summarise some of the points being addressed here.

- Whilst the writer has the final authority regarding the story, the process is guided and shaped by Colleen.

- Both the story-giver and the author of the story are women, friends and feminists in orientation.
- The writer's political and theoretical orientations have steered or shaped the course of the research (even if only unconsciously).
- Only data gathered for the purposes of the life story exercise are used in the weaving of the story and the final product.
- The relationship history outside of the story must have played a role in the selection of the story-giver and the latter's presentation of the narrative.
- An emancipatory framework is used in a processual way rather than presuming that analysis can enlighten the story-giver.

A participatory ethnography – Michele Moore

Methodologies that emerge out of circumstances

In these circumstances there was no time to make formal decisions about appropriate research methodology. I had entered the situation with no explicit research brief. I went to meet David knowing the ethnographic journey would inevitably offer rich theoretical insights for the social model of disability, and knew that engagement with his story would provide unique empirical evidence on the experience of living with spinal cord injury. But I did not premeditate an approach to my engagement with his life or foresee a strategy for 'collecting data'. I did not know how best to proceed and could not tidy emotionality out of the process.

There are principles which over the years I have struggled to make shape my research practice. I was guided by the desire to hold on to personally valued principles, to take the most open and honest and collaborative approach possible to finding out about his experience, and to seek to effect positive social change as part of the process. I knew my engagement would produce some sort of research account and that this would be problematic. I had written extensively about, and was familiar with, the difficulties of the ways in which real life intersects with methodological aspirations and practices (Moore et al., 1998; Moore 2000). But I had not faced the methodological tensions that were to surface in this project. I had not known the extent to which I would conduct 'life story research' and I had not known that one possible outcome of the research could be the prompting of a man to take his own life. I had a strong personal commitment to the project of finding out David's story but no idea of the personal – and collective – pain and fear, or determination of events, that the project would bring.

'Methodology in life story research', for this project, was characterised by struggle, uncertainty and multiple confusions. It can be argued that the methodological approach was heavily implicated in David's death.

I cannot decide who killed David Hope but I came to understand that methodological orientation in the job of researching life stories had to be very critically interrogated. Looking back, it is possible to recognise some essential ingredients of a formal methodological approach. Since the emergence of 'participatory' and 'emancipatory' frameworks as structural frameworks for disability research in the early 1990s I had been convinced that the only sensible starting point for advancing an understanding of disability matters is one of consultation. The premise of consultation was central to the way in which I approached David's story. I had learned from disabled people of the extent to which much of the research that goes on in the name of improving the quality of disabled people's lives has been done about them, without them and subsequently been irrelevant and a waste of time (Oliver, 1987, 1996).

Participation in relationships

Therefore from the outset I made considerable efforts in my engagement with David to make sure that he decided the focus of our dialogue and to ensure his meaningful participation in all matters relating to the way I built up his story, the sense I was making of it and the way it would be told. David established the discursive practices through which his story was revealed. He refused to be interviewed in any sense. He dismissed the possibility of tape-recording out of hand and obstinately monitored the notes I took. He was censorious of my engagement with others who were connected with his story. He had clear ideas about dissemination of his story but insisted that once he was dead, if his wishes were at odds with his mother's then hers should take precedence. Questions concerning methodological tools are necessarily subordinated alongside commitment to a premise of consultation. The whole principle of consultation is, of course, horribly contorted now that he is dead. This problem will be returned to later in the book.

The other chief ingredient of the methodological approach I took to finding out and communicating David's story, was defined by the core theoretical position which my work promotes, namely that disability is the product of social organisation and not personal limitation (UPIAS, 1976; Oliver, 1990). This committed me to researching David's story in an open and transparent way and to making sure the project turned on his perspectives and experience. The difficulties that prevented me from telling David's story in particular ways are entangled with the social origins of oppression and so the theoretical and methodological drivers in this work were very actively fused. All in all, the development of an apposite methodological approach to the researching of David's story proved a fraught and uncomfortable business.

Thus the discourse of struggle fundamentally shaped the methodological and theoretical approach I took to researching David's story.

Comparatively speaking, the tensions which came together in this project were – and continue to be – enormously challenging. The question of how to maximise the impact of David's story on policies and practices which shape the lives of disabled people is fraught with difficulty because the two principal characters in the story, David and his mother, had conflicting views on its destiny.

David wanted his story told so that life-threatening experiences faced by other disabled people are rendered more visible. Sheila asked not to be involved in telling the story. When David was dying she received anonymous hate mail. She lives every day with the pain of David's story whereas he chose death to escape the pain of the story. My original commitments were to his priorities, but David confused these with clashing positions – requesting both that his story should be told, and that this mother should be looked after, following his death. Polarity in his thinking put the methodological direction of the project against the central proposition of the emancipatory research paradigm. It has always been difficult to know what to do with the story. Some of the images in David's story create barriers to the dismantling of oppression for disabled people and for their care-givers. The ethical issues are deeply disturbing and will necessarily have to be revisited throughout the book.

The troubling nature of participation

Frequently I found myself having to creatively and flexibly negotiate difficult and sensitive boundaries in the researching and telling of David's story. Usually this has made my own voice too dominant and there has been the temptation to be judgemental and dogmatic. At the time of writing I feel very much at odds with David's expressed views on the protection of his mother which, put in the broader picture, seem to me an act of collusion in the oppression of disabled people and their families. Professionals in the story may wish to reconstruct aspects of their interventions. Casting David's experience as life story research offers some potential for disentangling resistive tensions, but the task is disturbing. The methodological approach I took demanded a critical purchase that at the time was unattainable and in retrospect has been inadequate.

David's story exposes a major question for me concerning the way in which we enhance professional and academic interventions in disabled people's lives through the telling of life stories like his. I had hoped that David's story would raise his voice and raise his issues, but his absence from its authorship is problematic. Ultimately, the extent to which David has been consulted in the researching and telling of his story has been obstructed by his death. The measure of the project's emancipatory prowess depends partly on the value one places on his death. But partly too on what difference the telling of his story can make. I wanted to tell David's story to advance an agenda for drawing up disabled people's futures on their own terms, but the premise of consultation which is commensurate with this agenda is thrown into disrepute by his death.

A non-participatory fiction – Peter Clough

'Frank' is a fictional narrative which arises – primarily – from Clough's desire to portray the complicated personal tangles and weaves which so often underlie various (more public) events in the professional lives of teachers. For purposes of distinguishing the analytical approaches of the four stories, we have introduced *Frank* as characterised by non-participatory and fictional methods of enquiry into the broadly similar phenomena which each story addresses. But it will be clear from reading the three previous sections of this chapter that as a composition *Frank* sits uneasily across the distinctions we have made, perhaps most importantly because it makes no claim to rest on data as conventionally understood. So although there may be considerable topical and formal similarities between the four stories, the distinct purpose of including *Frank* in this collection is to raise questions about the role of the author in the creation of stories (social scientific or literary) and about the nature of the data which are so created. How and where do ethnographic and literary composition segue into each other?

Composite narratives

As a composition, *Frank* is at its simplest one of a number of attempts (see Clough, 2002) to communicate research insights in a more direct, a more persuasive manner than is normally permitted by traditions of report. It doesn't exactly set aside important notions of validity and reliability and so on, but it assumes that readers attend primarily to writing as it 'speaks to' their experience, and that analysis is part of a later moment of explanation. So stories like *Frank* can be said to 'work' if readers are moved to say somehow: 'Yes, *that's* what it's like . . .' And the character Frank is a fiction, in so far as no such character ever had three-dimensional form, and the story might well have been prefaced with 'Any resemblance to actual characters living or dead is purely accidental . . .' This is, of course, one of the greatest lies ever told by writers (or their publishers), for a fictional character depends for its plausibility on the borrowings from 'real life' which their authors make (and, as Joan Didion (1968, p. xiv) says, 'Writers are always selling somebody out.', And Frank is indeed assembled from my own experience (as a teacher, researcher and writer) of people like him (or like parts of him). There are even – though I cannot show you the evidence – whole phrases and sentences taken from conversation and interviews with people whom I've met or worked with. But at the end of the day, Frank is all of a 'symbolic equivalent' (Yalom, 1991), a 'poetic composite' (Richardson, 1994) or a 'stereotype' (Booth and Booth, 1998).

Fiction and analysis

Frank is a work of fiction, if to write fiction is to say this is how I see the world; I believe these characters and events to be true of human experience; I believe – short of wishing to be didactic – that there is something to be learned from this story. Where *Frank* differs from *Gerry* and *Colleen* and *David*, however, is that the evidence for his existence will not be found outside of some posture of the nerves which allows you as reader to say 'Yes, that's what it's like . . .' You will not, therefore, *validate* the story with reference to its instruments and the (accessible) data they generated, but rather *verify* it as it accords with your own life. Does this begin to sound mystical? But look for one moment at what researchers – or at least those in social science guided by broadly qualitative principles – do to their data and their subjects. They seek to analyse – literally, that is to say break down into their smallest elements – subjects and situations so that single, temporal truths are generated with predictive validity. And, it is assumed, this is carried out without recourse to the 'subjective', the personal; thus methodology describes an unavoidable relationship between textual artefacts and their objective correlatives.

But we are a long way from realising that research in the social sciences will only find in its theatres of enquiry what it puts there. For social practices, and hence social researches, are pre-eminently worlds of paid-up meanings – as it were – and attributions; in experience they issue from and are set about with meanings which are always ready to hand. And as researchers of social practices, we ourselves give shape, weight and identity to these meanings: we do not come innocent to a task or situation of events; rather, we wilfully situate those events not merely in the institutional meanings which our profession provides but also, and in the same moment, we constitute them as expressions of our selves. Inevitably, the energies of our own psychic and social history fuel our insight, and leave traces of those earlier meanings. But because the institutional drive requires a publicly accountable knowledge, we resort to method to clarify – though in fact mostly obscure – our true involvement. Stronach and MacLure (1998, p. 35) suggest that even this methodological aspiration is deeply frustrated, and indeed that

> It is in those accounts which seem most 'natural', 'transparent', 'real' or 'rounded' that are most carefully wrought with a view to producing just those effects in the reader – that the writer is never more present in the text than when she seems to be absent, and the subject seldom

less audible than when he seems to be speaking for himself. . . . The appearance of artlessness is a rather artful business.

For we might suppose that we slip method between us and those events, a sort of prophylactic which will keep them distinct from us. But this is to misunderstand the nature of method and its seamless identity with what it only apparently treats of. '[Any] science begins', says Oakeshott (1933) 'only when the world of things opened to us by our sense and perceptions has been forgotten or set on one side'. The scientific way of seeing is identical with what it sees in its search for stability:

> The method and the matter of scientific knowledge are not two parties . . . they are inseparable aspects of a single whole . . . And the notion of the categories of scientific knowledge or the instruments of scientific measurement interposing themselves between the scientist and his object is a notion utterly foreign to the character of scientific experience. Without the categories and the method, there is no matter; without the instruments of measurement, nothing to measure. *'Nature' is the product not the datum of scientific thought.*
> (Oakeshott, 1933, p. 37, my emphasis)

The datum becomes, then, not the consequence of a way of seeing even, but that act itself (and as such, must be intentionally opposed to the thing in itself). And in just this way are 'social practices' produced by research. For there are no instruments, no methods prior to the function of consciousness, and all instruments and measures depend for their very existence on the way they serve this function. Consciousness seeks objects – indeed is knowable only by the moment and way of its finding them. And the whole of this experience is organised through an aesthetic.

Aesthetics and truth

Aesthetic attending to something is not a special or a marginal case peculiar to (self-conscious) artists, but one which can be systematically developed – and indeed marketed – by them only because it is the very foundation of intelligence. This is to say no more than that we attend primarily to objects in this way as a condition of our being in the world; we are here and embodied. Such a discourse takes us away from the responsibility of the author (of any report) to justify his or her claims to tell the truth, and shifts that responsibility to the moral and critical sensibilities of the reader. As Sandelowski has it,

> When you talk with me about my research, do not ask me what I found; I found nothing. Ask me what I invented, what I made up

from and out of my data. But know that in asking you to ask me this, I am not confessing to telling any lies about the people or events in my stories/studies. I have told the truth. The proof is in the things I have made – how they look to our mind's eye, whether they satisfy your sense of style and craftsmanship, whether you believe them, and whether they appeal to your heart.

(Sandelowski, 1994, p. 121)

If, as we said at the outset of this section, the notions of authorship and data are radically questioned by *Frank*, then equally some of the answers to these questions – the 'meta-story', perhaps – reach into the epistemological ideas represented by phenomenology and by hermeneutics. We return to these in later chapters (and particularly Chapter 7). What points are being addressed here? By introducing the notion of fiction, we suggest that there may be two parallel sets of claims:

It could be said that	*but . . .*
1 The writer is sole author of the story	the reader is 'co-writer' if the achievement of the story depends on the reader's 'evidence'
2 The characters are fictitious	they are based on 'real' people whom the author has met
3 There are no explicit data for the story	evidence is provided by the reader
4 This is an 'author-evacuated' text	the author has a clear purpose

An important factor in *Frank* (and arguably this applies to the other three stories as well) is its location in the field of social research. Is *Frank* research? Can it be regarded as, in any way, a form of research report? Clough and Nutbrown (2002) suggest that 'All social research sets out with specific *purposes* from a particular *position* and aims to *persuade* readers of the significance of its claims; these claims are always broadly *political*' (p. 4). So, by way of reflecting on *Frank* we can pose four questions:

- Is this a *persuasive* narrative?
- Is the *purpose* of the research and its report clear?
- How has Clough as the author demonstrated the *positionality* of the narrative?
- In what way is the story *political*, and might it have any political impact?

Reflecting on this chapter

The scene is now set for us to unpick some of the tensions, questions and choices of method that faced us as four life story researchers approaching the venture from four distinct methodological positions. The following chapter will explore how we went about our methods. We do, however, feel it necessary to pinpoint some key issues facing the life story research in the early – and ongoing – stages of method/ology:

- Method/ology creates visions of its participants/informants – some more real than others;
- Method/ology can be done alone and with others – though the former does not necessarily have more of a masturbatory feel;
- Method/ology grounds the researchers' reading of present and future research events, in ways that allow for/preclude possibilities;
- Method/ology in researching life stories is always itself a storied venture.

With these key ideas in mind we now turn to stories of our researching life stories.

Chapter 6

Doing

Method in life story research

Introduction

The aim of this chapter is to guide you through the research stories that produced the four life stories of this book. The structure of this chapter is different from the previous one. Here we consider different stages of the research process from four particular methodological positions. Our aim is to give some specific responses to the question commonly posed by those new to life story research: 'How do you do life story research?' Typically, perhaps, we want to throw in a disclaimer from the start. By attempting to explicitly account for the use of qualitative methods, the research stories we present below may present a vision of method that boasts a simple, smooth, deliberate, linear and unproblematic process. This is often far removed from the messy reality of life story method/ologies. In the final section of the chapter, we bring back into focus the researcher's own reflections on the doing of life story research: thus exposing some of the dilemmas and problematics of this approach to research.

Starting off

How did we come to know our characters and narrators? Let us tell you how we met.

Gerry O'Toole's life story

Gerry O'Toole is the embodiment of one particular 'real life' person known to the author, recast in a variety of ways, bringing in the stories of a number of other people with the label of learning difficulties. Tedlock (2001, p. 455) suggests that ethnographic writers combine personal and theoretical understandings. Meaning-making is located between the interiority of autobiography and the exteriority of cultural analysis (Tedlock, 2001, p. 455). In this sense, Gerry's story is as much about the making of one life as it is the modest analysis of a specific culture. As Tedlock

(2001) notes, ethnographic writers may conceptualise their positions as a 'marginal native' 'professional stranger' or see themselves as 'going native' or 'maintaining some distance'. The researcher here – Dan Goodley – worked from a position of 'ally and participant'. Much of the information drawn upon emerged from a long-held involvement with people with learning difficulties and the self-advocacy movement. 'Gerry' was a person I got to know through my voluntary work and research.

He had always intrigued me. Here was a person who boasted a rich and varied life. Unlike many of his peers, Gerry dipped in and out of service settings, professional cultures and institutional practices. While many people with learning difficulties inhabit these contexts from residential home, to day centre, to charity-organised disco on a Tuesday evening, Gerry entered these places only from time to time.

His life appeared to say something about existing differently from his welfare-located peers. Maybe he appealed because his ordinary life of family, friends and work seemed so extraordinary in view of many lives of institutional living experienced by so many of his friends. The words of Gerry's story derive from a whole host of voices and sources including:

• Research field notes from funded projects;
• Direct quotes from secondary sources;
• Anecdotes recalled by the author;
• 'Personal gems';
• Documents produced by people with learning difficulties;
• Vignettes shared by people with learning difficulties in self-advocacy groups;
• Formal individual and group interviews;
• Stories from academic, policy and practitioner literature in the field of learning difficulties.

How these data were brought together is considered later in this chapter. For now it is significant to state that the raw data of Gerry's story did not emerge from a systematically devised, timetabled period of empirical research activity. Instead, Gerry's story was a long time in the making; drawing upon a whole host of personal and professional experiences. Life story research can and should make use of stories that might not neatly fit into the empiricist view of data. Instead, we hope, readers will start to re-interrogate their own collection of narratives which may well form the basis for life story work. I had wanted to tell Gerry's story for a long time.

Colleen's life story

Colleen is a real character, a woman in her fifties who was and is known to her co-writer (Rebecca Lawthom). Her life story and the form of it arise from sustained collaboration and negotation between the narrator (Colleen) and the interviewer (Rebecca). The shape and form of the story were devised together.

> Narrative activity becomes a tool for collaboratively reflecting upon specific situations and their place in the general scheme of life. ... the content and direction that narrative framings take are contingent upon the narrative input of other interlocutors, who provide, elicit, criticise, refute and draw inferences from facets of the unfolding account. In these exchanges, narrative becomes an interactional achievement and interlocutors become co-authors.
>
> (Ochs and Capps, 2001, p. 2–3)

The life story presented is the finished product and contains Colleen's voice (clearly visible) and the interviewer's voice (implicitly visible). The life story begins with negotiation and agreement over the taping of the interview or 'chat' as Colleen called it. The topics of the interview and the form of the discussion were framed and agreed by Colleen. I asked her about life stories and she immediately talked about needing to give a historical context. The story is, then, both about the present and the past. I have known Colleen for around ten years and her full life story was not known to me prior to the interview. Her more recent past was underpinned by the rich account of her earlier life. Ochs and Kapps (2001) point out that we cannot credibly reflect upon ourselves in the moment, as we experience the present. Rather the non-present – the past and the possible – is the context for self-making, and the most suitable genre for this is personal narrative. How this material was brought together is considered later in the chapter. The shape, ebb and form of the story was the product of ongoing consultation and negotiation.

David Hope's life story

David and I (Michele Moore) are distantly related though we had never met before the occasion of this 'study'. Thus personal and professional boundaries in our relationship were always fuzzy and this greatly affected the research practice. It is probably fair to say that David would not have shared so much of his story with an outsider in a professional research capacity. It is likely that my involvement with his family was precariously situated in terms of conventional codes of professional conduct. These issues have to be acknowledged and evaluated in terms of their impact on the emergent data and acceptability of the ensuing account.

There were advantages and disadvantageous to our complicated research relationship. Without doubt the family ties were key to David agreeing to meet me in the first place, and then key to him not quite being able to throw me out in the way he was reputed to regularly bawl out home care staff and other professionals who had contact with him. Later on, in a period of considerable upheaval he had appealed to the family link as a way of pinning down my commitment to him *'Please, please ring. ... We're sort of related ... Please, please ring'*. In other ways the family tie was problematic, for example when David thrust me into confrontations with his mother. The senior social care worker seized on our family connection in different ways, sometimes as a way of undermining my credibility – and conversely, when David was dying, in order to exclude me from certain information: 'that would be confidential to the immediate family'.

Frank's life story

There are some empirical contexts for Frank. The most specific of these is a teacher whom I (Peter Clough) met during fieldwork investigating schools' perspectives on Special Educational Needs policy. This turned out to be an unusual respondent, for although working at the time as a classroom assistant, he had until three years before been headteacher of a large, residential special school and had taken early retirement on health grounds following chronic nervous exhaustion. Since we were of an age and had much to talk about in terms of some parallels in careers (and their policy contexts), I came to know him very well, interviewing him formally for some nine hours on tape before our clearly emerging friendship seemed to render him ethically invalid as a research subject. (It was then, of course – tape recorder strictly off – that I really got to know him!) (And the ethics of *Frank* are discussed in the next section). Frank was on a case; pursuing some inchoate connection between the events of his childhood, his masculinity, his sexuality and his choice of career – and hence, what could be called his moral career.

I should not have noticed 'Frank', I suspect, had his story not fed the hunch of an abiding interest in the subtle relationship between individuals – the 'inner person'? – and their professional careers. I was interested in the apparent consistencies which existed for some between 'what they were' and how they earned their living; and the different, perhaps inverse consistencies that related the two: I have, for example, worked for and with a number of people who have made their relatively distinguished careers bearing badges of social justice, equality, democracy, partnership and collaboration – yet whose own practice spoke only of autocratic self-interest bordering on the despotic.

'We all research our own weaknesses,' my Ph.D. supervisor had once said to me, and this resonated with the reflection that a majority of people with whom I trained for (mainstream/academic) teaching found themselves developing careers in special schools of various sorts, in mental health institutions and in social services departments. For all this, however, the primary empirical context must be, I suppose, my own life and experience. As the organising consciousness here I have created a set of devices to express a number of my own concerns. Frank is rather indifferently a vehicle to allow me to do this.

Ethics

Clearly, each of the research relationships outlined earlier bring with them significant ethical concerns. Some might be quite explicit and would no doubt be tackled well in an introductory text on qualitative methods (e.g. Bannister *et al.*, 1994). Other ethical considerations are more implicit and less easy to deal with. We will be coming back to these ethical questions throughout the book – particularly in Chapter 11 – but for now, here are some ethical starters.

Ethics with Gerry O'Toole

A non-participatory ethnographic approach to life story research raises a number of ethical considerations. Since the author is the writer of the narrative, issues of anonymity and confidentiality take a particular slant. Gerry O'Toole is a fictional name. He is based primarily on one person known to me (Dan) as a consequence of different research projects and involvement with a number of groups of people with learning difficulties. But, and there are many buts here, his ethnicity has been changed. His appearance described differently. His family details altered. As the story develops, so to does the making of Gerry. Although the original person on which Gerry is based dominates the characterisation, by the end of the story, there are remnants of other people (with learning difficulties) known to the author. He has moved, to some extent, from real to fictional – though he still feels very real. In terms of confidentiality, all the stories emerged in public settings. No experiences used were from confidential professional case notes or legal documents. Moreover, the finished narrative includes stories that were shared in desperate times. Tellers of some of the stories would never have known that their disclosures would become part of a public document. This raises uncomfortable issues for researchers. What right do we have to voyeuristically forage for neat soundbites and distressing experiences to inform our life story work? There are no clear and easy answers here – ethics are always open to debate and constant appraisal. There are three points here that may in some way tackle these concerns. First, as anonymity is maintained and fictional devices are employed, so the stories do remain confidential to the original tellers.

It would be impossible to unearth from where the accounts exactly came, unless the author was subjected to interrogation. Second, it should be remembered that stories are in a constant state of becoming (Turner, 1991). While a vignette may recall the indignities of, for example, being denied opportunities at school, who is to say that the person on whom the story is based is still in similar stifling environments? Third, and crucial to life story work that blurs research and practitioner roles, many accounts of discrimination recalled in Gerry's story originate from the real experiences of people who have, since the time of telling their accounts, challenged disablement through their involvement with self-advocacy. This point about resilience leads to a further consideration in relation to ethics.

Plummer (1983, p. 111) encourages life story researchers to 'get your subject's words, come to really grasp them from the inside and then turn it yourself into a structured and coherent statement that uses the subjects' words in places and the social scientist's in others but does not lose their *authentic* meaning'. This notion of authenticity is a key concern for non-participatory ethnographic approaches. One key aim was to capture the resilience of Gerry (and his peers such as Maddie Harrison) in the face of many disabling barriers. On writing the story, then, the author owned the narrative in ways that highlighted the human spirit in the face of some of the most appalling examples of discrimination. While the author's voice dominates, it is hoped that the resilient acts of people with learning difficulties are authentically articulated.

Ethics with Colleen

The ethics of an emancipatory interview approach are complex. Although the collaborators can work and piece together a negotiated narrative, issues of confidentiality and anonymity are key. Emancipatory interview approaches should always be guided by the interviewee in terms of focus and content. Moreover, the life experience that is being drawn upon is always owned by the interviewee and no amount of clarity, ethical undertaking and transparency can subvert the narrator's wish to tell a good tale. Ochs and Kapps (2001) make a distinction between narration – telling a good tale – and narratives: the latter can only be fragmented intimations of experience. Young (1987) notes that telling surely assists the construction of a tale but the tale necessarily lies beyond the telling. Bearing these point in mind, I (Rebecca) exercised some caution around family details, geographical attachments and employment history. Working with the narrator, we chose alternative names, places and workplaces. The length of the original life story gave many possibilities for paring down details. Working with the narrator, we omitted certain experiences and highly sensitive information and allowed others to stand unadulterated. Storytellers naturally wish to position themselves as moral persons

(Ochs and Kapps, 2001). However, this is tempered by the natural instinct to tell stories, experiences and encounters which are atypical. With these tensions in mind, we need to consider the sensitive nature of life story work and in particular the personalised and difficult experiences that we might unearth. For these reasons, the key 'ethics committee', so to speak, was the narrator herself. She moderated, omitted and changed details of her life that she felt uncomfortable in presenting. The finished narrative is woven from the reality of lived experience with sometimes fictional names and places.

Ethics with David

David would not let me (Michele) tape a single word of his story. His reserve was not simply that he did not trust my assurances of confidentiality, although lack of trust in me certainly figured as a real barrier. The reason he did not want tape recordings made was because he could not exert any physical control over the actual tapes. If I had left tapes with him, he could not prevent anyone who so wished from picking them up and taking them. He could not listen to them himself without someone setting up and operating his equipment and so had little possibility of keeping the material private. In addition to this, there was an intercom between his room and other rooms in the house to enable David to call for assistance if needed. However, he had no control over switching this on or off. He often felt the intercom was being used to monitor his conversation. He often spoke in a barely audible voice in order to avoid being overheard and tape recording would have been difficult because of this.

David could not open or hold his own letters. This meant he did not wish me to take verbatim or extensive notes because he could not look over or edit them in private. If I needed to write to him, I had to write my name on the outside of the envelope so that family and caregivers knew not to open it. He would wait for a trusted assistant to come on duty before allowing the mail to be opened. At first I thought the constraints he imposed on the research process were overly mistrustful but in time I came to realise the importance he attached to retaining control of that process. Retaining a position of power over the research process enabled David to occupy a position of resistance over potential misuses and abuses of his story.

The difficult ethical questions arise now that he is dead.

Confidentiality was always an impossible goal in this work. For reasons such as have already been given, his physical condition meant that no information could be imparted between us without involving a third party. I was not entrusted with his confidence for a long time during the story's unravelling and have only scraped together a feeling that he had entrusted me by default and observation rather than by explicit agreement. In addition, the uncommon nature of David's situation has always meant that his confidences would be revealed should his story be told, as his identity is instantly recognizable to those who know of him. I have never negotiated any agreement on confidentiality relating to David's disclosures with his mother. I have never disclosed to her most of what he actually told me because he said it would break her heart and she had to be protected from any sense that she was personally responsible for his demise.

I cannot check out with him the ethical questions that concern me over the construction and telling of his story. To summarise the overriding dilemmas:

- David said he wanted his story told.
- Sheila originally said she did not want his story told but after his death accepted that it should be told because David wanted it told and because she came to believe that the telling of David's story might help to alleviate tragedy in the lives of other families.
- Michael (Sheila's husband and David's Dad) told Sheila – but not me – that she is not to be involved in any writing about what happened to David. He wants the story buried.

I have never spoken to Michael about any of this. He originally ignored and later objected to my involvement in David's life to the extent that if he was due home for his lunch when I was with David then I was sent around the corner to sit in the park until he was out of the house. Ethical confusions like these do not magically resolve themselves. Instead I attempt to own up to them, sticking by my decision to tell David's story (A) because he wanted it told and (B) because to conceal the story would bolster up professional policies and practices which generate a death-making process in disabled people's lives. Ownership of *this* story has to be mine – because David is dead and cannot claim it for his own and Sheila is excluded both from telling this story, and in a very real sense from knowing this story, by Michael's opposition to its existence.

Ethics with Frank

What ethical questions surrounding the making and uses of fiction arise particularly in *Frank*? I (Peter) want to argue here that, since this is fiction, and claims to be 'about' no single person, but rather 'about' my own consciousness, the ethical issues which arise in the writing and publication of *Frank* are different from those attended to in the cases of *Gerry O'Toole*, *Colleen* and *David Hope*. I want to argue that, but I can't. For though I claim this to be fiction, there are sources and settings and events and words which belonged (some time ago) to other people. I have taken my relationship with a man who trusted me (first as a researcher and then as a friend) and used it as a device through which to work out some of my own 'streams of consciousness'. I have (earlier) referred to this life which I have called *Frank* as a vehicle – a writer's trick. I have decided to call him Frank, I have brought in bits of lives (others' lives), I have rendered this story this way. I have chosen those themes. My responsibility as a writer, if I am to 'sell anyone short' as Didion would say, is to ensure that they do not know I have done so.

As far as confidentiality is concerned, my chief concern in assembling *Frank* is only that no one should see him or herself in it. However, is there a question raised here? Is there a different – and arguably more important – ethical responsibility, as it were, to myself? Not least since this 'self' is created in a social world inhabited by my family and friends. This is further complicated by the positioning of 'me' in *Frank* as a character. Sometimes I wear a disguise – sometimes I am 'me' as others might know me – at other points I have used 'me' as another fictional character – another device with which to make a point. At the time of writing I am still exploring these ethical tensions, well aware of the difficulties experienced by writers such as Philip Roth, Hanif Kureshi, Martin Amis and James Joyce, to name but a few.

How we wrote the stories

Behind the writing of any story is a writer. An obvious statement, perhaps, but researching life stories asks questions of the in/deliberate hand of the researcher. Walker argued in 1981 that much is written about the processual nature of methods but very little about ownership, subjectivity and decision-making (often on the hoof) in the doing of method. We now aim to demystify some aspects of our storytelling.

Writing Gerry O'Toole's story

The process of writing started with typing up a whole collection of vignettes. This included drawing upon a variety of sources, following Clough (2002): see Table 6.1.

In bringing this material together, two concerns were addressed. First, the narrative had to answer the research question detailed in the previous chapter:

> *What can one story tell us about the social and cultural worlds inhabited by people with learning difficulties?*

This question directed the writing of the story. Secondly, I (Dan) had made decisions about how the narrative would look. There was a focus on producing a life story about Gerry, peppered with vignettes about some

Table 6.1 Writing Gerry O'Toole's story

Source	Example
Research field notes from funded projects	As I entered the outdoor market, Gerry was, as always, conspicuous. Red, white and black bobble hat that just hid his long straggly thinning hair.
Direct quotes from secondary sources	'We don't want to be called mentally handicapped. We're just as good as anyone – maybe a little bit better' (Maddie Palfreeman, 4th International People First Conference report) Names and reference changed
Formal individual and group interviews	'[Brid pushes David into the cubicle, David covers his face with his lower arms] David: No . . . Brid: Jano' shut the door. Story from interview now dramatised as script.
Anecdotes recalled by the author, including 'personal gems'	'These are my precious stories. Event that shaped me. You won't have heard of them. It's time to start listening to what we have to say. Sooner or later, you'll listen. You will have to' (Speech heard at Conference, Scotland, 1998)
Extracts from the author's own life story	'Frog', Ian shouted, 'Frog'. The gang fell about, giggling. ('Frog' was all Ian really said, that and 'I love Chris Tipping', much to Tipping's embarrassment. He once spent the day spray painting 'I love Tips' on lampposts around the town.
Documents produced by people with learning difficulties	'Dear Editor I am writing on behalf of Partington People First group . . .' Letter to a local newspaper, anonymised
Narratives from author's publications	'Imran found an old lighter in the supporter's car. He asked if he could have it. The supporter, Dan, gave it to him with a patronising warning, "Now don't go burning down your mother's house, will you?!" He looked at Dan with despair and retorted, "I'm not fucking stupid, you know"' Extracted and rewritten from Goodley, 2000
Vignettes shared by people with learning difficulties in self-advocacy groups	Sarah: I have finally moved from my group home. One of the other residents was 'touching me up'. That's how my sister's friend Julia explained it.
Academic, policy and practitioner literature in the field of learning difficulties	'But the reason you feel like you do is less to do with my "condition" or "label" . . .' A paraphrased version of Abberley, 1987, p. 18
Fiction to enhance characterisation	Gerry's account of his family and his father's death

of the real experiences of people with the label of learning difficulties. The author wanted others to enter his story: either directly through him 'remembering' the experience of a friend (in order to include research notes by the author) or indirectly through the insertion of another's experience to provide further background to an area of life alluded to by Gerry (allowing the author to present a personal anecdote). In terms of presentation, Gerry's life provides the backbone to the story, with other 'empirical material' being inserted in italics throughout to build up the narrative. This second concern focuses on how narratives are constructed: their literary qualities and readability. A number of strategies are employed. These include:

- Borrowing from writers such as Tony Parker (see Parker, 1963, 1990), whose style of opening paragraphs is to present answers to interviewer questions (though we never hear the question):

    'My background? What? Oh ... family. Ha! You've opened a can of worms there!'

- Importing theoretical literature into the narrative, for example through paraphrasing disability studies literature on the sociology of impairment (Abberley, 1987):

    'But the reason you feel like you do is less to do with my "condition" or "label" ... and more because of the world around us that creates me in its own vision.'

    This is a paraphrased version of Abberley (1987, p. 18): 'By presenting disadvantage as the consequence of a naturalised "impairment" ... legitimates the failure of welfare facilities and the distribution system in general to provide for social needs, that is, it interprets the effects of social mal-distribution as the consequence of individual deficiency.'

- Narrating the experiences of others, with these experiences appearing as stories in their own right within the wider narrative:

    'She never said much about her time there but I know from others that she was made to wear weighted boots in institutions and they used to drug and hit her.

    A zillion dormitory keys held menacingly by his side. My brave face as Mogadon kicks in. On to avant-garde dance troupes and loud meetings of comrades ...'

The aim here was to have a strong life story of Gerry with additional narrative components which added to this account, by capturing ethnographic moments in the frozen text of a life story (Sparkes, 1994).

Writing Colleen's life story

Schwandt (1997) notes that social enquiry 'is not a form of inquiry *on* human action as much as it is inquiry *with* human actors' (p. 63). The process of constructing the narrative began with knowing and identifying a collaborator or co-researcher. Having known Colleen for a period of time, I (Rebecca) approached her and asked how she felt about working together on a project. I outlined the way in which the process might work and the eventual outcome or product which would emerge. We met up to talk about the process and ideas about how to handle difficulties (should they arise). Once she had agreed to work together, I started to think about possible areas we could discuss and showed Colleen the possibilities. Certain aspects of her personal life (current relationship and sexuality) were considered by Colleen to be less central to her story. She wanted to concentrate on how she got to where she is today. This feature of linear storytelling is a common method of sense-making. The discussion on which we founded the life story took the form of a taped conversation. Clearly, this conversation had an explicit purpose and an implicit agenda for both Colleen and myself. The discussion took one hour and three quarters and focused on childhood, young adulthood and the present. Mischler (1986, p. 69) points out that

> we are more likely to find stories reported in studies using relatively unstructured interviews where respondents are invited to speak in their own voices, allowed to control the introduction and flow of topics and encouraged to extend their responses.

Following the loosely structured conversation, I transcribed the tape and sent the full, unedited transcript to Colleen. Before we embarked upon joint collaboration, she needed to make any edits she felt were compromising and/or identifying. Once this process had been completed (with no changes from Colleen) we met and talked about the data/story and its form. Colleen was surprised at how 'interesting' it was and how much change and transition had occurred in her life. I outlined how we might shape the raw data into an actual narrative by eliding questions and answers together and pasting experiences together. A few examples will make this process more real. The nature of the relationship between the author and narrator is close historically and made formal interviewing redundant and potentially false. The conversation we taped focused on

Colleen's life story but, at times, my voice would finish off utterances, check facts, agree verbally or join with her in laughter.

> *Colleen*: 'Certainly if you hadn't got married by the time you were 20 you were definitely thinking . . .
> *Rebecca*: . . . you were going to be left on the shelf . . .
> *Colleen*: and I remember when I got pregnant at 25 I was old. My mother definitely thought there was something going on.

A key thread throughout the story was the strong work ethic of her family together with some social kudos that this bestowed upon them. The work experiences of both her parents and herself were key resources in this tale, both as comparators of success and as indicators of difference. I worked with Colleen to extract these and paste them together at particular points in the tale. I showed Colleen the reworked version and she agreed that the changes made the story more coherent. Within an emancipatory framework, questions about ownership are key issues to be discussed and debated. I wanted a narrative that made sense both to the narrator and the researcher. Colleen wanted an interesting narrative. We reworked the original transcript into a lengthy story and then together edited it, both to avoid repetition and to make sense of her experience. At times, my desire to intellectualise comes across and is ignored (thankfully):

> *Colleen*: I just needed to see if I could do something away from there where no-one knew you. You could be a new person.
> *Rebecca*: What sort of person could you be, how did you present yourself?
> *Colleen*: I wasn't bothered about talking about family or what I did at home so I just had like another little life. I enjoyed it, I enjoyed it too much apparently because I split up with my husband and I think it was going back to work that really did it I think, realising what a big mistake it all was, really scary.

At other times the story shifts towards less central themes. Colleen at one point talks in depth about her current work situation and the position of her colleagues both at work and in the domestic arena. When reading this back together, Colleen noted that this seemed out of place and not very relevant to the story. We agreed to cut this section out completely. I was reminded here of Baker's (1995) comment regarding life story research, that story-givers know 'the whole iceberg, not just the tip'. Was Colleen satisfied with the account or simply attuned to the need to present the tip? Undoubtedly, at the end of the process of editing, we can discern the tip, but, hopefully, the transparent process also allows the iceberg to be partially uncovered.

Writing David Hope's story

The writing of David's story was a long time coming. I (Michele) had always known that the telling of the story would one day be necessary. Through the writing of David's story it was hoped to advance strategies of personal and social resistance for men with spinal cord injury through exposing and problematising the overriding medical construction of his 'problem'. But knowing David's story, having a key position in relation to the production, dissemination and maintenance of his story after his death, combined with the subsequent chapter of my own life and its entanglements with the story, placed a block on my capacity to write it and, sometimes, even to think about it.

I have always been afraid of writing David's story. Afraid of a moral reaction in relation to my own involvement, but more afraid of the implications of misrepresentation for him, albeit implications that would only ever impact on individual and collective *memories* of him. And afraid, too, of the way in which telling the story, particularly via the relatively fixed and permanent medium of print, could impact on the circumstances of his mother's life, and the lives of others implicated in my version of the story, my telling and my analyses. There is a regrettable source of solace in the knowledge that David's family and friends are unlikely to stumble across the story in this text. I admit to cowardice in this account of how I wrote the story.

As already explained, the material for this story was assembled through the adoption of pluralist and eclectic approaches to capturing David's words, his perspective and his experience. Many of the hallmarks of conventional research practice could not be adhered to in this work, for David placed conventional interviewing and observation strategies off-limits. He refused to allow recording of his words, objected to all but the most cursory of notes being taken and refused to allow me to access any sources which could offer potential triangulation or verification of what he told me. For example, I once asked him if I could scrutinise his medical records after his death, but he did not want this as he would be in no position to refute what might have been written about him. He did not want me to discuss his disclosures with other people.

Most of the notes were made about half an hour after I left him, usually in a nearby car park where I stopped to scribble as hard and fast as possible. Occasionally he let me write down something he had said verbatim, for example when he said, '*It wasn't breaking my neck that made me break down.*' I put in a plea to be able to quote him on that. The one exceptional source of transcription has come from messages David left on my office answer machine: '*You might have saved my life mate . . . or you might not*' is a straight transcription from tape. So is the dialogue quoted when he phoned to say '*Ring as soon as you can . . . Please, please ring*'. After the inquest, various relatives sent on a newspaper clipping. I made notes of my interactions with various professionals and with people who advised me. The *'having looked over the edge you owe it to all of us to look over again'* speech was transcribed word for word.

Many researchers do, in reality, work in a similarly ill-defined and nebulous way. For example, 'convergent interviewing' is a widely used method which deliberately begins in an open-ended way in order to maximise the extent to which the data can be generated by the respondent's experience and not led by the researcher's questions. Nevertheless, such methods usually involve some level of structured process even if the content is unspecified (e.g. Dick, 1990). Similarly, researchers often have nothing to do with systematic note-taking procedures, arguing that these distract from the ambience of research relations and is intrusive (Glaser, 1998). However, I wasn't familiar with these communities of research practice at the time and felt the way of working to be unprincipled and chaotic.

For a long time it was impossible to draw the material together. Then, within weeks of David's funeral, I gained new knowledge through my own experience of mothering which completely transformed my engagement with what happened to him. My new baby son could not feed and was fighting for his life in intensive care. Not being able to make him eat was devastating. Sheila had been legally obliged to prepare and offer David every single meal he refused over the four months it took him to die and this she had done. I came to glimpse her anguish through a different darkness and needed a great deal of time to grapple with the shifting landscape of my commitments in the story. Part of the struggle simply to begin writing, involved trying to reconcile my powerful position as a researcher and writer with a newfound powerless position as a mother and would-be children's ally (see also Moore and Dunn, 1999). This shift brought radical changes in the telling of the story.

Eventually I wrote *a* story chronologically. I tried faithfully to get across as much as possible about what David told me and what he prioritised, but the story is hugely contestable. I stuck to my original theoretical inclination, which was to tell the story in order to reveal the social construction of David's disablement, oppression and ultimate exclusion. En route, dramatic shifts in my own experience and understanding inevitably mean that I narrate the story differently today in contrast to when it happened. Hence the potential of a given theoretical framework as a resource for constructing and making sense of a story is not fixed.

Writing Frank

I (Peter) wanted to use 'Frank' – to open up three themes of 'method':

1. Is *Frank* a story?
2. The commission.
3. The conclusion.

Each of these themes is identified and illustrated in Table 6.2 in terms of three key facets of the writing of *Frank*: the literal (what appears in the story); the construction (the devices used to locate it in the story); the derivation (the events, experiences and thoughts that might have lead to this element being here).

Table 6.2 Writing *Frank*

Of method . . .	The literal	The construction	The derivation
Is *Frank* a story?	The *Frank* narrative is basically an edited version of diary entries.	I have chosen here to let the diary entries speak for themselves.	The diaries came from a creative writing course that I attended.
The commission	'Much of his diary was turgid – dry, yet these pieces – those that made me read on . . . they said something – might speak?'	'Frank' felt his jottings were important enough to 'do something with'. He had read one of my published stories – knew (I think) the character from which Rob (Clough, 2002) was derived.	My own reluctance to keep diaries; my own understanding of the use of personal writing – and my diffidence about 'doing something' with 'Frank's' diaries come together here.
The conclusion	There are two conclusions; Frank's (*I don't know why I never – really – loved other men*), and mine: I phoned him a few weeks later – said I couldn't make the diaries into a story. I told him they might speak for themselves – but that they needed ruthless editing. 'Do it,' he said. I had not warmed to him.	These two conclusions come together in my idea that this is 'Frank' seeking his own therapy.	The piece finishes with the two conclusions because I wanted to convey both 'Frank's' desperation to have his story 'told' and my reluctance to accept his commission.

Engaging with informants in the writing of the process

Researching life stories brings with it relational baggage. And when we cast our stuff around the methodological lumber room, we are reminded of the things that used to make us feel, of events that are hard to relive and, fundamentally, of how we were with others in our lives. This section aims to do a bit of relational spring cleaning.

Engaging with Gerry O'Toole: a non-participatory approach

One conclusion from reading the process of methodology and method already accounted for in this and the previous chapter is that no engagement took place with Gerry whatsoever. It has been argued earlier that in the process of writing the story he closely resembles one individual known to the author (Dan). This individual was never approached about the writing of a story. If I had approached him then I could have adopted, for example, the emancipatory approach detailed earlier. However, Gerry's story reflects a non-participatory approach to life story research that precludes the physical involvement of participants. But, in terms of engagement, I feel it necessary to reconceptualise the problem.

Booth and Booth's (1994, 1998) work is important here. In some of their interviews with parents with learning difficulties (1994) and their children (1998), they became increasingly concerned with the nature of voice in narrative research. In particular, they ask what is to be done with people who lack a 'voice'. While Plummer (1983) argues that articulacy is a necessary resource in narrative production, questions remain about how to articulate less strong voices. When we mention 'voice' we can be referring to inarticulate people or to people whose stories are not often documented, publicised, listened to and afforded significance. One aim of writing Gerry's story was to capture some voices from society that so often remain untouched. The terms of engagement involve utilising the medium of life story research to document the many voices that exist in the primary character's lifeworld. Fiction, as the Booths argue, permits the writer to communicate voices via plot, narrative and characterisation in ways that keep authenticity and permit access to ill-considered lifeworlds. Indeed, as fiction brings in many characters to the plot, so perhaps readers are drawn to other characters: Gerry permits the introduction of comrades such as Maddie. Here the multiple voices of the narrative raise another notion of engagement. Gerry was engaged with, but in ways that aimed – method/ologically – to voice his experiences and relations with others. The person on whom Gerry is based is not a chatty chap – though his busyness and full life cry out for words to articulate their energy. The aim was to breathe some words into lives that so often do not rely on the spoken word.

Engaging with Colleen: an emancipatory approach

My (Rebecca's) relationship with Colleen existed prior to the research and thus 'working' seems not to fit the encounters we had. Rather, we translated aspects of our relationship into a working alliance. We discussed the clear outcome for the author in terms of an academic output (the book) and also explored what Colleen might have gained. She talked about confidence and the cyclical nature of her life ('come round full circle') which allowed her to make sense of her journey. In true emancipatory approaches, the nature of the outputs are jointly decided by co-researchers. However, this differed slightly in our encounter, as I wanted to use the final story in this book and Colleen enjoyed the process of reflexivity. At no time during the process did I use the word 'emancipatory' or enquire as to Colleen's subsequent 'emancipation'. The focus of the story itself was emancipatory and this feature of change and growth was recognised by both parties. Here, I am not claiming any special power of enlightenment or empowerment – indeed power was not mine to give away. Rather, the process itself was collaborative and emancipatory in content and process.

The analytical work undertaken following the drafting of the story is informed by the voice relational approach developed by Brown and Gilligan (1992, 1993) and Brown *et al.* (1989, 1991). This method arose from extensive research on girls and women within education and developmental psychology. Rather than seeing the self as predominantly rational, unitary and independent, voice relational methods arise from a relational ontology. Ruddick (1989) and others have posited the notion of selves in relation to others, embedded in a complex web of intimate and larger social relations. Brown and Gilligan were concerned about the lack of 'voice' in their research work with girls and young women. They developed a collaborative approach which aimed to explore individuals' accounts in terms of the relationships to people around them, and their relationships to the broader social, structural and cultural context. The voice relational approach exposes the nature of the relationship between the researcher and the researched.

> It's an attempt to work as a writer would work, by giving people their voice, by giving ourselves a voice in our work and then thinking consciously about the orchestration of the pieces we write.
> (Kitzinger and Gilligan, 1994, p. 411)

This orchestration, this piece reflects the input of both Colleen and myself. Moreover, Colleen's participation has been key to the design, form and outcome of the process.

Engaging with David: a participatory approach

The ultimate goal of emancipatory research practice, as first advocated in a special issue of the international journal *Disability, Handicap & Society* in 1992, is that a project should seek 'to further the interests of "the researched"' (DHS, 1992, p. 162). In disability research, the interests of 'the researched' cannot be presumed by non-disabled researchers, but must be established by direct consultation with disabled people themselves. In my (Michele's) work with David he articulated his interests in 'the research' as being to help other disabled people avoid the pitfalls of his life. In a sense I have subjugated these interests by referencing the social model of disability and turning the central gaze of the research interest away from individual disabled people and towards other people who must act to resist the construction of disablement. Hence, the politics of emancipation are confused in this work.

Less ambitious claims, too, for disability research practice to be 'participatory' (Zarb, 1992) and to involve disabled people in projects in meaningful ways, whilst taken seriously in the beginning, have eventually been set aside. None of the key informants have been engaged in the writing of this story. I try to claim good reasons for the lack of participation in the story-telling – David is dead, Sheila would be upset by the intended revelation of aspects of this shared experience – but these are weak and unsophisticated claims. And so for all that I assert allegiance with participatory and emancipatory disability research paradigms in the production of David's story: involvement of the key informants has been at best uncertainly negotiated and at worst abandoned. However, as with the writing of *Gerry O'Toole*, while the here and now of method/ology might seem non-participatory, the end product (the story) aims to capture the participatory actions of David and others in the doing and telling of his life. While we return to these concerns later on in the book, it would seem unproblematic to say that participatory approaches are involved not simply in the doing of method/ology, but are also bound up in the wider project of researching life stories.

Engaging with Frank: A literary theory approach

Much of life history work (e.g. Goodson and Sikes, 2001) has at the very least an implicit social determinism. One of the things that is attempted in *Frank* is to move more towards an implicitly psychoanalytic stance (though this is clearly no less deterministic); so *Frank* highlights those 'truths' of hidden human consciousness. What is distinctive about *Frank* (in comparison to other life-historical work) is that it fits more with the genre of the modern novel: it is confessional, intrusive, introspective and, as Murdoch says (in Bradbury, 1975), 'quasi-allegorical and crystalline'. I (Peter) have already illustrated how the structure and devices of *Frank* have been created as a parallel text; but alongside the text to be found in the construction of the narrative which is *Frank* are – I think – four substantive issues:

- The father
- Religion
- Sexuality
- Roots.

Table 6.3 explains the literal, the constructional and the derivational factors of the four themes.

Reflections on the research process

This has been a long chapter. We now take stock.

Reflecting on the writing of Gerry O'Toole – Dan

The first thing to note about writing life stories is the author's intent. Tedlock (2001, p. 459) notes that since readers derive meanings from a text that are shaped by the discourse communities in which they are based, ethnographers must have some idea as to what discourse communities they are hoping to address. Gerry's story was written with an interdisciplinary audience in mind, who may not have previously come across (the stories of) people with learning difficulties. But there were also theoretical and epistemological intentions in mind – in relation to disability, impairment and resilience – which I attempt to unearth in the next chapter. For now it would be useful to reflect upon the method/ological venture that led to the writing of Gerry's story.

What about the role of participants in the process of research? Is it ethically, morally and politically right to treat our participants as passive elements of a culture to be understood by the all-knowing researcher? Various critics from feminism (Stanley and Wise, 1993) and disability studies (e.g. Oliver, 1996) have argued vehemently against such a non-participatory approach to research. It is sadly ironic to observe researchers (who are committed to making sense of social inequalities) adopting ethnographic research, which then reproduces other power relations (between the researcher and the researched). But such a view of power is rather simplistic. Life story research not only illuminates notions of method/ological power but also power as imbued in the representation of realities via a narrative. When Gerry's story succeeds it does so in ways that raise voices to the fore, out of hidden cultures, into the (supposedly) more hallowed arena of research text. Here, then, Gerry and his peers are permitted a place in such an arena without having to waste their time physically being in it. Who wants to do research? Is it really that crucial to ensure that everyone enters the research arena? Does it not segregate and categorise people even further when we aim to 'include the oppressed'? Perhaps Gerry's story demonstrates human character, resilience and determination that exist with or without the researcher. In this sense the life story is a testimony to a prior resilience and emancipation. Finally, Gerry's criticality hopefully shines through the narrative: here is a critical, reflexive, maybe articulate voice. While Gerry acts outside of the story, the story emancipates him as storyteller and critical visionary.

Reflecting on the writing of Colleen's story – Rebecca

A key concern for qualitative research and feminist work in particular is how to maintain voice while simultaneously recognising the impact of the researcher. Larson (1997) notes that narrative knowing is complex because we need to interrogate our own deeply held assumptions about research and the ways in which we conceptualise individuals theoretically. Colleen is for me a story of a feminist life (my interpretation) although I am not sure Colleen would label herself as feminist. Her story was constructed with a feminist (who would label herself as such) and this means that the story's frame and its development may well have been steered towards a feminist slant. Our prior relationship also gives Colleen some knowledge about my feminist beliefs. However, as Larson (1997) shows in her work, even feminist enquirers and collaborators need not share common assumptions about the methodology and methods of personal narrative enquiry. The shared political standpoint of feminism is a broad umbrella which allows for a multiplicity of meanings. The story is a coming-out story in many senses. Overtly, it can be read as sexual 'coming out' but this is no tale of passing or making do, constrained by dominant heterosexual discourse. The coming out also refers to the growing confidence and realisation both of Colleen's potential and of ways in which agency is constrained by structure. The voice of the story-giver, the narrator, is a powerful one and is maintained throughout the text as 'I'. Colleen positions herself as relational throughout the text and peppers the tale with the voices of specific others (e.g. family members) and a generalised other, symbolising dominant societal beliefs (e.g. being 'left on the shelf'). The dialogue we had throughout the process ensured that my feminist lens did not become all-pervasive. Borland's (1991) work demonstrates the ways in which stories can be disowned or distanced if researchers' lenses are not shared by their participants. The researched (a 70-year-old woman) disputes the interpretation of the story and disowns it:

> Your interpretation of the story as a female struggle for autonomy within a hostile male environment is entirely YOUR interpretation. You've read into the story what you wished to – what pleases you … The story is no longer my story at all.
>
> (Borland, 1991, p. 70)

Table 6.3 Engaging with Frank

Of substantive issues . . .	The literal	The construction	The derivation
The father	My father is there; he is dirty from work; in a rage he seizes me – this is the word I always use – he seizes me and all of one action pulls my pyjama trousers to the ground / has his belt off from his waist / pushes me face down onto the table / lashes my bottom with his leather belt.	I have put together here a series of 'hunches' about the father in relation to his sons, alongside other hunches as to why the father takes out his sexual frustration on the boys.	This – I think – comes from a multiple and complex memory of boyhood; it reflects my own indignity at the hands of my father and the perpetual feeling of indignity.
Religion	I was bound by so many rules; it seemed it was all rules. There were the rules of my damaged family, which of course were not so visible; the rules of the neighbours which my mother feared and whispered about; the rules of the fucking methodist church, and of school.	This has nothing to do with faith. I think I understand 'faith' – what makes things difficult in 'Frank's' heritage is 'religion' – and, more importantly, denomination. Methodism (with the capital 'M' of the time) was at the root of 'Frank's' father's readjustment.	The roots of this are in childhood experiences of organised religion (my own and those borrowed from others) that oppress and confine. They are experiences where the 'organisation' and 'routinisation' of religion are divorced from any experience of faith, or Christian love, or forgiving communion.

Table 6.3 continued

Of substantive issues . . .	The literal	The construction	The derivation
Sexuality	When he told me a few years ago that he was a nudist, what he said was: "I've a private yard here at the back I can strip off in summer' and later: 'o yes we used to strip off in the desert' and 'I spent the best part of four years bollock-naked in the desert'	What is being built here, through a series of entries, is a story in the story. The reader will find the various threads which point to male–male sexual experiences (it would not have been called 'gay' then); and the shame that the fact that they happened is shot through his subsequent life – with his wife and his boys – when he returns.	In suggesting that The desert love left no mark, I'm suggesting that this man (I can hardly bear to use that word and think of him) remained unchanged because of the desert nakedness – his male encounters which might have happened.
Roots	St. Annes-on-sea is nowhere to live a life. A man should rage and be foul there; a man should spoil it and foul it. It has no future and no past.	The entries about the 'roots' are mainly the reporting of facts – along with 'Frank's' thoughts about 'going back' and Frank's seeking a reason for the misplaced family.	This all works around the words in the last entry here, But he laid waste around him; already cut off, he cut off and cut off. The entries about family and roots are edited such that they eventually explain that everything he did was effectively 'cutting-off'.

The story-giver, Colleen, emerges from this story as a reflexive and critical narrator. She asserts that experience and age are important but allows genuine pride and emotion to be expressed ('I am happy now'). By engaging in dialogue with one narrator, we are allowed to make sense of a personal trajectory in detail. This rich journey is made possible by our engagement both with the minutiae of Colleen's life (e.g. her dad's car) and by the wider regulatory practices which may have engulfed her (the beliefs about sex and childbearing). Finally, the woman's voice is central throughout and her critical reading of her past allows us to be both critical of and delighted by a life full of change and transformation.

Reflections on the writing of David Hope – Michele

In this story, multiple confusions and controversies are unresolved. It would be misleading to see the research process as credible in terms of its engagement with the requirements for participatory research. The people whom the story is about had minimal input into its production and no input into its writing. Indeed if their participation in the writing of the story had been maximised then the story may well have been suppressed. Perhaps it should have been. Wherever participation of the key players identified conflicting interests I subordinated these to my own grandiose sense of the 'wider interests of disabled people and their families'. To some extent this is part and parcel of working with a theory-driven approach. Yet it also exposes a level of researcher arrogance that makes for uncomfortable reflection on both the research process and its outcomes. Elsewhere in my writing I have advocated 'a reflexive, self-analytical critical approach to disability research firmly grounded in human rights principles' (Moore *et al.*, 1998, p. 97) which I do see as underpinning the work with David, but clearly there is a long way to go in the demanding pursuit of critical, rights-based emancipatory life story research. Mistakes notwithstanding, I think I did the poor best that could be done in the circumstances to optimise participation, but still feel ill at ease with this. Clearly there is no room for complacency.

The question of whether research engagement with a person's story is ever justifiable if the act of engagement may itself generate life-threatening consequences can be unexpectedly much nearer to the surface than the researcher expects (see also Clough, 2002, p. 58). Moreover, engagement with any sensitive story profoundly affects the researcher as well as the researched and there has to be a refusal to collude in the maintenance of silence around the levels of pain and risk involved in life story research. These considerations remind us of the potency of stories but also suggest possibilities for the contestation of storytelling methodologies and practices.

The most vital point of reflection concerns the question of whether the telling of David's story affects positive social change. Was this research

worth doing? Is David's story worth telling? Will telling it make a difference that improves outcomes for men with spinal cord injury and their
families? Will telling David's story progress understanding of the politics
of disablement or, conversely, recycle negative images of disabled people
and their lives and thus have oppressive consequences? If we genuinely
seek to transform understanding of disability through life story research
then it is important to open up these debates.

Reflections on the writing of Frank – Peter

In *Frank* the architecture of the story explores the archaeology of both
the use of the fictional narrative turn to 'tell' a persuasive story, and the
archaeology (or perhaps 'fossils') of a life. Without doubt this story is
made and used to explore occupations of my own – with the mystery of
fatherhood, with my roots, with questions of belief and religious institutions, and of sex and sexuality. Lurking somewhere is a largely implicit
connection between Frank's troubled childhood and his choice of professional location, working with disturbed boys. I say 'choice' here, though
I don't think it's quite that, and is perhaps better understood by a subtle
teleology which offers the reader an open-ended reflection on the connection. In this respect, the story avoids the determinism which characterises
both the 'classical' life history and the (equally classical) psychoanalytic
case study. I was aware of doing this in earlier attempts to make patent
the latent (Clough, 1995, 1998, 2002; Clough and Corbett, 2000). *Frank*
is not didactic; it is, if anything, eristic.

Frank is a fantasy. It may not be a particularly good example of it, but one
of its formal ancestors is the classic Victorian novel – it is moral, realistic and
bourgeois and – above all – the author owns it (or so I say). However, since
it appears some hundred or so years later than its forebear, and what's more
masquerades as social science in a postmodern age, it needs some apology.
'What a strange claim!' you say; no self-respecting (and how they did!)
Victorian would want anything to do with the tub of guts which is assembled in the name of art as *Frank*. Surely your literary history is mistaken, and
you're thinking of Virginia Woolf, or certainly James Joyce (who certainly
knew about unseemly stains)? Wrong, I say.

> The characters in my novels are my own unrealised possibilities. That
> is why I am equally fond of them all and equally horrified by them.
> Each one has crossed a border that I myself have circumvented. It is
> that crossed border (the border beyond which my own 'I' ends) which
> attracts me most. For beyond that border begins the secret the
> novel asks about. The novel is not the author's confession; it is an
> investigation of human life in the trap the world has become.
>
> (Kundera, 1984, pp. 65–66)

The design and achievement of *Frank* springs out of resentment of the deluded, unwakened reader who believes in something called proof which will not disturb his epistemological slumbers.

Conclusions and further questions

Reading through this chapter, we are reminded of the popularised definition of the intellectual: 'somebody who finds an inordinate amount of questions, and little or no answers'. A forage into the use of methods in researching life stories opens up a whole host of debates connected with power, authenticity, ethics, stance, subjectivity and applications. We will return to some of these debates in Part 4 of the book, but for now we feel there are three key questions to keep in mind. First, what exactly is an authentic life story? Is it one that reflects in/directly the input and ownership (as with Colleen's story) – hence individual authenticity? Or should authenticity be measured in terms of the extent to which it meaningfully captures some of the artefacts of a culture inhabited by a narrator (as, arguably, with Gerry O'Toole's story)? Second, our consideration of method has demonstrated, we hope, the close connections of methodology and method. Often, the latter is presented in key under/postgraduate textbooks as a toolkit to be taken from to answer a particular question. However, this chapter has highlighted the ways in which a life story researcher's use of method and consideration of a phase of research are directly influenced by the methodological persuasion that they adopt. In this case, it may make more sense to talk of method/ology rather than methodology and method. Finally, methods are never used by researchers within a theoretical vacuum. Life story researchers approach their narratives and their narrators with key assumptions in mind. We hope that this chapter has at least implicitly demonstrated some of the ways in which authors' preoccupations have advanced particular visions of research. In the next chapter, we turn to an explicit consideration of the link between method/ology and epistemology.

Chapter 7

Informing

Epistemology in life story research

Introduction

The aim of this chapter is to revisit deeper concerns introduced in Chapters 5 and 6 and to consider how our theoretical frameworks came to impact upon the stories that we have written. Broadly speaking, this involves each of the four authors considering how their particular take on knowledge – their epistemological view – has influenced their writing of their narrative. We aim to unearth the often buried assumptions of life story researchers: to lay them bare on the grounds of method/ology and to consider how epistemology shapes method/ological terrains. Bannister *et al.* (1993) argue that qualitative research is part of an ongoing debate. Crucial to this debate is the role of epistemology in relation to the doing of qualitative research. Each of the authors of the life stories presented in Part 1 of this book came to their storytelling with particular epistemological baggage. Epistemology can be viewed as the grounds or structures on which we build up theories. In its crudest sense, epistemology is a philosophical orientation – which directs us to see the world in particular ways, and then make sense of what we see through the use of related theories. Following Goodley *et al.* (2002) and Clough and Nutbrown (2002), life story research is often viewed as having the following epistemological orgins:

- *idiographic not nomothetic* – interested in the private, individual and subjective nature of life rather than the public, general, objective;
- *hermeneutic not positivist* – preoccupied with capturing the meanings of a culture/person rather than measuring the observable aspects of a culture/person;
- *qualitative not quantitative* – focused on the wordy nature of the world rather than its numerical representation;
- *specificity not generalisation* – amenable to the specific description and explanation of a few people rather than the representative generalities of a wider population;

- *authenticity not validity* – engaged with the authentic meanings of a story and its narrator rather than devising measures that measure what they purport to measure;
- *language as creative not descriptive* – recognises the constructive effects of language rather than language as a transparent medium for describing the world.

While life story research can be seen as a post-positivistic approach to research that eschews long-held traditions of positivistic approaches to social science, the epistemological leanings of life story researchers often bring with them a host of other, more specific considerations.

Poststructuralist approaches to life story research – Dan Goodley

Gerry O'Toole's story was created by the author through the employment of an ethnographic approach. An ethnographer's theoretical position will noticeably influence the ways in which they choose their methods, deal with their material and later conceptualise their analyses. Indeed, acknowledging theoretical agendas and frameworks is a key part of ethnography's engagement with the generation/construction of meaning. Gordon *et al.* (2001) identify a number of epistemological persuasions, each generating particular theoretical accounts. They note that the postmodern turn in the social sciences has had a major impact upon the ethnographic approach. In this section, we will consider the ways in which Gerry O'Toole's story was the product of an engagement with a postmodern method: that of poststructuralism.

Postmodernism and narrative

Postmodernism is a subject ripe for social scientific debate. It continues to receive passionate support and scathing criticism. For some, the notion of a postmodern world smacks of defeatism: giving up the modernist agenda of progression, seeking truth and associated emancipation, most notably embodied in scientific progression (Assiter, 1996). For others, recognising postmodernism is itself part of a radical political and philosophical agenda: challenging a host of 'grand narratives' that serve the needs, actions and demands of omnipotent social groups. Moreover, postmodernity is used as a term to describe the twenty-first century's move towards late capitalism, post-Fordism and the knowledge society. Lyotard's (1979) *The Postmodern Condition* provides one useful inroad into the phenomenon. He suggests that postmodernism involves incredulity towards metanarratives or grand narratives. Modernist societies are – or were – typified by the promotion of grand narratives. These have three specific features. First, they aim to be *overarching* and all-encompassing. Scientific narratives on 'learning difficulties' are posited in ways that purportedly can be imported into studies and practices that aim to make sense of, and treat, people so labelled. Second, these grand narratives boast *foundationalism*; they desire to base knowledge on claims that are 'known' with certainty. Scientific knowledge about 'learning difficulties' utilises concepts and claims such as 'objectivity' and 'scientific method' which seemingly have a given certainty to them (not least through the use of intelligence and psychometric testing). Third, they have an optimistic faith in *progression*. The 'truths' of these grand narratives are implicitly held to be part of the modernist agenda of progression, which for people with learning difficulties is often associated with their 'cure', 'rehabilitation' and 'care'.

For Lyotard, these elements of grand narratives are increasingly open to question. Indeed, by using the term 'grand narrative' instead of 'truths', we are encouraged to question the very status and function of these narratives and, accordingly, to offer alternative narratives. Following Assiter (1996, p. 17), how can we still unquestioningly hold up the foundationalist, all-encompassing and progressive qualities of grand narratives – enlightenment projects such as science – that foundered on the rock of tragedy that was Auschwitz? Grand narratives are not and never were benevolent offerings for all. They served a variety of institutional interests, were located in a host of performative acts and led to constructions of many members of the human race as the 'objects' of knowledge to be assessed, measured, treated and in some cases wiped out. In its most radical anti-foundationalist moments, postmodernism escapes these modernist horrors to leave us with a collection of alternative, and possibly more empowering, narratives.

Poststructuralism and narrative

In terms of turning to more empowering narratives, one possible route is offered by what may be termed poststructuralism: the discourse or methods of postmodernity offered by writers such as Judith Butler (1990, 1993), Michel Foucault (1973a, 1973b, 1977, 1980, 1983), Jacques Derrida and Jacques Lacan (see Stronach and McLure, 1998). Poststructuralists interrogate the workings of knowledge and grand narratives in a number of ways. First, grand narratives reflect the manipulative powers of 'discourses'. Entities such as 'learning difficulties', 'abnormal', 'criminal', 'insane' are created within and by institutions of society through words and actions – discourses – which serve particular societal and institutional functions. They should, therefore, be viewed with scepticism rather than as truth. Second, the universalising theories of grand narratives are rejected. Poststructuralist analyses have shown that 'universals' or 'truths' actually marginalise certain groupings to the status of 'other', such as women, black, gay, mentally ill, working-class and disabled people. Grand narratives are clearly not universal when so many groupings are afforded a deficient, lacking and other position. Knowledge and power are intertwined. Third, poststructuralists are suspicious of modernist values of justice or freedom since they have their roots in oppressive discourses – where some groupings benefit from these values and others are ignored. Consequently, the disciplines/disciples of scientific progress are viewed with cynicism, including psychiatry, psychology, sociology, social policy, politics, medicine, and so on. Fourth, the *raison d'être* of modernist knowledge – understanding human beings – is problematised. Following Foucault, there is a price to be paid in understanding – or more accurately, constructing – the human subject. Hence, the liberal notion of the embodied, agentic, humanist human subject is deconstructed. Attention is paid to the very ways in which this view of human beings is itself a reflection of dominant discourses of modernity (Butler, 1990). Instead, poststructuralists highlight how 'subjects' are fragmented, decentred and multiple. Following Foucault, Assiter argues that the individual self is a fiction, an historically contingent construct:

> The individual is not a pregiven entity which is seized on by the exercise of power. The individual, with his identity and characteristics, *is the product of the relation of power exercised over bodies* [my italics].
>
> (Assiter, 1996, p. 9)

This radical rewriting of the human subject calls into question how we view ourselves and others. Poststructuralism suggests that our selves are constructed via a host of discourses and grand narratives. The individual human being, or human subject, is not a biological or natural given. A human subject and associated sense of self is created through power and knowledge. Selves and individuals, the available objects that are used to talk of (and therefore constitute) the self, emerge from the discourses of a culture in which they are created.

For some individuals, their selves are particularly open to constitution by 'expert' bodies of knowledge. Hence the selves of people with 'learning difficulties' are often constructed through reference to discourses and objects of human services such as 'lacking intelligence', 'behavioural incompetence', 'maladaptive functioning' and 'immature development' (Ryan and Thomas, 1980/1987). Within the grand narrative of 'science' there is a tendency to view these objects as part of the embodied unitary human subject: they make up the selves of people with learning difficulties. For poststructuralists, these very objects are the stuff of a grand narrative that requires dismantling.

Poststructuralist storytelling

Poststructuralist storytelling aims to excavate the power and knowledge that are used to construct versions of humanity. This contributes to *social constructionist* critiques in the social sciences (see Burman and Parker, 1993; Burr, 1995). Klages (2001) argues that a key aim of poststructuralist feminist theorists is the study of how gender is created and/or destabilised within the structure of language itself. Similar things could be said about Gerry O'Toole's story. A key concern emerging from the ethnographic research, and discussed in Chapters 5 and 6, was the way in which people with learning difficulties' 'handicaps' appeared to be less the consequence of their 'impairments' and more the product of disabling experiences. In this sense, Foucault's consideration of the discursive construction of deviance and abnormality resonates with the ethnographic experiences collected from the life worlds of people with learning difficulties. The subjectivities of many of Gerry's peers were often locked into the meanings that were afforded them in institutionalised and segregated settings. The aim of the life story was to capture the socially constructed nature of these experiences, the language of the wider culture and their accompanying subjectivities:

> Language is the place where actual and possible forms of social organisation and their likely social and political consequences are defined and contested. Yet it is also the place where our sense of ourselves, our subjectivity, is constructed ... Subjectivity is produced in a whole range of discursive practices – economic, social, and political – the meanings of which are a constant site of struggle over power.
>
> (Weedon, 1987, p. 21)

This sense of struggle over power, subjectivity and knowledge can be viewed in the life story. A strong narrative thread is that of Gerry resisting (or perhaps escaping) many encounters with oppressive discourses, in contrast to the vignettes of others. A sense of discursive oppression and resistance runs throughout the narrative.

Furthermore, Derrida's method of deconstruction enters Gerry's story. Eagleton (1983) and Hedges (2000) provide a useful overview of this poststructuralist method. Deconstruction aims to demonstrate how something represented as completely different from something else exists only by virtue of defining itself against that something else. Therefore, the alienation experienced by some people with learning difficulties can be understood only when the opposite of their experiences are demonstrated: being disabled exists only in relation to not being disabled. Hence, David (who enters Gerry's story) is viewed as abnormal only when his socks are removed to show his 12 toes, which are so different from his abusers' 10 toes. And Gerry's ambition and achievements as an 'ordinary' chap take on resonance only when the 'extraordinary' experiences of disabled others are accounted for. There are a number of contrasting stories that demonstrate the potentially fluid and mutable nature of living with the label of learning difficulties: the story (hopefully) destabilises the naturalised notion of 'learning difficulties'.

In terms of ownership, postmodernism problematises traditional ethnographic visions of the ideal 'objective' ethnographer's account; it attaches significance to the narratives of 'human subjects' whose voices may have been ignored or spoken of by grand narratives. Malinowski's maxim of capturing the 'native's vision of their world' is directly contravened by postmodern demands for researchers to openly and critically write themselves into their ethnographic accounts. If we accept the presumption that life is only a collection of narratives, then researchers need to own their narratives of a given part of the social world. The turn to the text has led to the death of the subject. The reflexive, embodied, agentic human being is replaced by an attention to the ways in which (human) subjects and (social, cultural) objects are constructed through a variety of interrelating stories and practices: or discourses.

Gerry O'Toole: a postmodern subject

Gerry's story is a research(er)'s ethnographic story that develops a discourse about a given culture and characters of a discursive tale. Gerry is a subject in a postmodern tale of disability discourses. The term 'fiction' can be applied in the poststructuralist sense: to fictionalise a host of practices that are often seen as inevitable and 'the right' practices for disabled people. Via the narratives collected during ethnography, the resultant story aims to destabilise common-sense understandings of disability and impairment; to challenge 'truths' that occupy and dominate the lives of some people with learning difficulties; to blur the words of writer and character and to illuminate how 'abnormalities' such as 'learning difficulties' exist only in relation to opposite conceptions of 'normality'.

Feminist standpoint approach to life story research – Rebecca Lawthom

The first thing to recognise is that there is a plurality of feminisms (Mama, 1995). We use the term 'women' to refer to a diverse collective of females, differentiated by 'race', class, age, disability and sexuality. Feminisms, whilst still other to dominant discourses, need to retain a collective identity in order to work together to transform dominant power relations in society (Yuval-Davis, 1993). Feminist standpoint epistemologies in research emphasise the perspectives of those whose lives are shaped and constrained (or marginalised) by the dominant social order. Ussher (1997) notes that a central concern for feminist psychology today is to theorise and explore the ways in which women's experience is gendered, both through the material conditions and the symbolic discursive processes of social life.

Feminist narratives

Certain narratives emerge from feminists themselves that shed light on the gendered nature of, for example, academic life (Ramazonoglu, 1987; Kagan and Lewis, 1989; Lawthom, 1997). Alternatively, narratives are often used by women with women. A good example of the ways in which feminists use narratives with women is demonstrated in a bicultural study (within Aotearoa/New Zealand). Here, women's experiences of recovery from disabling mental health problems are cast as stories of recovery. The stories show both their agency and struggle within mental health care provision:

> Their texts of illness are social texts, gendered and raced, and so are their recovery texts, yet the latter drew on the more empowering cultural resources available to them as women and men, Maori and non-Maori, rather than disempowering stereoptyes which had once defined them more fully.
>
> (Lapsley, Nikora and Black, 2000, p. 422)

Hunt (1998) similarly has used storytelling with women to generate critical thinking about mental health and emotional health care. Indeed, stories, as rich valuable data, are key to understanding womens' experiences. Mauthner's work with women who are diagnosed as postnatally depressed, uses a voice-relational methodology and subsequently presents the accounts as post-natal tales (Mauthner, 2002). Zhang's (1999) work with women in China emerged from her own experience of termination in a country with a one-child policy. She found in women's stories a clear relationship between pregnancy, abortion and the one-child policy. Concern about health, job absence and 'face' (important in Chinese society) impacted upon women's menstrual cycles. Zhang's research not only had emancipatory policy-making implications regarding contraception and counselling but led her into feminist theory and academia. The relationship between women and words has not always been an easy one. Women's ways of knowing as celebrated (e.g. Belenky *et al.*, 1986) are not always viewed as privileged accounts of experience (even within the feminist community). Though there may not be agreement between diverse representations of feminism (separatist, liberal, Marxist, etc.), there is common agreement over women's relative standing in relation to gendered power (taking into account 'race', class, sexuality, ability). Diversity across method/ologies seems an important feature of accessing and telling stories which may, otherwise, remain untold.

One of the crucial impacts of feminist epistemology on research has been the paradigm-shifting analyses of 'malestream' method/ology. The arguments of Salmon (2003) are symptomatic of feminist critiques of research in the social sciences. Salmon (2003) argues that methodologism is a limited epistemology. It is a forlorn belief that quality can be guaranteed simply by following procedures. Following Feyerabend (1975, 1978), justification for the value of scientific methods cannot logically emerge from the methods themselves. Investigators should be explicit about the epistemological basis, but two problems emerge:

1. epistemologies describe the use to which methods can be put, not which methods should be used;
2. post-hoc retrospective epistemologism.

Feyerabend's view is that the anarchist scientist is playful rather than precious with method/ology. This provides an epistemological rationale for recently emerging views in social science that 'good' research is playful; that research which slavishly follows methodological rules stultifies research; and that real scientific progress results from imagination, creativity and common sense, rather than merely deduction and induction (Rennie, 2000; Robinson, 2000). These arguments, taken from a feminist perspective, are reminiscent of Oakley's (1981) classic paper which argues for relationality over methodologism in terms of working with women, instead of on them. Though this paper has been critiqued for inadequate consideration of representation issues (e.g. white academic feminists representing black women's experience), the issue of relational engagement still seems important to feminist emancipatory research.

Colleen – a feminist tale?

Colleen's narrative is fundamentally a feminist tale. In form, it gives voices to one woman and her story; in process, the research was undertaken in an emancipatory framework; and in context, the story tells of a woman's realisation that patriarchy is present, both at a macro and personal level. What makes this tale feminist is not the realisation of the patriarchal dividend – men hold power in exchange for domestic capabilities – but that Colleen survives this, and is cognisant of the need for a way of understanding that could be called feminist:

> Whether this will ever change, whether ever anyone will ever think it is a really wonderful job that women do, I don't know.

Colleen's feminist tale might not fit into a unitary vision of what feminism is. McNay has argued for a relational idea of identity, which encourages us to think of difference in terms of its construction through the social realm ... a theory of identity as relational, and therefore open-ended, provides the basis for a theory of resistance based on a politics of difference.

(McNay, 1992, p. 110)

As feminists, we may share diverse priorities while accepting, in practice, a set of 'relational ethics'.

A social model of disability approach to life story research – *Michele Moore*

The extent to which a particular theoretical framework impacted on the story about David and of how a particular epistemological stance led to the writing of a particular kind of narrative is plain for all to see. I have not tried to disguise the power of the social model of disability in the framing of the story or to gloss over its associations with emancipatory research practice. The social model of disability – the British Disability Movement's 'big idea' – shifts attention away from the 'disabling consequences of impairment' to the disabling consequences of society's exclusion of people with impairments (Oliver, 1996). Emancipatory research practice aims to genuinely involve disabled people in research and meaningfully capture their understandings of themselves and the disabling world (Zarb, 1992). Both of these dimensions of the research agenda were influential in shaping the thinking and processes which led up to the writing of the story. Barnes (2003, p. 14) explains that 'when directly linked to disabled people's ongoing struggle for change, doing emancipatory disability research can have a meaningful impact on their empowerment and the policies that affect their lives', and this is the position to which I was committed at the time. Yet the circumstances were such that an emancipatory research agenda could not be pursued with any faithful reference to the essential criteria of that approach – processes of consultation were, for example, wholly inadequate and arguably the project is not recognisable as emancipatory research practice because its commitments are frequently muddled. The processes of the project might not best be described as having a *'meaningful impact'* on David's empowerment or on the policies that affected his life and the lives of his peers. But the driving theoretical and associated methodological principles were unshakeable, hence explicit acknowledgement of the ways in which these bias the life story project is imperative.

While one of the chief purposes of research is to support the generation of theory, it is also true to say that in life story research, as soon as you have identified the life you are interested in, your project is bound up with your theoretical predispositions, and is subordinated to your personal theoretical inclinations. Questions of whose life you research and why you are subjecting that life to research throw the matter of theoretical neutrality into dispute. When methodological and analytic choices are then also mapped onto the process of researching and writing a life story, both the focal life and the ensuing story are necessarily transformed. In the field of disability research there is a requirement for the transformative power of combining theoretical preferences and methodological processes to be maximised in the project of emancipation; hence it emerges that it is not possible or productive to separate theoretical persuasion from the narrative. The narrative *should* be underpinned unequivocally by the aim of empowerment; and the aim of empowerment is fundamentally underpinned by the social model of disability.

All of this raises familiar debate about 'objectivity versus subjectivity' in research and exposes a large part of the methodological struggle which all life story researchers face. Even before I met David my partisan position was fixed. I had formulated questions out of a deep professional engagement with the experiences of disabled people and out of personal knowledge of his family situation. For example, I was interested in finding out about his experiences of living in his parents' house *because* in an earlier study of experiences of spinal cord injury I had witnessed immense difficulty in mixed-generation families obliged to negotiate boundaries of independent living within one household (Oliver *et al.*, 1988). I wanted to know about his perceptions of medical and social services *because* I had repeatedly observed failures of service providers to confront the conceptual inadequacies of community care policies and services shaped without reference to the social model of disability (see also Priestley, 1999). My personal experience was material to the shaping of the story: '*I think I made up my mind what was wrong with David's life before I was even out of the car . . . I knew him to be about my own age . . . I was saying to myself . . . I'd be wanting to commit suicide too*'.

The life story research that I do explicitly seeks to optimise the relationship between life stories, an agenda for empowerment and inclusion and the everyday contexts in which exclusions of people with impairments are played out. I have said elsewhere that my work is 'fundamentally antithetical to the possibility of objectivity in respect of this commitment' (Armstrong and Moore, 2004). Of course we all have many vested interests, and this is why ideally life story researchers should, in my view, place emphasis on consultation with insiders to check the elaboration of our theoretical discourses and to offer alternative perspectives and guidance. In the context of my story of David, however, these aspirations are hugely compromised. His experiences of life and culture were very far from my own. Recognising David as the expert on himself and his experience means that a construction of a story about him and his experiences which has been constructed without him obviously runs counter to a focus on disabled people's own starting points.

Critics will always be able to dispute whether I have presented the 'real story', but arguably this does not actually matter. For me, the hallmark of life story research is that it should prompt positive social change : 'it can be partial, it can be disturbing, it can raise more questions than it answers, it can be contingent, provisional, ideological even, but it must advance an agenda for inclusion that is – as far as possible – prioritised by those at risk of exclusion, and it must be centrally informed by those who live with the reality of exclusion' (Armstrong and Moore, 2004).

A focus on points of disagreement about the purposes of life story research concentrates attention on the experiences of disabled people and can throw up glimpses of alternative theoretical positions that could be adopted. It is invariably helpful to think about the issues you are in danger of neglecting if you view the world in a particular way. Sticking firmly with the social model of disability as a tool to guide research processes and analyses will undoubtedly lead to the discounting of other theoretical perspectives and there is a danger that the life story is being hijacked through research as a means of *imposing* change. In this sense, life story research can be seen as an arena in which struggles take place over values, applications and change. Our own habits and patterns of thinking and behaving as life story researchers need to be examined all the time.

So, in conclusion, the story about David is entirely prejudiced by a particular theoretical and epistemological stance, which has led to its construction in a particular way. My emphasis has been on demonstrating how a social theory of disability can be intrinsically tied to life story research methodology and to claim that this fixture is an essential feature of life story research that seeks to advance the project of inclusion. Arguably it is vital that life story researchers make no attempt to tidy their theoretical baggage out of their writing. We cannot erase our personal commitments from life story research, nor can we feign objectivity. Nevertheless we can offer life story research as offering a way in to different ways of 'making the familiar strange' and contesting normative assumptions.

A literary theory approach to life story research – Peter Clough

This section sketches out the contribution of literary theory to the development of life story research in social science. Robert Scholes argues that narrative is 'a place where sequence and language, among other things, intersect to form a discursive code' (Scholes, 1974, p. 200). He puts forward the idea of 'iconic and indexical dimensions of language'. For 'narrative is not just a sequencing, or the illusion of a sequence . . .; narrative is a sequencing of something for somebody' (ibid., p. 205). For Scholes, real events happen, and they happen elsewhere – apart from the narrative. Such 'real' events can then be symbolised by narrative.

A narration is the symbolic presentation of a sequence of events connected by subject matter and related by time. Without temporal relation we have only a list. Without continuity of subject matter we have another kind of list.

(Scholes, 1974, p. 205)

There is work for the reader/audience too, for 'the difference between drama and narrative is not that characters speak in drama but that we hear them; not that they have bodies but that we see them. Drama is presence in time and space; narrative is past, always past' (ibid., p. 206). So narrative is about 'selection' *for* 'telling' and the selection and presentation of these events must connect, have contiguity, with the subject matter so that their occupation of space is significant. As Scholes continues:

When the telling provides this kind of sequence with a certain kind of shape and a certain level of human interest, we are in the presence not merely of narrative but of story. A story is a narrative with a certain very specific syntactic shape (beginning–middle–end or situation–transformation–situation) and with a subject matter which allows for or encourages the projection of human values upon this material. Virtually all stories are about human beings or humanoid creatures. Those that are not invariably humanise their material though metaphor and metonymy.

(Scholes, 1974, p. 206)

The portrayal of lives through life story research could be said to have three elements: the telling of *events*, the creation of *text*, and the *interpretation* of those events. In the case of fictional narrative in life historical research, events are not only *told* but are also *created*. What is interesting – perhaps taken for granted – is the (pre)existence of *events*. Something had to have happened to bring about the story. Scholes's analytical framework can be applied in the analysis of all stories:

Events came first, the text second, and the interpretation third, so that the interpretation, by striving toward a recreation of the events, in effect completes a semiotic circle. And in this process, the events themselves have become humanised – saturated with meaning and value – at the stage of entextualisation and again at the stage of interpretation. Our customary distinction between historical and fictional narrative can be clarified in terms of this structure. History is a narrative discourse with different rules than those that govern fiction. The producer of a historical text affirms that the events entextualised did indeed occur prior to the conceptualisation ... It is certainly otherwise with fiction, for in fiction the events may be said to be created by and with the text. They have no prior temporal existence, even though they are presented *as if* they did. As Sidney rightly pointed out four centuries ago, the writer of fiction does not affirm the prior existence of his events, he only pretends to through a convention understood by all who share his culture.

(Scholes, 1974, p. 207)

So what are we to take from this conceptualisation? How might we use it to interpret the four stories in this book and to create other stories at varying points on the 'truth'–'fiction' continuum? Richardson (1994) offers us some help here by pointing to the complex relationships of freedom, audience, constraint and (self-)consciousness in any story.

Although we are freer to present our texts in a variety of forms to diverse audiences, we have different constraints arising from self-consciousness about claims to authorship, authority, truth, validity and reliability. Self-reflexivity unmasks complex political/ideological agenda hidden in our writing. Truth claims are less easily validated now; desires to speak 'for' others are suspect. The greater freedom to experiment with textual form, however, does not guarantee a better product. The opportunities for writing worthy texts – books and articles that are a 'good read' – are multiple, exciting and demanding. But the work is harder. The guarantees are fewer. There is a lot more for us to think about.

(Richardson, 1994 p. 523)

Doerr (2002), in his collection of short stories, seems to be working out a set of personal concerns, about freedom, restriction and intrusion. His style is to end his fictional stories with single poignant (often short) sentences which, arguably, are the reason for the story. His political, moral or emotional message hangs at the end, and it is only at this point that we know what the story, as far as its author is concerned, is *about*. But to return, finally, to the distinction between fictional and the fictionalised. *Gerry O'Toole* and *Colleen* are fictionalised accounts broadly 'truthful' and, in *Colleen's* case, agreed with their informants/participants. *Frank*, however, is fiction – agreed with no one – out of the author, no negotiations, no vetos. 'Frank' (as he is portrayed in the story) has traces in him of other teachers and students, in addition to the one man who came to mind when I wrote *Frank*, but in the end 'Frank' is a character, not a person, and he is brought together to embody an insight of the author's; for, as Kundera has it,

characters are not born like people, of a woman; they are born of a situation, a sentence, a metaphor containing in a nutshell a basic human possibility that the author thinks no one discovered or said something essential about.

(Kundera, 1984, pp. 65–66)

The 'basic human possibility', or the 'something essential', is subtle and calls for evocation rather than description, for this is not a didactic text; rather, the intention is to assemble a moral milieu in which – guided by the craft of the author – the reader finds himself or herself. The story 'works' to the extent that it creates such a moral space. Robbe-Grillet says of this process:

> Fiction writing, unlike reportage, eye-witness accounts or scientific descriptions, isn't trying to give information – it *constitutes* reality.
>
> (Robbe-Grillet, 1955, p. 89)

Thus, the literary approach to life story research can stand apart. It can stand on its own bed of complexity of ethics and morals. Values, when we consider fictional narrative in social research, are unprotected; they are at the mercy of the author. So, this approach is essentially about language, using language to *create* events *through* texts which are then open to the multiple *interpretations* of their readers. As Postman has it:

> Both a social scientist and a novelist give unique interpretations to a set of human events and support their interpretations with examples in various forms. Their interpretations cannot be proved or disproved, but will draw their appeal from the power of their language, the depth of their explanations, the relevance of their examples, and the credibility of their themes. And all this has, in both cases, an identifiable moral purpose.
>
> (Postman, 1992, p. 154)

Reflecting on this chapter

Michele Moore argues earlier that 'the story about David is entirely prejudiced by a particular theoretical and epistemological stance which has led to its construction in a particular way'. This point about persuasion, positionality and particularity is crucial to all qualitative research, though perhaps even more so to life story research. All writers of stories are driven by particular visions of the world, which lead to the types of narratives that unfold. It is our hope that we have exposed at least some of the ways in which epistemology informs the writing of stories and the vision of the social world in which those stories take place. We now move from method/ology to interpretation.

Part 3

Making sense of life stories

Part 3 contains our engagement with analysis. Chapter 8 describes four approaches to analysis – discourse analysis, voice relational analysis, grounded theory and literary analysis – which will be used to analyse, respectively, the stories in Chapters 1–4. You will note that these analytical approaches reflect the four distinct epistemological stances of the authors described in the last chapter. Epistemology links method/ology and analysis. Chapter 9 presents four analyses of the stories – each story being analysed using one analytical approach. Our aims with this chapter are twofold: to analyse the stories through locating them in wider theoretical considerations and to demonstrate how analysis appears in the text following a particular approach. Chapter 10 critically reflects upon analysis. We pay particular attention to the impact of analysis in terms of its fit with our original aims of writing life stories and its impact upon the integrity of the life story.

Chapter 8

Frameworks

Analysis in life story research

Introduction

This chapter begins our analytic journey of life stories. One of the authors of this book has written elsewhere:

> The meanings of a narrative arise out of the interaction of story, storyteller and audience (Reason and Hawkins, 1988, p. 86). What audiences do with stories is often unclear. Consequently, an argument may be made for analysis that points out to readers themes within stories. Goodson (1992) suggests that analysis should increase the wider benefits of narratives by opposing unsympathetic, conservative or hostile readings . . . analysis strengthens stories.
>
> (Goodley, 2000, p. 57)

In this chapter we introduce you to four approaches to analysis. You will note that each analytical position fits neatly with each of the four epistemological positions articulated in the previous chapter. So, for example, a poststructuralist epistemology adopted by the writer of Gerry O'Toole's story is now taken further in terms of a poststructuralist approach to analysis (discourse analysis). We would like to flag up a health warning here. Often, during a research project, different concerns may mean that there is no logical link between a given epistemology and a directly resultant approach to analysis. However, we have kept with such a direct relationship for reasons of continuity and to clearly demonstrate the ways in which particular analytical frameworks have specific epistemological priorities.

Discourse analysis – *Dan Goodley*

I have argued in this book that Gerry O'Toole's story reflects a non-participatory ethnographic methodology, drawing upon a poststructuralist approach to narrative and the phenomenon of learning difficulties. In this section, I will consider how I attempt to make sense of the story. What is needed is an approach to analysis that allows us to answer the original research question posed by the author: *What can one story tell us about the social and cultural worlds inhabited by people with learning difficulties?* In addressing this question, we will continue with our engagement with a poststructuralist epistemology, by drawing on a poststructuralist method: discourse analysis.

Discourse, subjectivity and self

As we saw in Chapter 7, poststructuralism alerts us to the multiple, fragmented and socially constructed nature of the self and the individual (Burr, 1995). Burman and Parker (1993) argue that discourse analysis is a poststructualist method that provides a *social account of subjectivity*. Rather than viewing subjectivity as being in the heads of individuals, discourse analysts turn to the practices, texts, assemblages of knowledge, documents, experiences and narratives of given social and cultural locations in which subjectivities are constructed. Discourses are social phenomena in the sense that whenever people speak, listen, write, read or act, they do so in ways that are determined socially and have social impacts (Fairclough, 1989, p. 23). Sidell provides a rather literal view of discourse:

> How a discourse exerts power is through individuals who become its carriers by adopting the forms of subjectivity and the meanings and values which it propounds. This theory provides an understanding of where our experience comes from and can explain why so many of our experiences and opinions are sometimes incoherent and contradictory.
>
> (Sidell, 1989, p. 268)

Sidell's use of the term 'individual' here is problematic. You will recall from the previous chapter, that a poststructuralist epistemology challenges the notion of the a priori existence of an agentic, embodied, humanist human subject. This view of human beings is itself a creation of dominant discourses of modernity (Butler, 1990). Discourse analysis furthers this critique by interrogating those powers and practices that *create* human subjects. Discourse analysis deals with conflicting, subjugating and institutionally founded discourses that posit particular versions of self, personhood and subjectivity. Discourse analysis may allow us to make sense of the ways in which human beings are shaped and moulded, via the power of discourses, in given social and cultural backgrounds. This links directly with the original research question of the author: to investigate social and cultural meanings in the lives of people with learning difficulties through the analysis of one narrative.

Discourse, power and regulation

For Cicourel (1980), discourse analysts need to make explicit reference to broader cultural beliefs. Such an approach typifies a particular view of discourse analysis – that discourses are tied to *socio-cultural and political dominance and regulation* (Burman and Parker, 1993). While some discourse analysts have aimed to unearth inconsistency, variability and contradiction in talk (e.g. Potter and Wetherell, 1987) and others have illuminated the argumentative qualities of rhetoric (e.g. Billig, 1996), those of a more critical or political leaning aim to engage explicitly with the relationship between discourse, power and regulation (e.g. Henriques *et al.*, 1984; Burman and Parker, 1993). This latter stance draws heavily on the work of Michel Foucault (1973a, 1973b, 1977, 1980, 1983). Foucault was interested in the ways in which social and cultural locations fed upon discourses which masquerade as 'truths'. Discourses are also practices that fit particular societal needs: to rehabilitate the offender in a prison setting; to cure the irrational madman; to enforce normalised notions of sexuality in schools; to subject patients to medical expertise and interventions. These discursive practices are particularly noticeable in what Rose (1999) terms the *psy-complex*: those psychological, educational, human, welfare, health, rehabilitative and knowledge systems associated with 'the abnormal'. Within the psy-complex, Foucault suggests that it is possible to investigate elusive practices of power such as 'technologies of the body', 'disciplinary powers' and 'professional gaze'. Foucault was interested in those stories that illuminate some of these discursive practices in given cultural places. Such an approach fits with the original research question of interrogating social and cultural worlds through the story of one person with learning difficulties.

Governance, subjectification and resistance

All human subjects are open to a gamut of discursive regimes that 'allow' them opportunities for making sense of themselves. While common sense may have us believe that increased knowledge of ourselves is a good thing – it results in enlightened individuals and developed societies – there is a price to be paid. The increased production in knowledge in late capitalism has given rise to many versions of self. We feel free to understand, to better and to develop ourselves. Alas, Foucault argued, *we are free only to govern ourselves*. The power of discourse works in elusive ways. We know how we should act in given settings. We are aware of the limits of where we can appropriately go in our identity construction. We are free, but only to act in ways that we know we should act. Discourses inform our thinking about how we should be at given times and specific places. The final product of this process is that of *subjectification*; experienced as an inner consciousness, it is created by drawing upon available repertoires. Certain institutions and their members are particularly open to forms of governance and subjectification. People with learning difficulties – such as Gerry O'Toole – are regulated, closely observed and controlled by professional intrusions. Complementary discourses such as 'medicalisation', 'psychology' and 'individual' are brought to bear on the professional and self-governance. These discourses are especially accepted – and become almost commonsensical by nature – in institutions of group home, day centre, special school and segregated workplace. People with learning difficulties are allotted subject positions of 'client', 'patient' and 'service user' and the associated discourses are replenished outside of institutions by others' usage of them. This fits with the original research question: to interrogate the workings of cultural and social worlds of people with learning difficulties.

Foucault famously wrote that where there is power there is also resistance (Foucault, 1977). At its most radical, a poststructuralist discourse analysis exposes the categories of 'person' and 'learning difficulties' as entities formulated in power relationships of language by key knowledge-producers of the psy-complex. However, things that are 'man-made' can often be demolished and rebuilt. While there are individuals and institutions with more access to discursive raw materials, possibilities exist for rebuilding versions of humanity. The discourse analyst not only examines the wider socio-cultural origins and impacts of discourses (and the consequent subject positions, objects and possibilities for subjectification) but also explores opportunities for resistance to dominant governing discourses. Discourse analysis is a resistant approach to analysis: resisting static, structuralist and immovable views of discourse while embracing resistant performative acts of human subjects. Following Wilkinson and Kitzinger (1995, p. 3), it aims to explore what it means to be a person with learning difficulties in the modern tale, by interrogating those discursive practices that constitute versions of self and ways of being for people so labelled. Discourse analysis allows us to interrogate the social construction of Gerry O'Toole and his peers.

Voice relational approaches – *Rebecca Lawthom*

Colleen's account of her life is analysed drawing upon voice relational approaches. Here, I (Rebecca) present the facets of this approach and how it may be used in an emancipatory fashion.

Introducing a voice relational approach

The voice relational approach arises from a long feminist tradition of engaging with women and for women. Brown and Gilligan (1992, p. 22) point out that

Recasting psychology as a relational practice, we attend to the relational dimensions of our listening, speaking, taking in, interpreting, and writing about the words and the silences, the stories and the narratives of other people.

The method has its roots in clinical and literary traditions, interpretive and hermeneutic theories and relational understandings. Hermeneutics – the study of scripture or meaning – ensures that the analyst attends to the meanings held by informants of their worlds. This positioning of voices as relational *within the analysis*, is an explicit step in feminist research, which has traditionally listened to women to understand lives 'in and on their own terms', and thus to ground theory in women's own experiences (Du Bois, 1983; Finch, 1984; Brown and Gilligan, 1992; Henwood and Pidgeon, 1992). Much of the feminist work within the qualitative tradition has problematised the notion of 'voice' and power within research. What this approach offers is multiple readings of an account, potentially offering richness and complexity while retaining a self/person/individual within the story. Larson (1997, p. 456), following her experience as a story-giver, suggests that:

> We rethink traditional monological practices in narrative inquiry and use dialogical processes that assist story givers in untangling the complex meanings of their own lived experience.

Feminist thinking about reflexivity has elucidated the need to address two aspects of the research process: first, the nature of the research relationship and second, its relation to theory construction and epistemology. Haraway's (1991) notion of 'situated knowledges' acknowledges that theory production can only be a social activity embedded in culture, society and history.

Doing voice relational methods

Voice relational methods can and should be used collaboratively to, first, tease apart and then make sense of narratives. Broadly, the analysis takes the form of a number of distinct readings of the narratives. Four readings are undertaken: first reading for plot and our responses to the narrative; second, reading for the voice of 'I'; third, reading for relationships; fourth, placing people within cultural contexts and social structures. A more detailed description is given in Box 8.1 (after Brown *et al.*, 1989; Brown and Gilligan, 1992; Mauthner and Doucet, 1997).

Box 8.1 Voice relational methods: an overview

Reading 1: Reading for plot and our response to the narrative
What are the story, the characters, the sub-plots? Recurrent images, words and metaphors are listened to. The reader is encouraged in this reading to read for herself in the text, placing herself in relation to the person (background, history and experiences). This allows the reader to examine how her assumptions might affect interpretation. Both social location and emotional responses allow the reader to use reflexivity to track one's own responses to the text.

Reading 2: Reading for the voice of 'I'
In this reading, we look for 'I' and how this shifts to 'we' or 'you' when discussing perceptions or experiences. Brown and Gilligan (1993) term this discovery 'how she speaks of herself before we speak of her'. The analysis here aims to stay with the respondent's multi-layered voices (I/we/you) rather than slotting them into single-layered themes or memos (as with other qualitative analyses).

Reading 3: Reading for relationships
In this reading, we look for the way in which respondents speak about interpersonal relationships with other people and broader social networks. There is a conscious reading for relationships that examines connections, autonomy and dependence.

Reading 4: Placing people within cultural contexts and social structures
Here the narrative is explored in terms of broader political, cultural and structural contexts.

Clearly, there is some overlap between these four readings, as they constitute reading and re-reading of the same account. However, each distinct focus aims to span and track the individual's agentic voice together with the voices of those in relationship with the individual, through to shared societal discourses. The focus on voice aims to transform the act of reading into an act of listening as the reader takes in different voices and follows them through the narrative.

The readings undertaken in voice relational analysis can be done (and were by Brown *et al.*, 1989, 1991) in group settings. This allows diversity to emerge. For my analysis, to ensure that an emancipatory stance was taken, Colleen was involved in all stages of the analysis. The written finished product is the result of a collaborative analysis. The four readings were presented to Colleen and we then discussed and shared how we saw these analyses working on the data. The more detailed discussion of this process is found in Chapter 9.

Grounded theory – *Michele Moore*

Grounded theory (Glaser and Strauss, 1967; Glaser, 1995, 1998; Strauss and Corbin, 1990, 1997) was chosen as the best analytic tool for making sense of David's story because it offers a well-established approach to ensuring that ideas and recommendations which the researcher develops and makes emerge *from* the data, are *grounded in* what key participants have contributed through their words and experiences. Grounded theory gives an analytic qualitative approach explicitly concerned with seeking out theoretical explanations for what is going on in any given research situation, and is sufficiently adaptable to be fitted to projects in which both the research methodology and the process of analysis are developing in unpredictable ways.

In addition, grounded theory analysis is not dependent on any particular methodology and even data collected at the limits of standard research practice – such as characterised researching with David – can be subjected to analytic scrutiny using this approach. For instance, it is not imperative to have detailed notes made *in situ* for grounded theory analysis. There is no requirement for transcription or verbatim recordings and frequently leading grounded theory analysts advocate against the use of extensive note-taking and tape-recording *in situ*, arguing that these are distracting and intrusive habits. As explained elsewhere, note-taking was prohibited in the research with David – occasionally he allowed a few jottings, which of necessity turned out to consist at best in a few words hurriedly pulled together to try to capture an important emerging theme. All in all, grounded theory provided a congenial strategy for handling the irregular material that this peculiar research journey had called forth.

Grounded theory is often described as an 'emergent process' in the sense that theory is envisaged as surfacing through assembled data. In fact, from the outset I was using Oliver's work on the social model of disability to shape the theoretical persuasion of the project, so in this sense I was predisposed to 'force' the data into a theoretical framework rather than to allow alternative theoretical explanations to unfold. I claim to have kept a realistic eye on the necessity for reconstruction of the chosen theoretical position. But following this adaptation of one of the defining dynamics of grounded theory means that the application of grounded theory in this project could be seen as misappropriated. This adaptation need not, however, be taken to imply that the theoretical framework developed is any the less robust. Glaser and Strauss (1967) place emphasis on theories as being generated from observation and from logical assumptions – in the case of this study both were made from both within and beyond the focal project.

The process of making analysis using grounded theory at all times overlapped with the processes of collecting the data. From the very first time David was brought to my attention, as I was seeking to make sense of what was happening to him and to gain insight into how he was experiencing what was happening, the social model of disability unavoidably sprang to mind. The opening gambit 'No one knows *what's wrong with him*' provoked me to research action precisely *because* I was fiercely committed to resistance of individualised and pathologising images of disabled people's lives and the data very quickly began to fit neatly with this commitment. The social model of disability provided the theoretical foundation of the study and also rendered analysis and data collection more than overlapping processes, for they were integral to one another. There is a good chance that somewhat improper use has been made of grounded theory in this study by forcing data to fit a preconceived theoretical agenda, but an alternative reading is that this approach to analysis served to cross-validate important theoretical understandings already offered.

For the analysis I sought to identify categories of data which encapsulated important themes. As our meetings proceeded and a dialogue built up, I became increasingly conscious of barriers that were underpinning David's experiences of disablement – 'disabling barriers' became a core category or organising theme. I then identified sub-categories such as 'environmental barriers', 'social barriers', 'service provision barriers', 'financial barriers', 'barriers to personal relationships', 'personal assistance barriers' and so on and wrote notes to myself under each of the headings. For example, under 'environmental barriers':

> *David doesn't have his own entrance . . . can't get to the front door without assistance.*

> *He mentioned the intercom and worrying that people switch it on to eavesdrop.*

> *Talked about the intercom [again] and not being able to switch it off independently.*

New categories were added as time went by. Some categories generated new categories as they grew and the sophistication of the debate became clear, so that entries under 'service provision barriers', for example, were further divided and recoded to make use of a new category, *'silencing and collusion'*. In the margins of the notes I added links to literature that came to mind, or needed to be looked up, and made notes of any connections to other research of which I knew. This is called 'memoing' by some grounded theory writers (e.g. Dick, 2002). I was constantly on the lookout for experiences or data that *could not* be coded with reference to the social origins of disablement, but there were none. This meant that the analysis began to feel 'safe'. There is a kind of integral rigour built into grounded theory as you search for evidence which disconfirms your favoured theory – the fewer 'discarded observations', i.e. observations falling outside the theoretical framework being used, then the more confidence you can have that the theoretical explanation is 'working'.

'Constant comparison of data' with other sources is a key ingredient for validation in grounded theory analysis. There was constant comparison from moment to moment in conversations with David, comparison across conversations between David and others, comparisons to be made from one day to the next and of course comparisons to be made between what was coming up *in situ* and what was being said in the relevant research literature. All of these comparisons, without exception, endorsed a theoretical explanation that looked to the social origins of disablement.

In this study I did not have any expectation that it would be possible to engage in additional sampling to take stock of whether David's situation was 'like' or 'unlike' others, and I was not optimistic of finding people in similar situations whose experience could strengthen the theory being generated. However, a fellow researcher I was in contact with at the time was involved in discussions about planned suicide with a disabled woman in another part of the country. We made ongoing comparisons of the situations of David and the woman Tina. What happened to Tina is, as they say, another story. But it was instructive to note at the time that Tina's experiences cross-validated David's and the explanatory powers of the social model of disability entirely fitted her story too. Other cases of disabled people seeking suicide as a 'positive' option have since been reported in the press and these too have offered up points for comparative analysis. The final aspect to building the analysis involved gaining familiarity with research literature and other writings which could be connected to the emergent data and categories.

The analysis I constructed is presented in the next chapter. It shows the theoretical explanations derived from the orgnasiation of the data into categories and provides a new body of knowledge on disability and the life course that is uniquely grounded in David's story.

Literary criticism – *Peter Clough*

Of the many frameworks which might be employed in the 'analysis' of life story research, we might call upon the structures and ideas of Plato. It goes without saying, I think, that it is somewhat presumptuous to believe that one *can* analyse a life story. What *is* a life story, but something already rendered and interpreted? That said, there are structures and frameworks at work in us as we create and/or read life stories, and the positions set out by the discipline of literary criticism come into play when we seek to identify the themes and structures at work in the stories. In the third book of Plato's *Republic*, Socrates posits a distinction between two ways of rendering speech: diegesis and mimesis. The characteristic feature of diegesis is that 'the poet himself is the speaker and does not even attempt to suggest to us that anyone but himself is speaking' (Plato, 1963, p. 638). In mimesis, on the other hand, the poet tries to create the illusion that it is not he who speaks (ibid., p. 106) (see Figure 8.1).

←——— diegesis ————————————————————— mimesis ——→
poet as speaker   'other' as speaker

Figure 8.1 Representation of the diegesis/mimesis polarisation

The polarisation of diegesis and mimesis reappears under the names of 'telling' and 'showing' in Anglo-American criticism of the end of the twentieth century and the beginning of the twenty-first. 'Showing' is the supposedly direct presentation of events and conversations, the narrator seeming to disappear (as in drama) and the reader being left to draw his own conclusions from what he 'sees' and 'hears'. 'Telling', on the other hand, is a presentation mediated by the narrator who, instead of directly and dramatically exhibiting events and conversations, talks about them, sums them up. Figure 8.2 represents a combination of the polarisations of diegesis and mimesis with the modern notions of 'telling' and 'showing'.

Percy Lubbock (in 1921) erected 'showing' into the highest ideal to which narrative fiction should aspire:

> *The art of fiction does not begin until the novelist thinks of his story as a matter to be shown, to be so exhibited that it will tell itself.*
> (Lubbock, 1963, p. 62, orig. pub. 1921, author's emphasis)

←——— diegesis ————————————————————— mimesis ——→
poet as speaker   'other' as speaker

←——— 'telling' ————————————————————— 'showing' ——→
narrator as 'mediator'   narrator 'disappears'

Figure 8.2 Representation of the diegesis/mimesis polarisation of Plato and modern structures of 'telling' and 'showing'

On the basis of this norm he attacks novelists such as Fielding, Thackeray and Dickens whose narrators opt for 'telling' – they tell, sum up and comment (Rimmon-Kenan, 2002, p. 107). We can take this framework for thinking about stories further. Iser (1971, p. 285) argues:

> No tale can be told in its entirety. Indeed, it is only through inevitable omissions that a story will gain its dynamism. Thus whenever the flow is interrupted and we are led off in unexpected directions, the opportunity is given to us to bring into play our own faculty for establishing connections – for filling in gaps left by the text itself.
>
> (Rimmon-Kenan, 2002, p. 127)

So, when in this book you read the stories – of Gerry O'Toole, Colleen, David and Frank – you bring to the reading your own structures of analyses. Your own literary criticism, your own preferences for 'being told' or 'being shown'. Readers of the most difficult stories are asked to do some of the analytical work themselves. *Frank*, for example, asks much of the reader; even though subsequent sections of the book 'unpack' parts of the writing and generation of the story, the story itself 'tells' little. *Frank* leads the reader to a place where they might begin to search for the meanings and issues which lie behind and surround the story.

Where the 'art' of the literary is concerned, there is a strong argument that the structures and analytical frameworks are – actually – unimportant. What matters is what works, what appeals, what persuades. And if we are to make stories which push at the boundaries of the narrative turn and challenge their readers to create their own meanings from them (using their own personally informed structures of analyses) then should we not be creating new frameworks, new structures and new positions from which we make meaning from those stories? This is a difficult but essential task, for, as Sterne has it:

> Shall we for ever make new books as apothecaries make new mixtures, by pouring only out of one vessel into another? Are we for ever to be twisting, and untwisting the same rope? For ever in the same track – for ever at the same pace?
>
> (Sterne, 1977, p. 167)

Conclusions

Too often, social and educational researchers launch into analysis without exposing the frameworks they are drawing upon. In this chapter we have seen how very different frameworks will disrupt the narratives they are trying to understand in ways that lead to particular types of knowledge production. We toyed with the idea of analysing each others' stories with our own analytical approach in mind. This would have provided some interestingly different interpretations of the four stories presented in Part 1 of this book. For now, we hope that you have some understanding of various analytical approaches and their impact upon the reading of stories.

Chapter 9

Findings

Four analyses of life stories

Without further ado, we now present four analyses that draw on four analytical approaches.

A discourse analysis of *Gerry O'Toole: A design for life* – *Dan Goodley*

Back to our research question, posed in Chapter 5 by the author of Gerry O'Toole's story: What can one story tell us about the social and cultural worlds inhabited by people with learning difficulties? Discourse analysis allows us to answer this question by examining the ways in which Gerry and others are moulded by the power of discourses. Following Wilkinson and Kitzinger (1995, p. 3), analysis aims to explore what it means to be a person with learning difficulties in this post/modern tale, by interrogating those discursive practices which constitute versions of self. While Gerry has told *his* story, this is the analyst's supplementary story. Three discourse analyses are offered.

The construction of people with learning difficulties as objects

Learning difficulties are often considered to be objectified naturalised phenomena. They are something people are tragically born with. Organic, unchanging and resolute. Yet, Gerry's stories demonstrates what Titchkovsky (2002, p. 105) calls the thingification of the world, persons and experience, which produces a phantom objectivity and denies and mystifies the body's fundamental nature as a *relation between people*. If we take the stories of Bant and David in Chapter 1 we can see a continuum of objectification from person with learning difficulties as plaything through to person with learning difficulties as object of abuse. Bant's friend and Brig's workmate are no longer human subjects: they are objects to be reacted to and objectified further. Note, also, the unspoken elements of how impairments such as learning difficulties are constructed: 'You feel it inappropriate to catch my eye,' writes Gerry, not because others' lack social skills but because of the performative awkwardness of reacting to troubling objects (Butler, 1990). Following Titchkovsky (2002), the observer is caught between seeing the object ('the learning disabled') and subject (a passer-by on the street). Gerry is clear about where these contradictory understandings reside: in a world where groups of people 'bat for different sides': the objectifier/signifier and the object/signified. Such an understanding of impairment-as-object is significant: crucially, *people with learning difficulties are objects*.

Impairment construction, through objectification, has contributed markedly to the exclusion of people identified as those objects: they are literally and metaphorically unable to open doors, as with Gerry's peers at the conference in Scotland. People with learning difficulties are aware of the consequences of objectification; hence, the move towards the label 'People First' suggested by Gerry and his peers who organised their group under such a banner. This choice of name speaks of a history of being viewed solely as an object of understanding, ridicule, intervention and control. And, often, as a disposed object. As Tremain (2002, p. 42) puts it, disability has been impairment all along. A crucial part of the exclusion of people with impairments – what may be defined as 'disability' (Oliver, 1990, 1996) – is the very construction of their impairments and therefore their selves as objects. Gerry O'Toole's narrative displays the remnants of being constructed as an object of intervention and the often horrendous consequences of such interventions. This life story tell us that the social and cultural worlds inhabited by people with learning difficulties are often ones in which they are liable to be constructed as objects – as opposed to the 'people first' that they want to be.

Governance and subjectification

Gerry's story can be seen as a tale of the psy-complex (Rose, 1999). Many of Gerry's peers are continuously monitored and disciplined by professional chaperones. There is a sense that Gerry is very much aware of the psy-complex's location in the institutions of special schools – 'funny buildings, strange places, labelled as soon as you got there'. However, the psy-complex is not limited to professionalised institutions. The psy-complex is part of wider society. From Ricky Lake and Oprah to self-help books, counselling and everyday self-reflection, domineering discourses of our 'selves' – and how our selves should be – are felt and experienced in everyday life. Versions of self do not remain in institutions, but are formed and reformed in everyday contexts. People with learning difficulties are 'village idiots', 'the funny backwards chap', 'the special needs kid' – the easy piss-take in the working men's club. As part of our wider 'need' to understand ourselves – a key progressive aim of a civilised, modern society

– power is afforded those, at given times, who utilise discourse's explanatory and regulatory qualities. We know a 'handicapped person' just from looking at them: we have the available knowledge resources, and consequently, we often feel we have the power to know; and the power that comes from knowing. This knowing of self – and how self should be – has been termed governance. This can range from governing others (such as gazing at the abnormal in the vignette of David) through to more elusive self-governance ('now things are a lot more subtle'). David was free to make a choice, to go on holiday, which then resulted in long-term exclusion. In making sense of ourselves, we draw upon available discourses, which may give us a sense of agency. However, we are free only to govern ourselves. As Kurtz (1981, p. 14) puts it, 'acting like a retarded person [*sic*] can soon become second nature'.

Essentially, modern human subjects are open to a gamut of discursive regimes and practices which allow them opportunities for making sense of themselves. The final product of this process is that of subjectification – experienced as an inner consciousness, created by drawing upon available discourses (governance). While common sense may have us believe that an increased knowledge of ourselves – and resultant subjectification – results in enlightened individuals and developed societies, there is a price to be paid.

Box 9.1 Subjectification in Gerry O'Toole's life story

Subjectification for people with learning difficulties appears to be associated with their bodies and minds being rendered in the following ways:

- *docile* (students fell asleep in Gerry's class);
- *passive* (the staff insist on Maureen leaving the door open when she is having a bath);
- *controlled* (Katy is not allowed to come to People First meetings if she behaves badly);
- *incompetent* (not to be trusted with a cigarette lighter);
- *pawns* (to be moved from group home to group home);
- *unknowing* (not informed about the death of Maddie Harrison).

Gerry knows his place in the cooking class at the day centre, and excuses it as an opportunity to see friends – but is this a knowing acceptance? A politics of pity for the member of staff? Or a subjectification of his subject position as client to be taught by the staff member? For people with the label of learning difficulties, such as Gerry O'Toole and his peers, their daily lives are regulated and controlled by professional intrusions. Education is increasingly multi-layered in terms of the increasing forms of professionalisation. While the ambulances and large-scale institution-alisation of Gerry's childhood might have disappeared, the advent of a host of specialist services (psy-complex), discourses of self-knowledge (governance) and their application (subjectification) create a new horrific realisation: at least when institutionalised in the old hospitals, inmates' minds had wings. We learn that the social and cultural worlds inhabited by people with learning difficulties are ones that are closely policed, moni-tored and controlled, which in turn may subject people to ways of seeing themselves that are worthless and incapable.

Resilience and resistance in the midst of the psy-complex

Gerry's story is ordinary in the face of extraordinary experiences of other people with learning difficulties, but still has the threat of disablement. Discourse analysis is a resistant approach to analysis: resisting static, struc-turalist and immovable views of discourse while embracing resistant, performative acts of human subjects. Foucault famously wrote that where there is power there is also resistance (Foucault, 1975). At its most radical, a poststructuralist discourse analysis exposes the categories of 'person' and 'learning difficulties' as entities formulated in power relationships of language by key knowledge-producers of the psy-complex. Now, things that are 'man-made' can often be demolished and rebuilt. While certain indi-viduals and institutions have more access to discursive raw materials, pos-sibilities exist for all to rebuild versions of humanity. The discourse analyst explores opportunities for resistance to dominant governing discourses.

One key origin of resistance lies in the multiple selves and identities of a discursive world. During the day we may move between the subject positions of parent, partner, colleague, consumer, player and lover. Each of these positions has power connected to them. What is so telling about Gerry's narrative are the very different subject positions he holds – from day centre user, to worker, to key member of the family, to member of the pub team, to memberships of the working men's club. The character of this narrative is someone allowed to move in and out of institution-ally created *subject positions*. Often, there are very direct acts of resistance with tremendous symbolism – none more obvious perhaps than that Gerry wanted to dig himself out of school! So characters in the narrative found that external (material) barriers challenged their subject movement. It is therefore even more remarkable to see people who are so objectified by the professional gaze finding spaces to escape subject positions – such as Gerry O'Toole and comrades like Maddie Harrison. For some their new subject positions might have to take place away from the professional gaze: such as setting up the self-advocacy group outside of the day centre, dispensing with the services of a member of staff as the group's supporter. Perhaps this is key to Gerry's narrative – to enter contexts away from the professionally populated spaces of learning difficulty services. It is interesting to note that self-advocacy groups affirm positive visions of self – People First – often in non-service, non-professionally led contexts. While we should be wary of how the psy-complex can enter a whole host of seemingly enabling spaces (Goodley, 1997), we are reminded that resistance often takes place in invisible, hidden places.

In the market, Gerry's learning difficulties are invisible, though in the curriculum of the special school they are exposed. Following Oppenheim (1998) and Milbourne (2002), the school allows assessment of skills and abilities only through a host of dominating governing principles, which may ignore wider skills that show up only in other institutional spaces (such as the market). Gerry is a remarkable character. He slips in and out of service settings and boasts a rich and varied experience of life. For some of his peers, the opportunities are not so available. Here the actions of potential resilient allies are thrown into sharp relief. Far from us denouncing professional practice, we should be aware of the many professionalised cultures where professionals are resisting. When Gerry talks about 'broken teachers' he highlights the ways in which professional subject positions are not all-encompassing and that professionals themselves are caught up in the disabling world of the psy-complex. For resistance to be read as meaningful, cultural exchange has to take place between participants in a social setting (Davies and Watson, 2002, p165). It is no surprise that members of the People First movement, which Gerry and his peers are part of, have spoken about those members of staff who have broken the professional mould to offer alliances and comradeship (Goodley, 2000). Gerry's story is one of resilience and success as a consequence of the conditions in which he has found himself. Other characters – real people who are real friends and comrades of Gerry – enter the fray. Often their stories are situated in more oppressive and exclusionary practices and institutions. Indeed, one of the key things for Gerry is his relative freedom and occupation of a space outside of disability service work, care and welfare. Intriguingly, his narrative ends with the final act of resistance – lost, in love in Rotherham.

A voice relational analysis of 'I'd never met a vegetarian, never mind a lesbian': Colleen's story – Rebecca Lawthom with Colleen Stamford

Following the principles of voice relational methods outlined in the previous chapter, the analysis of Colleen's story is set out below as the analysis was undertaken – in four separate readings.

Reading 1 – Reading for the plot and our responses to the narrative

Reading for the plot

The main events in this story illustrate development, progression and a largely heterosexual mainstream trajectory. By this, we mean the growing up of girl into woman and mother. The main plot is one of personal change and growth, at first perhaps within a boundaried community, yet at the same time distinct within this community. The sub-plot is perhaps one of otherness, of not being the same, being different. Recurrent words and images are 'hard workers', 'work ethic', 'working class'. The whole family worked hard (a mother with two jobs, a dad who worked hard and did housework, a husband who worked hard and Colleen, for whom working was also important). Money is a key image linked to this – the family had more money and could go on holiday. Colleen took on Saturday jobs in order to get money to buy nice things and later got a posh salaried job in town. As a nuclear family unit, Colleen's immediate family should have been happy with what they had – owning their own house. They had already exceeded the previous generation's council house dwelling.

Expectations are a key feature of the story – it didn't matter what else Colleen did, she would get married and have children (everyone did). Pressure from church and family were subtly exerted (you did certain things in a certain way). Work was only a temporary situation as absence was expected – once you got married, you paid a smaller insurance stamp and once young children came, work inevitably stopped for a while. Roles and relationships were framed by expectation – Colleen's mum reminding her that her husband was 'not going to stand for that' regarding separate sleeping arrangements. Confidence (sometimes its lack) and subsequent choice enters the story in distinctive ways. Colleen 'daren't' do O levels, she wouldn't have her pick of the crop in terms of boyfriends – both due to perceived attractiveness and confidence. 'Mum said I was too big for my boots.' She found working in a mixed-gender environment difficult (as being used to all girls). She was proud of her place at secretarial college and this extended to her family. Colleen felt confident with voluntary work settings such as those involving older people and people with learning difficulties. Overall, she was not particularly confident in her early years – 'I was mediocre, not a sparkling personality, not particularly attractive'. She also recognises the role of feedback in this – 'Children grown like flowers with praise.' Success is a key concept Colleen uses (to judge her own competence). College, a nice job with smart people and owning a house – are all markers of achievement (externally at least). Emotionally, the children and later her new-found career bring happiness. The new job brings personal success and being good at something. She chose to do nursing and loves it.

Family dynamics and women at home are featured throughout the tale. The expectation is that women will do housework and it is of no importance in this closed-off world. However, if men do this work, like childcare, they are wonderful. Colleen's family was different in terms of gender division of labour – 'my dad just loved my mum' and thus did do household tasks (also because she was ill, depressed?). For Colleen, there is a reversion to traditional roles – she and her husband did their own jobs but she says 'I did work plus on top of other things'. The roles of families and dynamics are also present in the new nursing job – much is going on even if you can't see it.

Reading for the sub-plot

The sub-plot is largely framed in terms of difference – Colleen's difference from both her family and her changing self (her own difference). Her early memories are of her father doing housework and the childcare being maintained by the male side of the family. Her father realised this wasn't normal, he 'wouldn't put the washing out' as this was a public display. Colleen comments 'he was a New Man too soon'. Colleen feels she had to dress differently as she mixed with people from 'posh parts', perhaps overdressed at times as she misjudged the dress code. Kudos came from this proper job (not shop or factory work) and again this was different from the other girls on the estate. Colleen says she was late getting married and late having children (five years after marriage). She consistently feels not up to scratch – being brought up where she was. 'I hope I wasn't a snob but wanted to think I was better than some.' Colleen's parents did not understand why Colleen wanted to work, following the children going to school, but Colleen says, 'you could be a new person.' Colleen also talks about her married life and her change/her difference in terms of growth from a quiet person to having an opinion and voicing it. From her 'working-class' life, she feels the difference and had 'never met a vegetarian let alone a lesbian'. She finds people at her new workplace 'alternative', very complimentary and very different. She recognises her own difference when she says, 'I am good at interaction, I have come full circle.'

Reader response

Reading my own response into the analysis is interesting. Colleen's childhood is not like mine in certain ways. There are similarities such as both parents working and a nearby grandparent, but a very different set of expectations surrounded me. As for Colleen, coming from a working-class area was not an issue until leaving it and recognising the difference. For me, it was leaving for university; for Colleen, it was mixing with 'posh people'. I (Rebecca) assumed I was always going to go to university and unlike Colleen felt praised for things and confident. It was painful to hear some of Colleen's self-description as being mediocre and not attractive. I find myself wanting the tale to 'come good'. Emotionally, it was a warm interview and a warm tale. Theoretically, while reading it through, we are thinking of early relationships and learning how to get praise (developmental frameworks). Using a feminist lens, I am also seeing women as often disadvantaged (by patriarchy) and therefore more limited in choices. However, working mothers (which we are) are not given a panacea with better childcare provision and I find myself agreeing with Colleen regarding women's unequal domestic load. Reading the tale as a narrative of change and transformation (from a feminist orientation), are we attributing Colleen's 'freedom' from domestic heterosexuality to the remedy provided by a woman partner? I find myself engaging with the change aspects of the tale – but on re-reading again and again, see much in the story that is stable and being engaged and fulfilled at various points in her life.

Reading 2: Reading for the voice of 'I'

The second reading follows the method suggested by Mauthner and Doucet's (1997) adaptation of Brown and Gilligan (1992). Using a coloured pen we traced Colleen's use of the pronouns 'I', 'we' and 'you'. Looking at this allows the space between an active 'I' or where 'I' is struggling to say something to shift to a 'we' or a 'you'. This second reading for personal pronouns allows the narrator(s) to speak for themselves – attending to 'I'. As listeners, we try to hear the person and the way she speaks about herself. For Colleen, reading for 'I' was really important in displaying the tension between what she did, liked, felt proud of and a wider dominant set of voices about what should be done. Personal expectations and interpretations of events are inextricably linked to the cultural values and norms which surround them. Colleen talks of achievement, 'I would never have gone to do nursing training', 'I would have thought it was far above me anyway' and the tension with others regarding expectations, 'You never thought about whether you'd be happy doing that or what would happen if you didn't' and 'if you had no expectations of yourself you could easily be left out and done nothing'. At key points in the narrative the active, agentic 'I' switches to locating herself in a dominant culture where behaviour is prescribed:

> I had never had a long-term boyfriend at all and already you were beginning to think that maybe it wasn't going to happen and then what would you do?

At other times the narrative is informed by social and structural contexts and then turns to the personal:

Certainly if *you* hadn't got married by the time *you* were 20 *you* were definitely thinking *you* were going to be left on the shelf and *I* remember when *I* got pregnant at 25 *I* was old.

This kind of analytical reading retains the individual (across ambiguous discourses) rather than distributing and reconstructing them across themes (as in thematic analysis).

Reading 3: Reading for relationships

In the third reading we listened for the ways in which Colleen spoke about her interpersonal relationships – family, relatives, children and the broader social networks. Again, using a coloured pen, we traced words and phrases that related to this. This reading placed Colleen amidst a complex set of competing needs. There is much sense of positive relating: 'My Dad, he's really proud', 'it brought the entire family a lot of pride', 'I think he just loved my mum and would have done anything for her'. Moreover, there is also evidence of mixed emotions regarding rights and responsibilities in Colleen's domestic setting versus work.

> I think it was just a thing of being Danny's mum, or Rosa's mum, I was sick if being someone's mum or someone's wife, I just needed to see if I could do something away from there where no one knew you.

Later she talks of the home – work boundary:

> But then I saw the light then and I am thinking, 'Oh, hang on a minute, why should I work and do the housework, and do the shopping and do the ironing and do everything, and all he had to do was go out to work?

There is also, throughout the narrative, a sense of the inevitability of being a mother and the pleasure gained from that:

> I have to say when I got the job, I always thought in the back of my mind that it didn't really matter what I did because it wouldn't be for long, I would get married and have a baby.

> I had had the children . . . and I was happy staying at home, I think that I liked doing it and I did it well and I felt confident with that.

There is a sense of growing confidence with regard to being competent at relationships:

> I didn't feel good at interaction so I picked jobs purposefully to avoid that contact. I have ended now in a job which has huge amounts of that, and more of that than anything else. Actually, I am finding out that I like it.

Reading 4: Placing people within cultural contexts and social structures

For this reading, we looked at Colleen's position within the broader social, political, cultural and structural contexts. There is evidence in her account of a shift in terms of both values surrounding age – 'Nowadays people can do whatever they like at whatever age they want whether retraining or going to uni, this is a good thing. I sound like an old crock but times have changed and my life has gone full circle in some ways' – and values surrounding class – 'Where I lived it had a very bad reputation whereas now it is quite trendy to be working-class, isn't it? Interestingly, her perceptions of gender imbalance, particularly in relation to women and sharing childcare, demonstrates more continuity than change:

> still women do exactly the same thing (as I did) they are just under a different guise now. If the husband manages to pick them up (the kids) a couple of times from the childminder or something. I work with women who do it, who do a job, arranging the childcare and the shopping. I am sure a lot of women think they have come a long way. The childcare has improved and that is about it, I think.

This reading also allows a focus on institutions, structures and ideologies, as providing strong enabling or constraining messages. Colleen talks of expectations:

> we had everything – our own house which me mam and dad had never done (you know council houses were the norm really) so I had made it in their eyes. Yes and that were it, your life stopped then, you'd no need to bother doing anything else.

> You weren't meant to use birth control because we were both Catholics ... so yes, there was a lot of pressure on from church and it is surprising what you take on board yourself without anyone actually saying. You just like mini clock what you see.

The four distinct readings allow analysis to take place from diverse perspectives that focus on action, characters and wider social settings. It is an approach that seems to value and give prominence to voice, while allowing the voice to be changing and shifting.

A grounded theory of *The death story of David Hope – Michele Moore*

The analysis was built up using grounded theory to formulate a set of theoretical explanations derived from David's story following steps described in Chapter 8. To recap briefly, the point of the analysis is to reduce the data to manageable proportions and a central organising theme was quickly identified as 'disabling barriers'. Data were then sorted into various categories of 'disabling barrier' – for example 'environmental barriers', 'barriers to social provision' and so on. The sorting process enabled an extensive sweep of the principal themes in David's story. In grounded theory studies, data analysis and the development of theory are iterative processes, and as the data were organised into categories and themes a common thread could be readily identified and substantiated. Observance and interrogation of disabling barriers exposed the dominance of medical discourses in everything that happened to David. This led to a shaping of the analysis around the problem of 'conceptualising resistance to disabling barriers'.

As the categories are looked over and put together to construct a core set of findings, a narrative starts to be developed that examines the properties and meanings of the categories and looks at the theoretical implications they generate. This examination of the material pulled together as 'data on David's story' comprises the development of the theory based on the data. The theory emerging from this analysis is that what happened to David can be understood with reference to the absence of a focus on the social origins and significance of his disablement. Shifting the focus towards social barriers would arguably have produced very different outcomes for David.

The analysis raises questions about how to conceptualise David's reactions to the immensely powerful medical discourses that structured his life following spinal cord injury. It seeks to open up new possibilities for the sharing of his experience and knowledge. It shows that while he was silenced by oppressive medical discourses he was not subdued; he was systematically overwhelmed because no credibility was attached to his signposting of the multiple social barriers to a better life and his viewpoint was given little respect.

An overview of the data suggests that these claims relate to three main findings: fixation on a causal relationship between impairment and disablement by providers and other key allies, disabling responses to David's resistance to oppressive discourses, and the impact of services operating coercively. As said before, I make no claims about the significance of these findings but present them to prompt debate that will hopefully affect positive social change.

Fixation on a causal relationship between impairment and disablement

The dominance of an assumption that there is an inevitable relationship between impairment and disablement in everything that happened to David exposes the power of the medical model of disability in his life. It meant that service provision was specifically focused on impairment and far less concerned with the problem of dismantling barriers to his participation and inclusion in an ordinary life. The focus of key service providers was always unbendingly fixed on the body–impairment dyad as the key determinant of David's experience and this was compounded by nearly universal acceptance of a causal and unchangeable relationship between impairment and disablement. An ever-present medical discourse meant that David was predominantly viewed as an impaired body rather than as a whole person. His spinal cord injury was seen as the source of personal tragedy necessitating a high level of support to be prescribed and regulated according to the medical beliefs of the day. People thought about the impairment and its presumed negative consequences much more than they thought about him and his potential for transcending the limitations imposed by impairment, given an adequately supportive community and culture.

It can be seen from the data that medical discourses were constantly presented as authorative in David's life, yet the prescriptions of the medical profession constituted an entirely regulative and oppressive source of disabling barriers. Problematising impairment (rather than social barriers) made it – and David – the key site of scrutiny and blame throughout his life, as typified by the report of his inquest where commentators all looked to David himself for an individualised construction of what had happened. It was reported in the press that *'he had come to the conclusion that he couldn't stand living with his body'*. Failure to critique the medical model of disability within social services led to an automatic presumption that David's body was problematic to him; he was automatically pathologised *because* he had a spinal cord injury. In fact David's body was *not* the major focus of concern to him. Inadequacies of service providers, which subjected him to daily abuses of his body, violations of his dignity and corrupted his relations with loved ones *were* at the centre of his despair, but these factors were not interrogated and the individual blaming philosophy enabled providers to place the locus of responsibility for what happened beyond the failings of their services.

At David's inquest, emphasis was placed on medical opinions and these were treated as being clear-cut: *'the GP said the full impact of his condition began to be clear to Mr Hope . . . and he was assessed as clinically depressed'*, *'the doctor said . . .'*, *'the district nurse said . . .'* and so on. The privileging of medical models in discussions throughout his career as a person with a spinal cord injury was such that the bearing and authority of assertions went unquestioned – making the prevalence of the medical model both more powerful and more dangerous. When David begged for something to be done about unrelenting eye pain, his experience of pain was negated by the GP's view that nothing was wrong. His expressed and unbearable pain was denied by diagnosis. Other people then endorsed the perception of the medics – so that his mother would not 'bother' the GP with David's requests for new opinions. The favouring of medical opinion can be seen over and over again, such as when Sheila made it clear that she believed David should have stayed longer in a medical health institution and subjected himself to the views of medical practitioners, or when people pointed out the fine line to be navigated between seeking change and being sectioned.

The assumption that impairment causes disability had leaked beyond the medical world and into wide-ranging cultural impressions of the meaning of spinal cord injury. David, who did not accept the view that he was pathologised by his injury per se, risked being further pathologised by his own point of view, as the next part of the analysis shows. He was clear from the start: *'It wasn't breaking my neck that made me break down,'* but the more he said this the more firmly he was condemned.

Disabling responses to resistance of oppressive discourses

David's personal perspective was invariably treated as problematic and pathologising. His experiential knowledge of what was happening to him was viewed as what Foucault calls 'subjugated knowledge' – it was afforded less credibility than other sources of knowledge, considered far less credible than the knowledge of professionals, less credible than the knowledge of non-disabled family and friends, less credible than my knowledge as someone who knew him only very briefly.

Whenever David refuted other people's views of what was happening to him, or refused to accept disabling recommendations, internalised psychological explanations were sought to account for his resistance; he was *'lacking in positive mental attitude'*, *'making immense demands'*, *'uncooperative'* or *'attention-seeking'*. There was rarely an attempt to look at the social factors – and other people's responsibilities – implicated in David's position. For example, the family GP said that David *'lacked the positive mental attitude to fully investigate the possibilities of work in the computer field'* adding *'he could use a mouth-stick and move around using a chin-operator on his wheelchair'*. This neglect of personal ambition sweeps over the possibility that David was actively resistant to a coercive discourse that failed to take any account of his personal ambition. If we place the locus of responsibility elsewhere, David might equally have said that 'the GP lacked the positive mental attitude to fully investigate the possibilities of a fulfilling life after spinal cord injury'. It is plain that the GP could have chosen to use his professional networks to convene some imaginative joined-up working that might have harnessed David's personal ambitions.

Similarly, when the GP said that David *'had a feeling that he had no future and there was no point in living'*, it is not out of the question that providers had made David feel as if he had no future and there was no point in living with their one-horse suggestion of work in the computer field. Besides, in the ten months I knew him it proved impossible for the entire entourage of family, friends and providers to fix David's printer – which casts a different light on the view that David was the intractable factor in the problem.

The expectation that David was 'the problem' again stemmed directly from the nearly universal treatment of his spinal cord injury as a determinant of disability – and could only produce outright defiance. He was unwilling to take on a one-dimensional identity to enable service providers to swing in around his impairment and then consider their job done. He wanted recognition of the other parts of his individuality, he wanted enablement of his identity as a son, an uncle, a friend, a lover, a writer and so on, but he was objectified in the singular terms of his impairment and this exhausted his personal powers of resistance to disabling barriers.

To me, the data suggest that the assumption of a causal and inevitable relationship between impairment and disablement was exploited to validate a focus on David's personal psychological capacity for generating personal enablement or, conversely, constructing his own disablement. The upshot of this was that the more he felt himself to be disabled the more this was explained as 'because he was lacking in positive mental attitude', 'too depressed', or accounted for with reference to any other individualised inadequacy that could be brought to mind. The more distance other people were able to place between David's experience of disablement and external sources of oppression – many of which were perpetuated through their own gift – the less likely they were to be drawn into the – albeit uphill – task of dismantling disabling barriers. I am not suggesting that David was deliberately and systematically oppressed, but it seems clear that responses to his resistance to oppressive discourses were disabling – and, moreover, changeable. The notion that David's resistances constituted *reasonable* abdication of personal responsibility was never mooted. Thus the analysis identifies many unanswered questions about why David died.

Impact of services operating coercively

Ground floor access, respite, hoists, body braces, antidepressants, home care attendants and so on comprised familiar and legitimate sites for intervention in the eyes of service providers, and they focused their efforts for David on the provision of services essential specifically for impairment. Appointments could be arranged for refitting a spinal brace (eventually), but action on the provision of a new printer so that David could produce his own letters was beyond the bounds of possibility. He could be admitted to a respite facility, but would be left to lie alone in bed for the duration. His life was defined entirely in relation to management of a C4 spinal lesion and without any reference to his entitlement to services which would support him to do the things he wanted to. According to Morris (1997) this is disempowering service provision that does not seek 'to cut through boundaries set by budgets, organisations and professional expertise' (Morris, 1997, p. 28). The boundaries that were set closed off the possibility of looking at David's whole experience. Arguably he was starved to death by a lack of attention to 'budgets, organisations and professional expertise'. David was given only two choices: to accept a causal link between impairment and disablement that was being presented by key providers, or to reject the dominant discourse and be thereafter seen as resisting advice, stubborn, ungrateful, abusive and 'abnormal'.

David was expected to reconstruct himself following his injury from being 'independent, happy-go-lucky and challenging' to being 'dependent, passive and compliant', in order to minimise support difficulties for local providers. Yet it was accepted even at the inquest that *despite his paralysis* David's *'mind and intellect remained the same'*. Observance of the tension here comes from focus on 'barriers' in the data. Time and time again, difficulties facing service providers were turned into sources of oppression for David. An obvious example can be seen in the refusal to permit David to have adequate choice or control over decisions relating to respite – support difficulties for providers were used to justify his oppression. His only choice was to have no choice – a situation that 'is indicative of the disablism in society' (Wareing and Newell, 2002). Another invidious glimpse of how the provider agenda usurped his own can be seen in the response of the case conference to his wish was to die at home. Social services reserved the right at all times to decide whether they would allow him to stay at home. This decision was motivated by a concern to protect home support staff who felt compromised by David's actions. So the difficulties social services faced in deployment of staff were allowed to ride roughshod over his entitlement to personal choice and control – even when he was dying.

The business of the spinal brace appointment provides another case in point. With his back already bruised, blistered and bleeding, David dreaded making the battering and agonising journey to be refitted over hundreds of miles in a speed-restricted ambulance. He feared this journey so much that he chose not to make it even though he knew not going would make it impossible for him to get out of bed ever again. Within the parameters of the chosen analysis it will by now be clear that the construction of rehabilitation that the brace-fitting service was offering was unquestionably a causal factor in David's death. There was a gulf between service providers and David which left him on the receiving end of services and practices that determined his desire to commit suicide. But all this was changeable – the brace fitters could have travelled down to where he lived in half a day. The presumed sticking point here brings to mind a point made by Alldred, who noticed that invariably accountability is individualised 'when questions about financial obligations are raised' (Burman *et al.*, 1996). This same discourse takes a different form in the senior social care worker's view that David made his decision to commit suicide because he was shocked by the cost of independent living. The narrow focus of the medical model on the physical site of the body works most destructively when used to account for inadequacies in service provision.

Much of the advice and guidance David received was coercive. There is no question about this, for example, in respect to the instruction that he would have to convince hastily convened committees of his capacity to cope with an independent living situation. The sanctions implied were real: the case conference committee would not have taken David's request seriously if he had not complied with this directive, but to construe David as lacking the capacity to cope with an independent living situation is to seriously neglect the impact of an entrenched, individualised view of disability and to misapprehend the origins of disablement. To me the data show that all of the social, community and health services around David operated coercively. They frequently operated both against his will and also in opposition to his entitlements. I would confidently say that the disabling politics of community care made him commit suicide. And though he was coerced through fear and pain and neglect in the relatively short term of nine years living with spinal injury, ultimately he was not coerced. He is, however, a long time dead.

Conclusions on analysis

In order to support other people in David's situation this analysis suggests that it is important to find ways of acknowledging the ramifications of the medical model and the possibility of resistance to it. When it was said that David *'had come to the conclusion that he couldn't stand living with his body'*, an alternative reading is that David *'had come to the conclusion that he couldn't stand living with an oppressive medical discourse that constructed his life with reference to his body as the sole determinant of his identity and destiny'*.

The medical occupation of David's life was conveniently forgotten when it came to apportioning responsibility for his death:

> A narrative verdict was recorded which was 'David Hope died from starvation after electing not to be fed after severe injuries suffered following a swimming accident.'

Once again an analysis, using grounded theory to interrogate David's side of the story, exposes sufficient social explanations to warrant possible reconstruction of the narrative verdict:

> 'David Hope died from neglect after service providers elected not to support any aspect of his life which was not solely to do with impairment after severe injuries suffered following a swimming accident.'

The analysis that emerges, from grounding theoretical development in the social model of disability, gives clear reasons for opposing the construction of men with spinal cord injury through deficient and pathologising views of impairment. It undermines the analysis of what happened to David agreed upon at his inquest and exposes strong reasons for criticising the medicalised discourses of disability which shot through every aspect of his life and death – including the final inquest and the philosophies, policies and practices of the organisations and agencies meant to be supporting him. It illustrates that David chose not to be a disabled person. He was willing to live with impairment but he was wholly resistant to living with disablement.

A literary criticism of *Frank* – *Peter Clough*

I have already outlined (in Chapter 6) how I wanted to use *Frank* – to open up three themes of 'method': (1) Is *Frank* a story?, (2) the commission, (3) the conclusion. Each of those themes is briefly considered in terms of the literal, the construction and the derivation. I have also previously identified four substantive issues from *Frank*: (1) the father, (2) religion, (3) sexuality, (4) roots, in relation to the literal, the constructional and the derivational factors of the three themes. In this section I want further to 'unpack' the creation of *Frank* in order to lay bare the structures that might be used to analyse the fiction which is *Frank*. This section is also structured around the literal, the construction, and the derivation and provides a more comprehensive consideration of the themes of 'method' and of 'issue' which have already been briefly introduced in Chapter 6.

Analytical contexts of Frank

In this section I discuss the contexts of *Frank* – both the literal story and the parallel text to be found in the construction of the narrative which is *Frank*. There is some small repetition here because the brief introductions to these ideas in Chapter 6 cannot be excluded from this fuller analysis. There are seven themes in this section:

1. Is *Frank* a story?
2. The commission
3. The father
4. Religion
5. Sexuality
6. Roots
7. The conclusion.

Each of the above themes is discussed under three headings: the literal (what appears in the story); the construction (the devices used to locate it in the story); the derivation (the events, experiences and thoughts which might have lead to this element being here).

(1) Is Frank a story?

The literal

The *Frank* narrative is basically an edited version of diary entries. In themselves they 'tell' a particular story of the heritage of one man. It is, in its whole, an uneventful story, but, as 'Frank' tells it, the story of his childhood, his father, his religious upbringing, 'out-of-place' geographical location – all account for his later-life difficulties. (At least I think this is what he is trying to say; though he never, actually, gets around to it.)

The construction

I have chosen here to let the diary entries speak for themselves. This becomes evident, first of all, when ' Frank' declares his pseudonym at the outset of the narrative account.

The derivation

The diaries that make up the story came from elsewhere, a Creative Writing course that I attended a couple of years after I met 'Frank' – we were encouraged to keep our own diaries, to record our thoughts – anything – unedited. I have never kept a diary, as such, but I have always kept a notebook (often several). And so, this use of diary entries – written and read, at random, from 'Frank's' diaries – are a device from my own method of reflection and recording. I write things down. I don't always know that what I write is important – much less *if* it's important – but I do know the usefulness – indeed, the necessity – of 'writing something down'. I never write things for an audience – never 'do' anything with much of my personal writing – but I *do* write.

(2) The commission

The literal

Much of his diary was turgid – dry – yet these pieces – those that made me read on . . . they said something – might speak?

'I must go soon' – I said. How could I tell him that I couldn't (wouldn't?) write his story?

'You'll write it? Do something with it? Interview me? Let me see a draft?' He was keen, disgustingly keen.

The derivation

This narrative is derived from edited diary jottings which 'Frank' felt were important enough to 'do something with'. He had read one of my published stories – knew (I think) the character from which Rob was derived (see Clough, 2002). I still have a sneaky feeling that, although the story of Rob was terrible, 'Frank' was in awe of the fact that Rob's story was made public – in a book, reviewed, used on courses (apparently a student in his last school quoted it).

The construction

My own reluctance to keep diaries, my own understanding of the use of personal writing and my diffidence around 'doing something' with 'Frank's' diaries come together here. I write personal notes – but they are just that – and this notion that I should 'do something' with some others' diaries is somewhat absurd. I have chosen here to build into 'Frank's' desire to 'be published' the idea that he thinks he knows who 'Rob' might be. I am implanting here a sense that 'Frank' is seeking some kind of fame (or at least affirmation of his life) through the publication of his story. Perhaps 'Frank' thought he knew who 'Rob' was . . .

(3) The father

The literal

2nd November

I am seven, eight and on this light summer's night I can't sleep; maybe I have been down two or three times already but I am not prepared for what happens. My father is there; he is dirty from work; in a rage he seizes me – this is the word I always use – he seizes me and all of one action pulls my pyjama trousers to the ground/has his belt off from his waist/pushes me face down onto the table/lashes my bottom with his leather belt.

My brother says my father put him to bed one night as my mother worked and Colin remembers this: violation, my father tearing off Colin's clothes and Colin's shame at standing naked before him; the impropriety of it all; rough hands pushing

My other brother – my older brother – says he has no memories like these.

The derivation

This – I think – comes from a multiple and complex memory of boyhood; it reflects my own indignity at the hands of my father and my perpetual feeling of indignity. Whether or not I (or my brothers) were stripped and flogged – or (what could you call it?) abused, pulled on, however brought down to our naked vulnerable selves, whether or not this happened – is not the point. The point here is that young boys can feel stripped and penetrated at the hands of their fathers (if those fathers do not know how to be fathers to their sons)*. Elsewhere in the story it is made clear that the mother is not a part of this degradation of my boyhood man.

The construction

I have put together here a series of 'hunches' about the father in relation to his sons, alongside other hunches as to why the father brings out his sexual frustration on the boys. He misses those desert nights. His wants those gentle pullings in the desert tent. He is ashamed of the 'desert-love' (the Methodists made certain of this).

(4) Religion

The literal

18th September
I was bound by so many rules; it seemed it was all rules. There were the rules of my damaged family, which of course were not so visible; the rules of the neighbours which my mother feared and whispered about; the rules of the fucking methodist church, and of school. The whole thing, the central principle, was containment, no growth, conservatism ...

I've thought hard about this, and I think the whole thing ...

---

*I write a story on this theme also (see Clough, 1995).

The derivation

The roots of this are in childhood experiences of organised religion (my own and those borrowed from others) that oppress and confine. They are experiences where the 'organisation' and 'routinisation' of religion are divorced from any experience of faith, or Christian love, or forgiving communion. Hence: fear, whispering, rules, containment.

The construction

This has nothing to do with faith. I think I understand 'faith'. What makes things difficult in 'Frank's' heritage is 'Religion' – and, more importantly, denomination. Methodism (with the capital 'M' of the time) was at the root of 'Frank's' fathers readjustment. He has – in the desert – (perhaps) found pleasures which did not fit with his own 'roots'./This only mattered because it mattered to 'Frank' – and I only knew that when I read his last entry –

> *3rd January*
> *I don't know why I never – really – loved other men.*

Perhaps this is what 'Frank's' story is about.

   Perhaps this is the motivation for the telling.

   Perhaps *Frank* is a different story after all – which, had I interviewed him, would have been told . . .

(5) Sexuality

The literal

13th December
When he told me a few years ago that he was a nudist, what he said was:

'I've a private yard here at the back I can strip off in summer' and later: 'o yes we used to strip off in the desert' and 'I spent the best part of four years bollock-naked in the desert' and later: 'I go to Gresham you know, a sun-club in the baths there'. He was sixty-eight when he told me this.

The derivation

In suggesting that *The desert love left no mark*, I am suggesting that this man (I can hardly bear to use that word and think of him) remained unchanged by the desert nakedness and any male encounters that might have happened. But there is no suggestion of a 'relationship' here – in that tent, any cock would do: *This is a six-man tent but he shares it only with Bill; or Trevor. And to lie warm next to another body and – often gently, tenderly – to hold each other's penis, to pull gently ... And the next day and the next day and all the nights are the same: Trevor, Ralph, Harry. O this is life. And if there is jealousy; and if a sergeant demands, and is rough and hurts, then this too is life, life far from all things mean.*

The construction

What is being built here – through a series of entries – is a story in the story. The reader will find the various threads which point to male–male sexual experiences (they would not have been called 'gay' then); and the shame due to the fact that they happened is shot through his subsequent life – with his wife and his boys – when he returns. The story of his sexuality – the disgust at his old-man's nudity, and the roughness with his sons – comes together in the explanation that he found something in the desert that both excited and repulsed him.

(6) Roots

The literal

7th May
St. Annes-on-Sea is nowhere to live a life. A man should rage and be foul there; a man should spoil it and foul it. It has no future and no past.

So here I was born into a town with no future and no past. It was birth into the day-care room of an old people's home; an affluent day-care room maybe, but beneath the deodorant spray and the daffodils the smells are the same: old flesh, old gums. (Or: birth into a perpetual January on one of those retirement coasts of Spain; or – this is worse – born on a perpetual cruise.)

12th May
My family should never have strayed into this place; they were the decent poor, and in neither respect should they have been housed here. St Annes should have been better policed at the boundaries, and they should have turned him back up the road to Blackpool or Preston.

14th May
I never heard my cousins or other relatives referred to but they were bloody this or they were bloody that bloody weedy Earnest – my mother's loved brother – that bloody oily Jimmy; your mother's bloody lot in Wakefield or my mother's bloody lot in Blackpool; Ernest-bloody-know-all; what's-her-name, that do-bloody-gooder in Clayton?

But he laid waste around him; already cut off, he cut off and cut off.
The neighbours were bloody know-all bloody Jenkins, Harry bloody
Rowlay; that smart bugger Sanderson, that bloody weed De Freitas. The
men he worked with were Buckethead or Little Zem; or, at best, bloody
Ken or plain Barker. And they were too clever by bloody half; or else
bloody idle or messy buggers

The derivation

This all works around the words in the last entry here *But he laid waste*
around him; already cut off, he cut off and cut off. The entries about
family and roots are edited so that they eventually explain that everything he did was – effectively – 'cutting-off'. The fact is – I think – that
'Frank's' father had to despise everyone – because – really – he despised
himself. He 'cut off' because he *was* cut off – hated everyone because he
carried (from the desert) a loathing and a frustration.

The construction

The entries about the 'roots' mainly report the facts – along with 'Frank's'
thoughts about 'going back' and Frank's seeking a reason for the misplaced
family. I think there is a point here when 'Frank' is – himself – misplaced,
and these entries are, in a sense, a working through of his own 'place'.

(7) The conclusion

The literal

(i) 'Frank's' conclusion
But you have to understand that my father was so damaged too. His
father – the story goes – was a ne'er do well; and gassed in the war; and
seldom worked, maybe even drank. And his mother worked severely. I
suppose you have to understand that, to understand anything of the rest.

3rd January
I don't know why I never – really – loved other men.

(ii) 'My' conclusion
'You'll write it? Do something with it? Interview me? Let me see a draft?'
He was keen, disgustingly keen.

He insisted that I took the diaries with me when I refused the fourth
pint. Inside the cover of the first he wrote his phone number.

I phoned him a few weeks later – said I couldn't make the diaries into
a story.

I told him they might speak for themselves – but that they needed ruth-less editing.

'Do it,' he said.

I had not warmed to him.

The derivation

Two conclusions come together in my idea that this is 'Frank' seeking his own therapy. He is appealing to the present age of therapeutic self-healing. *You have to understand. . . .* This comes from a suggestion that there has to be some reason why we are like we are. There has to be a reason why 'Frank' is like he is. In this story, my reason for 'Frank' being as he is – finished – is partly explained (or at least constructed) by my dislike of him. I don't want to write his story. I want to tell him that there are many more interesting stories to write.

The construction

The piece finishes with the two conclusions because I wanted to convey here both 'Frank's' desperation to have his story 'told' and my reluctance to accept his commission. Perhaps he should have offered to pay me – yet, I think, his attempt to buy me is conveyed suitably through the constant flow of beer – which I refuse. Clearly there was a narrative of some kind to be told – but I was not prepared to take the raw data of the diaries and create a story. That, I think, is what Frank would have wanted. So, in a sense, Frank gets his story published – but not as he had planned. Not the one he would have bought. *I had not warmed to him.* And so the story is constructed so as to detach 'my' 'voice' from his.

The preceding analysis is a sort of 'deconstruction' of *Frank*. It lays bare the means by which it was created and the influences which led me to write it as I did. There are works of fiction in this account too. For as the writing of *Frank* created the story, so does the discussion of an analysis of *Frank* lead to new stories.

Conclusion

We have come some way from the life stories presented to you in Part 1 of the book. We have attempted to supplement these narratives with analyses that demonstrate the telling nature of stories. Indeed, perhaps this is the main offering of the social researcher – to read stories, to illu-minate them and to demonstrate the analytical content within them. But this analytical 'need' of social research is not without dilemmas (or ironies). It is to these concerns that we next turn.

Chapter 10

Reflexivity

Reflections on analyses

Introduction

The role of analysis in life story research has been questioned. If, as Thomas and Znaniecki (1958) argue, stories constitute the perfect socio-logical material, then why the need to analyse? Whittemore, Langness and Koegel (1986) and Booth and Booth (1994) debate whether or not analysing actually works against the key aims of storytelling; to bring the disappearing individual back into social theory. For too long, they muse, social theory has created structuralist versions of the world that hold no place for the subjective realities of social members. In contrast, good stories provide vivid individual accounts of personal experience that implic-itly disclose underlying socio-structural relations (Bertaux, 1981). To analyse stories takes away ownership of the primary narrators and masks the qualities of a narrative with the abstract interpretations of the theo-rist. The best stories are those which stir people's minds, hearts and souls, and by doing so give them new insights into themselves, their problems and their human condition (Mitroff and Kilman 1978, p. 83).

While we accept that storytelling can do all of these things – without the analytical skills of the researcher – we also recognise that researchers have a responsibility to take further what stories might tell or tacitly acknowledge. The role of analysis is crucial particularly in postmodern times where the author has died. Caught up in a hermeneutic whirlpool (Toone, 1997), readers may access a host of meanings in making their interpretations. We feel uncomfortable, therefore, in leaving our stories open to a relativistic audience, who can do with the stories what they want. Analysis aims to offer a helping hand in guiding readers to the theoretical significances of a narrative. As one of us has said elsewhere (Goodley, 2000, p. 58):

> The emic ['insider'] view of the narrator and the analytical and report-
> orial skills of the researcher are combined to draw out broader socio-
> structural, cultural, political and theoretical points ... Drawing out

> points of convergence in a number of stories shows the relevance of a few accounts to many similar others . . . Stories cannot stand alone.

Simultaneously, we also feel uncomfortable with the analyses we have made. We have come to really own our life stories (often with others who have shares in them) – and no one likes their baby to be prodded and poked by an over-analytical hand. Therefore, in the spirit of reflexivity, this chapter exposes some of the misgivings we have with analysis and what has been done to our life stories.

Critical reflections on discourse analysis – Dan Goodley

Deconstructing Gerry

I experience mixed feelings when reading Chapters 9 and 10. In one way, the analyses take Gerry further – into the adult world of theorising and philosophising – where his story is taken seriously for what it can offer (albeit in some small way) to the postmodern and 'learning difficulties' literature. In another way, I am reminded of the 1997 Woody Allen movie *Deconstructing Harry*, where one of the characters (played by Robin Williams) has become temporarily hazy to the eye. He exists as a fuzzy character, a worrying ghostly apparition to friends and family, in search of some kind of cure from his psychotherapist. Just as Gerry – originally the embodied, clearly defined hero of the tale – is now rendered foggy by the analysis of a poststructuralist discourse. I started off the story wanting to present a man so extraordinarily ordinary: extraordinary because so many of his peers had succumbed to the disabling artefacts of the segregated institutions they occupied. The human essence had been lost in the discursive mire. Gerry's extraordinary ordinariness becomes lost in the discourse analysis.

The death of the subject and the end of stories

In a piece sympathetic to postmodernity, Hughes and Paterson (1997) conclude that poststructuralism replaces one form of structuralism with another: where once neo-Marxists rendered human beings the ensemble of material conditions, poststructuralists depict their humans as merely the objects and subjects of discourse. Fundamentally, such an approach casts a weary, cynical eye over the phenomenological aims of qualitative researchers who hold misplaced realist and humanistic views. The spectre of Foucault reigns supreme: you know that person you want to relate to? Whose story you want to tell? Well, they are a myth. 'People' – like 'science', 'love', 'care', 'emotionality' – and don't quotation marks get a lot of hammer in this postmodern world – are just products of (post)modernity. We are not the closed, embodied individuals we like to think we are. Instead, we are fragmented entities with fractured identities. Schizophrenic by nature, contradictory by design and consumerist in the final analysis. The postmodern/poststructuralist subject is at best an ensemble of available resources, at worse a mere object of discursive practices. Indeed, Gerry and his peers are no longer characters with agency, choice and ambitions – which people all have no matter how hard life gets – they are simply objects of sophisticated knowledge systems best seen in institutional settings. The postmodern narrator/analyst does away with the characters within the narrative and renders them mere objects and subjects in a discursive tale belonging to the researcher. So much for the emancipatory potential of story telling.

Discourse analysis deconstructs a narrative's characters, obliterates the plot and does away with the moral of the tale. This form of analysis would seem to be opposite in character to life story research. As the story crumbles, so we are left with sedimentary, witless, artless discourses. Perhaps we have some element of the plot, but gone are our characters. Perhaps we have some form, but little content. But are these the misgivings of an unreconstructed realist? Of someone who still wants to see his data intact? Or are they the doubts of a researcher committed to the very real people with whom he is involved? Who feels that analysis has done away with the people he is so close to?

Poststructuralism and life stories as real artefacts of society

Poststructuralism is not about embracing a Blairite 'third way' of theorising some elusive middle ground between structure and agency, or subverting the real and replacing it with spin. Instead, just as Mitchell (1974) suggested that Freudian psychoanalysis was a description not a prescription of gendered identity development in Victorian families, and if we take Marx's (1845) thesis that human essence is the ensemble of social relations, then poststructuralism can be viewed as a methodology that is in tune with the contemporary knowledge societies of late capitalism. Similarly, life stories reaffirm that which we have left – our stories, our constructions and our constructions of others. Life story research reaches into the heart of the postmodern condition and pulls out the only real thing we have left: our narratives. When we accept this then we can move on – towards a place of emancipation. Armed with the knowledge of the storied nature of the world, we become streetwise and in tune with the bogus or kosher stories that we are told. When Gerry tells of his peers' oppression, we feel its truth, we know he is talking about real things. Stories are there to be grabbed, to be told aloud, to be shared and

– crucially – to be acted upon. Indeed, the People First movement that Gerry is part of has often been ridiculed by other political organisations for 'only telling stories'. In contrast, storytelling has been an essential part of adding to counter-hegemonic understandings of disability and learning difficulties. Yes, they are socially constructed – yes, people with learning difficulties are written onto, so that they are made incapable of enacting the most basic of human rights – yes, these stories of oppression are real and so are the stories of resistance.

The real is dead, long live the real

Is poststructuralism real? Does it do a disservice to the real experiences of real people? Perhaps discourse is more real than real. One of the myths of modernity as that we attach such significance to the real, present world. Stories do not do this. They take us to places – often from the past but also from the present – that are both familiar and alien. Whether or not they are real is the wrong question to ask. Modernity's obsession with the real has finally given rise to an interest in belief and knowledge which can be hopeful and useful:

> Marxism must be read in its spectrality: that its particular modernist project is more alive (and more necessary to keep alive) as a spectre than it was as a living and somewhat disgracefully embodied dogma (Derrida, 1994, Stronach and Maclure, 1997, p. 26), the spectre of the communist manifesto; what manifests itself in the first place is a spectre, this first paternal character, as powerful as it is unreal, a hallucination or simulacrum that is virtually more actual than what is so blithely called a living presence.
>
> (Brown and Jones, 2002, p. 97)

Gerry O'Toole is as real as real can be in this postmodern age. All we can do is add to his realness by pointing out the possible knowledges at play. We need to ask, therefore, whether or not Chapter 9 adds to the understandings of the truths that Gerry tells us in Chapter 1. I would suggest that if we keep with a storied vision of the world, then poststructuralism and discourse analysis can neatly slide into this view. They should complement and enhance the discursive qualities of a tale. They must supplement the analyses already being made in the life story. As Daniel Bertaux (1981) points out, all stories are imbued with the nature of the world in which they took place or in which they are told. Behind every individual story is a socio-historical and political landscape. While stories start with individuals and end with the landscape, analysis finishes up the landscape and reminds us of individual stories that exist, often against the odds.

Critical reflections on voice relational analyses – Rebecca Lawthom

The voice relational approach provides a rich and detailed analytical reading of a narrative. Working within one narrative, but using several very different readings, highlights both the depth of the story-giver's experience and the richness of using diverse interpretations. Tracing the story per se it is not surprising to find a classic linear tale, but reading one's own responses into this highlights how my own theoretical focus impacts upon the collaborative analyses.

The many voices of voice relational analysis

Feminism blends both the personal and the political, and it is precisely this juxtaposition which is writ large in both Colleen's account and my reading and engagement with it. However, I am sure that a developmental trajectory, based on early care-giving experiences and schemas regarding self-esteem, could be provided by an interviewer/co-researcher with a developmental theoretical background. However, the other three readings (for 'I', for relationships and for social structures) position the narrative and the story-giver firmly as enmeshed in other arenas (psycho-social, historical and cultural). Insider perspectives have been well explored within the feminist literature (e.g. Wilkinson and Kitzinger, 1996). The voice relational approach not only privileges voice but can potentially destabilise the researcher's authority. The notion that research can ever 'give voice' is contested by critics who argue that participants are positioned as ' silent victims'. Burr (1995) has renamed the concept of the voice relational method as the opening up of linguistic dialogues, which acknowledge agency and resistance prior to researcher intervention. In its purest form, proponents of voice relational methodology suggest that analysis be done with groups rather than individuals (as might occur with other qualitative approaches). This analysis undertaken by the group is not about verifying or agreeing on what is seen but is another way of allowing alternative voices to consider the narrative. Doing the analysis using this process allows the shaping of the story to be discussed and contested. Critics may argue that interpretation in this way simply adds other voices (often privileged academic ones) to the fray. Yet, as Ochs and Capps (2001, p. 25) point out (using Bakhtin),

> the influence of others' ideas on the shape of the narrative is invisible. Taking the logic of revoicing to the extreme, every word, expression, and genre, we employ in a narrative has been co-authored in the sense that they have been developed and used by others before us.

The transparency with which voice relational methodology is undertaken helps to demystify the analytical process. Non-dominant groups, who are often the passive recipients or at best participants of research, often claim that analysis appears as a mystical process, and removes voice (the self) from the tale (Langness and Levine, 1986).

Easy analyses? Or collaborative analyses?

For Colleen's analysis, working towards an emancipatory approach, we analysed the narrative together. This process was interesting, as analysts occupied different understandings, frameworks and ownership of the data. Bird (1999) talks of distributed competence (in classroom settings) where learning occurs across diverse understandings. This concept might be of use here. I come from the academic, intellectual world, whilst Colleen is immersed in the activity of everyday settings – how might these differences unfurl? In Larson's (1997) work, both women are feminists and academics and still find huge differences in their approaches to and understanding of the narrative. I have touched upon the idea of alternative frameworks earlier, under the banner of feminism. While I am clearly a feminist (self-labelled as such), Colleen is more cautious about using the label (as in Griffin, 1989). Our understandings of how data work and are worked upon are vastly different. We embarked upon the analysis together after I had shown Colleen brief summaries of the readings (and how they were to be done). Clearly, here I am imposing an intellectual structure on the analysis, but the approach does allow for negotiation and accommodation. The first reading was easy and Colleen (ever mindful that a tale needed to be told) quickly discerned the plot and characters. The sub-plot about difference was suggested by me, but Colleen agreed, searched and found the relevant examples. For the second reading, the process of using coloured pens easily identified where 'I' shifted to 'you' or 'we'. Colleen first wondered whether this shift was a product of dialect, but after looking at the shifts could see a pattern of hidden 'others' – the generic 'you'. For the third reading, Colleen was surprised at how many relationships she had mentioned (and how many had been left out). She felt the story already had complexity and did not want to add more people. An interesting (and emancipatory) reflection upon her tale was the way in which interaction with others had been key (throughout her life). Whether these relationships were born out of respect (the convent school), embarrassment (mixed workplaces), reluctance (dating), confidence (parenting), lack of confidence (charity work) or finally realisation of esteem (new partner, new workplace), the key driver here was relatedness. Colleen could see and reflect upon how good she was at relating and the pride this brought.

For the last reading, the gap between academia and everyday life became apparent. The placing of people in social contexts, reading institutions, ideologies and discourses as influences, is a process learnt in many social science degree studies. Colleen focused on immediate and local influences, which were particular to her. We talked about the continuity of gender roles (women she worked with taking the lion's share of domestic tasks) and the rich patterning of this across class and area. Colleen could grasp this commonality with ease and found examples (the church, heterosexual pressure) without needing academic jargon! What is interesting about voice relational analysis is its accessibility – informants/storytellers can both see how it works and participate fully within it. Unlike some other processes (e.g. discourse analysis or poststructuralist readings) where the analysis has to be undertaken by the theorist, here the analysis is collaborative. Hence, the knowing is constructed by the researched and the researcher. Colleen was surprised at the apparent simplicity of the analysis and thought that 'science was just for experts'. Kagan (2002) talks of a liberated psychology being able to work with people, making psychological information and insights freely available. Emancipatory approaches should be about accessibility and inclusion. Colleen as the narrator and co-researcher was fully included in this process.

The dominance of some voice(s)

Criticisms of this approach originate from different epistemological stances – the notion of 'voice' or self is problematic within postmodern discussion of discursively constructed or fragmented selves (e.g. Butler, 1990). Mauthner and Doucet (1997), to counter this, suggest using Plummer's notion of listening to stories:

> somewhere, behind all this storytelling there are real, active, embodied, impassioned lives. Is this a process of peeling back stories to reveal better and better ones? And if so, when do we know a story is better?
>
> (Plummer, 1995, p. 170)

Another criticism may be the way in which reflexivity is used in the analysis. Whilst it is possible to explain the context and the assumptions on which interpretations are made, it is not possible to neutralise the social nature of the interpretation. It is plausible that researchers' views and theoretical frameworks may overwhelm the voices and perspectives of the researched. It is also plausible that data analysis itself could be disempowering. As researchers, we can dissect, cut up, distil meaning and portray readings in particular ways. Are we taking voice, agency and ownership further away? Good research (in an ethical and collaborative sense) involves negotiating these concerns and allowing collaboration and participation to shape the project. Questions remain, however, over whose voice dominated the analyses of Colleen's story.

Critical reflections on grounded theory –
Michele Moore

How do I feel about the analysis? The difficulties surrounding an analysis of David's story are familiar to qualitative researchers. Hollway and Jefferson (2000) discuss the difficulties in making a distinction between description and theoretical interpretation in qualitative research analysis that has clearly beleaguered the attempt at analysis presented in Chapter 9. In addition, breaking the story down to produce an analytic structure has necessarily led to fragmentation. But arguably, without the attempt to produce some kind of analysis, there is no clearly articulated starting point for a juxtaposition of interpretations on what happened to David. So perhaps some analysis is better than no analysis. Nevertheless I suffer now from what Lofland and Lofland (1984) called 'ethical hangover' – feelings of guilt and betrayal which, according to Homan (1991), are common for social researchers.

I am appalled at the analysis and its reduction of David's experience, though I do not attribute this specifically to the decision to take a grounded theory approach. Obviously any analysis is reductive and the confines of a grounded theory approach do the story a routine – but probably not especial – disservice. Going back a stage, I am appalled at the story from whence the analysis came, because it reduced David's experience to bones in the first place – both literally and metaphorically. The analysis is upsetting because it patently shows the needlessness of David's death. Producing the analysis involved a stark look back at the futility of what happened to him. The analysis will make no difference to David. I am ashamed of it having been so long in the making – in the meantime other people have died in comparable circumstances. I am apprehensive about David's surviving family members knowing or not knowing about it and embarrassed about the interpretations and judgements that will be made about my construction of the data. I am long past worrying about the likely criticism that the analysis might not be 'proper' grounded theory; it is eclectic, it is messy, but importantly it does prompt evaluation of David's experience from some previously suppressed angles. I only hope there is no lingering sense that the analysis in any way seeks to be 'objective' or 'reliable'.

The hangover is very painful. It is unnerving to know that producing an 'analysis' has obscured David's voice and would quite probably persecute him if he knew about it. It hasn't been possible to prioritise David's preoccupations in the analysis; these have had to be presumed and fused with my own. If he had his own agenda for the telling of his story, it is far from foregrounded now. Making the analysis has at times been stressful because it has involved returning to the most extreme and disrespectful arenas of the disabling society in which we live, stating what has always seemed to me to be obvious about the menace of disabling barriers and recognising that for many – probably most – disabled people and their families the social model of disability is still unknown. Making the analysis has involved raking over the pain of my relationship with David (Moore and Skelton, 2000), wondering if I let him down, missing him, wanting to explain, owning the fact that my involvement led to no positive outcome.

Any value to the analysis lies in its powers of strategic persuasion. My personal goal for the analysis was that it should persuade the reader that if service providers had been willing to shift the focus of their interventions towards social barriers and away from an insistent focus on 'what was wrong' with David, then the outcomes might well have been different. I am happy for the jury to be out on whether this proposition is acceptable, but I do not want there to be any ambiguity about my own feeling about the data. I purposely intended to guide the reader's interpretations. Herein lies the potential for misuses and abuses of analysis. I have not shied away from its overtly political nature – the theory may be grounded but the grounding has been a highly selective and deliberate process. This leads to one of the chief drawbacks of grounded theory analysis, namely that it can blinker the analyst and lead to an interpretation of evidence entirely within the confines of the selected theory; it can shut down the possibility of noticing other possible theoretical directions.

I chose to ground the analysis in the social model of disability and the material can be fitted within this theoretical agenda. But arguably it could equally be fitted to other theoretical frameworks and the social model of disability focus has meant that the analysis ignores other theoretical propositions (Corker, 1997; Corker and Shakespeare, 2002). There are aspects of David's experience for which the social model of disability does not account. It does not provide for examination of multiple aspects of David's identity, for example, and does not get to the heart of what was going on in his mind. It does provide a simple way to make sense of some of the key determinants of his experience that transcends his personal struggle and calls others to account. For the purposes of this publication this has been deemed adequate, but it is not a 'complete' analysis. There are competing theoretical agendas which, had these been built into the grounded theory analysis, would have shed a different light on the data.

Moreover, however the analysis is interrogated, there is no getting away from the fact that it has made no difference. The power of any analysis is determined by the extent to which it gets noticed by relevant – and multiple – audiences. I have had the courage to take only small steps to reach relevant audiences, for example, mentioning David's story in professional and academic publications. Fear of personal consequences and repercussions for his family has swayed me away from disseminating the story or its analysis widely. Holding back analyses is not always easy; it was, for example, very tempting to respond to misleading newspaper coverage of David's death with my own account, but this would have afforded a platform for those already sending letters of condemnation to the family, and could have jeopardised future relations between the family and key providers, and Sheila's overriding concern was for family privacy. Nowadays the heat may have declined for some of the more harrowing aspects of both story and analysis, but realistically the delay has diminished the potency of the critique. It is difficult to know how to open the gateways that will ensure that analysis gets communicated to relevant audiences in ways which are not damaging to informants, but finding ways of pushing analysis through critical gateways is vital if research is to affect positive social change. Ideally an 'in process' surfacing of issues with a wide group of people involved in the research promotes interest in engaging with analysis and dissemination (Dunn, 2004), but this presupposes that those *in situ* know and accept that research is going on in the first place, whereas in this life story project this was never so.

Strong possibilities for making alternative meanings can come from analysis of life stories. This reminds researchers of the importance of enhancing the relationship between the academic world in which those stories originate and the actuality of everyday lives lived by the people whose stories are told. It is vital that we improve this relationship in order to best advance an agenda for social justice. Analysis that is confined to university library shelves or esoteric journals makes little difference to many social service providers and doesn't assist ordinary families. If we genuinely seek to transform understanding of disability (or any other social issue) through life story research, then it is vital to examine the relationship between the actuality of people's lives and the academic production, analysis and dissemination of stories about those lives.

Critical reflections on literary analysis – Peter Clough

In this section the character 'Frank' is the organising structure. I begin with a résumé of two important influences on the story. There are two influences behind my construction of *this* story in *this* form. First, I have had to deal with the notion of 'the commission' from people who really want me to tell *their* story – usually because it is terrible and they want it 'out' but don't want to be identified – and so feel they cannot tell it themselves. It's hard to deal with these 'commissions' for they often come from people I like – love even – and so I have to find ways of avoiding the task. I can't simply write stories that others want me to write. (Well, I can – any writer *can* – but that is not what the use of narrative is *for me at least*.)

The second influence on the construction of *Frank* as it is here is Yann Martel's *Life of Pi*; in his preface to the book the author argues that the power of story and the novel leaves the reader with two versions of the story and the question as to which one they prefer. Two stories, two endings – the choice is the reader's. But *Frank* can be considered as part of a much broader picture, and the important task here is not simply to subject *Frank* (or any other story for that matter) to critical literary analysis but to argue the importance of literary analysis and the functions of language in the creation of objects and meanings. I have written of this elsewhere, and the remainder of this section consists of an extract which sets out my thinking in relation to these topics (for a fuller account see Clough, 2002, pp. 76–77).

A major aim here is to argue for a view of fictional writing not as 'alternative' (or even particularly new), but rather as issuing from the same *radical* concerns and processes as those of other social scientists. As Postman puts this,

> Both a social scientist and a novelist give unique interpretations to a set of human events and support their interpretations with examples in various forms. Their interpretations cannot be proved or disproved, but will draw their appeal from the power of their language, the depth of their explanations, the relevance of their examples, and the credibility of their themes. And all this has, in both cases, an identifiable moral purpose.
>
> (Postman, 1992, p. 154)

Of course, we shall not in the end arrive at an account of truth-in-fiction which will meet the orthodox criteria of a social science. Such an account would be absurd, much as we might rigorously argue the existence of God. (In both cases, surely the question of existence is already answered, and the question is rather *how* this exists than *whether*?) It remains, however, in the examined world in which we live – where evidence genuinely matters – to offer some justification for the uses of fiction in social science which will help students to scoop with a scholarly confidence – 'without self-importance or self-consciousness' (Inglis, 1969) – deep into their personal resources for persuasive writing which cannot be dismissed as 'mere fiction'. To do this calls for a methodology that can deal analytic justice at the same time as experiential truth. This is a tall order.

But: when I turn on the radio or television; pick up a newspaper, a journal article or a novel; listen to a seminar presentation or watch a theatre play – in each case I attune myself quite precisely, yet with minimal effort or art, to a form of truth. That is to say, I am located in a version of truth whose engines are so far hidden from view that they are silent. It is, of course, only when I sense that there is some fault that I begin to hear the noise of those engines, and reach perhaps for a set of tools that will detect, analyse – correct, even – the fault. For strings of words don't mean something because they're stuffed or laid out with propositional knowledge. They mean because those words glance off much more regressed knowledges – vapid certainties – which are only in later moments made angular with the furniture of analysis (the pixels of experience as it were suddenly organised with actual purpose from a dense galaxy of possible meanings).

The problem of evaluation

We are led from this consideration to ask about an enquiry, not 'Is it qualitative or quantitative?' but 'Is it moral?' There remains a problem of evaluation. For even if an enquiry is 'open to its objects', if it declares the values and unique method of its author, how do we know that, and what yardstick can we possibly find that will qualitatively determine its morality? And anyway, if it deals in such a particular way with the particular, what can we compare it with and what relevance could it have for general experience? Is this not likely to be the very worst of 'subjectivity'? By opposing subjectivity to objectivity we distinguish persons from objects in such a way that their relation cannot be described without recourse to extremes of mentalist or behaviourist philosophy. If, on the other hand, we understand the terms as continuously related ways of *having* objects, then we take the vital step of involving persons with objects by necessity. *Subjectivity is defined, then, not by the particular which it dwells in by virtue of its own uniqueness, but by the concern it shows to give that particular a general recognition.* Such recognition completes the act, and the particular becomes an object constituted by sharing.

This process is not susceptible to validation. Because it has not explained subject–object relations for its schemes, the 'research attitude' – to which validation as a technique belongs – naively assumes this relation and is to be found acting in the firm reality of *noemata*. Of course, this research attitude is right when it speaks of demanding validation in terms of the object and not of the enquirer; it is right in supposing that the object is firm and, even if constituted, that it pre-exists characterisation. But the real meaning of its 'objectivity' is revealed when, in its provision of the validation it required, it fails to distinguish between the object proper and the characterisations given by what are yet more *noemata*. Again, validation needs endless shoring up with ever-regressing devices because it is not object-directed.

We have said that a phenomenology can be known by its revelation of the author's engagement with his or her objects. But how precisely do we know that? This is still the question. And what is it that we recognise and affirm or dispute?

If we return to the genesis of the phenomenology, we observe that there is a researcher and there is a *situation of objects* which s/he must constitute. At this point there occurs a critical *moment of characterisation* that determines these objects for the researcher and for the researcher's audience. This is the moment normally referred to as methodological, and which as such is the correlate of the later process of validation; indeed, it is all that validation can reveal: is the *method* what it set out to be, what its author says it is? For validation is based, as we shall see, on a limited model of truth that either takes for granted, or else ignores, the earlier process of *verification* that guarantees its coherence. Validation depends on further regressed devices in quite the way that truth of statement and truth of things – conceptual and pragmatic truths – depend on things being already what/as they are (Hofstadter, 1965). We are able to proceed to their statement or demonstration only because of some earlier moment of our knowing them. Things as they are must, on pain of ceasing to exist, be already partially revealed. This is what I take Heidegger to mean by *a-lethia*:

> Not only must that in conformity with which a cognition orders itself be already in some way unconcealed. The entire realm in which this 'conformity to something' goes on must already occur as a whole in the unconcealed. ... With all our correct representations we would get nowhere, we could not even pre-suppose that there is already manifest something to which we can conform ourselves, unless the unconcealedness of beings had already exposed us to, placed us in, that lighted realm in which every being stands for us and from which it withdraws.
>
> (Heidegger, 1971, p. 52)

> Verification stands in relation to validation as does understanding to explanation. Validation, then, is a gloss on verification; or, in Husserlian terms, it is the provision of other *noemata*, which abundance may yet avoid the thing itself. Attention to validation is in effect an attention to method at the expense of attending to the object which the method should reveal.
>
> (Clough, 2002, pp. 81–83)

Space here does not permit a further consideration of verification, characterisation and 'truth' (for this see Clough, 2002), but the final analysis lies in the reader's own 'reading' of the story – be it 'told' or 'shown' rooted in the tradition of diegesis and mimesis.

Conclusions

The critical reflections we present should not be viewed as the neurotic word-salads of academics with too much time on their hands. Well, they could be seen in this way. But, we are very much aware that the project of *Researching Life Stories* is one full of strange ironies and contradictions. Surely, the strength of a good piece of storytelling lies in its ability to convey a host of analytical viewpoints and prompt the reader to other ways of seeing. We would argue that when life stories are used in social research, researchers have a host of responsibilities and concerns that they do not share with a Martin Amis, Steven King or Iris Murdoch. Often researching life stories involves many potential audiences who may use those stories in professional and policy contexts. Meanwhile, the labour of researchers, which may be termed intellectualism, involves engagement with theorising and knowledge production. These concerns are examined further in the final part of the book.

Part 4

The age of biography: personal and political considerations

In this final part of the book we revisit researching life stories with some further questions in mind, related to how we might teach life story research; how life story researchers conceive of their audience and the effects of their narratives; and the wider implications and applications of our stories to theory, policy and practice. Chapter 11, *Teaching*, considers the craft and ethics drawn upon in the writing of the stories presented in Part 1 of this book. While we have considered in depth the method/ological workings and posturings that led to the stories and uncovered some of the analytical groundings that informed our understandings of them, we want to go further here in terms of outlining some general considerations for the novice life story researcher to keep in mind. Chapter 12, *A/Effecting*, outlines how we conceptualised our audiences and how these concepts influenced our approach to researching life stories. We distinguish and elaborate on a number of qualities inherent in the stories in terms of the reactions they may (hopefully) elicit in the reader – demonstrating further, we think, the power of stories. Chapter 13, *Applying*, finishes the book by illuminating a number of theoretical, policy and practice considerations in light of the four life stories and the researching processes described in this book. We argue that our trans-disciplinary, multi-method/ological and cross-analytical view of researching life stories provides a number of applicable findings.

Chapter 11

Teaching

Craft and ethics in researching life stories

In this chapter we ask how researching life stories can be taught. Our starting point is that a textbook version of how to do life story research undermines the possibilities for creativity and originality. We hope that the reader has been struck by the very different narrative styles employed by the authors of this book, and, perhaps, is motivated to borrow some ideas in thinking about his or her own research stories. Rather than attempting to come up with a toolkit version of life story research, this chapter offers some hints and thinking points. It is our view that learning about life story research can be done only when we consider the ethical, personal and political positions of the researcher.

Lessons from Gerry O'Toole – *Dan Goodley*

The craft of writing stories – drawing upon a non-participatory ethnographic approach, later subjected to (subjugated by?) some form of discourse analysis – would seem inevitably to involve some long-winded artful exposé of the merits of such an approach. However, with the story and analysis (which together we could call a narrative) now captured in frozen text – immobile and lacking in dynamism and so far away from the busy life of Gerry O'Toole – I am permitted some necessary breathing/thinking space to consider some moments that led to the narrative as it stands. Hopefully, reflections on these moments will be useful to you, the reader, in your employment of life story research.

Get to know your subjects from the inside

Too much research activity is based upon minimal involvement with a given group of people (referred to as participants), often over a short period of time allotted by funding (usually, if you are lucky, about three years), before the researcher moves on to another hot topic in order to enhance their research résumé (see the Research Assessment Exercise for details or not as the case may be). The current climate of research production is in danger of missing out on the gifts of longer-term – perhaps voluntary, non-funded and non-vocational – relationships with people who can enhance a researcher's knowledge of the world. When Plummer (1983) argues that we need to get to know our informants from the inside, he is hinting at the need to work relationally, emotionally and empathically with the people whose stories we are helping to tell. In my own case, my understandings of 'learning difficulties', disability, exclusion and inclusion have really been understood when I am involved with people whose lives are a constant struggle against the associated socio-emotional ailments of being given some spurious label. Gerry's story is informative – at least for me – because it is a (mere) product of a number of my long-term and ongoing relationships with others. Crucially, while such involvements have often given me a host of grounded intellectual 'Aha!' moments – when I feel like a disability studies researcher – it has also demanded that I make a number of emotional and personal affiliations and decisions. If I had understood Gerry and his peers as passive handicapped people, the subsequent story would have been very different from the one emerging here. My own epistemological view of people – which may be grandly termed poststructuralist – only ever made sense to me on a personal level: Gerry and his peers were/are clearly being created by the institutions (and associated knowledges) in which they were placed. Getting to know our informants requires personal and political investment in them. This raises issues connected with truth – if we know them, we will speak their truths. I know that Gerry and his peers are not the pathological victims of impairment that society expects them to be; they show this to me during all our interactions. But I know they are not those victims because our relationships would soon change and die if I were ever to view them in these ways. Getting to know our subjects – and let's hope we actually start using words like 'friend' or, maybe, 'comrade' – demands real knowing on the levels of emotion and intellect.

Getting to know yourself from the in/outside

As important as knowing others is knowing yourself and, perhaps, taking yourself seriously. Much research training – especially qualitative research – involves giving up on the things (people, knowledges and commitments) we know and aiming to embrace the communities of practices or paradigmatic peculiarities that go with being a researcher. I remember touting the idea of using stories in research to a postgraduate seminar a few years ago and being told that if I did take the narrative turn, I needed to expose my multiple selves in an explicit way so that others would know my position. But what of attending to that self – or collection of selves – we already know but which, often, remain un/der-exposed? I am consistently amazed by the number of practitioners and activists I meet – often in educational, health and social welfare contexts – who have years of experience in their trade but who, when faced with a research project to implement, forage away in the library for a topic of interest. When asked about the work that they do and then demonstrating many important considerations that need to be changed in their work contexts, so often they do not treat their own stories and experiences as the very stuff of research. Researching life stories offers opportunities for drawing on our own and others' narratives in ways that can illuminate key theoretical, policy and practice considerations. Researching life stories allows us to bring in parts of us. There would be no Gerry without my involvement with him. My hanging around with him – that I have termed non-participatory ethnography – gave me the raw material from which his story was created. Getting to know ourselves would appear to be a crucial part of life story research – in terms of considering the subject matter, the significance of that subject and, most importantly, the objects of our subject whose voices are so often lost in paradigmatic debate and intellectual pretentions.

Pushing forward the boundaries of ownership and partisanship

I sent a version of Gerry's story to a colleague of mine. He knows Gerry well – or at least the character on which Gerry is based – as well as some of the others mentioned in the narrative. He was critical:

> I must admit I had problems with this piece. I wasn't sure whose voices I was hearing, whether they were real stories or ones someone had compiled for effect. But the biggest difficulty I had was that the main character, Gerry, had, in part, become you, with your ways of thinking and some of your actions imposed on him.

This colleague is – to use his words – more of a 'grounded researcher', who would want to re-present only the *real* stories of *real* people as they *really* took place. But this is as much a position as one where the researcher takes over and speaks on behalf of others. To say that one is *allowing* their informants to *really* speak for themselves is, in my opinion, as much a power position as those taken by the authors of *Frank*, *David* and *Gerry* in this book. Researchers are always pulling strings. When someone's interview response is re-presented in a story – accents, mistakes, pauses and inarticulate spoken word as static, finalised text – the researcher has owned a position in terms of storytelling. I personally have massive problems with authors who feel it is perfectly acceptable to use academic-speak of the written text when writing in the 'I' and then pepper it with the fumbling spoken words of their informants (always the 'other'). As I found to my cost when constructing the life story of Joyce Kershaw, in which I wrote her story as she spoke it, she later instructed me, 'Danny, don't write how I speak, write as you write' (Goodley, 1998, 2000). Stories are not simply methods for transparently capturing real worlds and real people; they are always constitutive methods (Potter and Wetherell, 1987). The question of ownership is also one of partisanship. Researchers can allow their informants to speak, but whose side are they on (Barnes, 1997)? At least, in joining up with a person in collaborative storytelling – or allied storytelling in the case of *Gerry* – I had to make a decision whose character I was going to build up (and who else I was going to assassinate): I chose Gerry for the former (and professionals for the latter). Owning a person's story will lead to very different narratives depending on our affiliation with that person. My hope is that Gerry's story is authentic to the vision I have of him: as a quiet revolutionary. He may be embarrassed by my sad sixth-form politics view of him, but never mind; as some would say, it is my story not his.

Everyone has a story to tell, everyone can write a story

I am still not sure if Gerry's story is that good. What a thing to admit, eh? But I'll lay my anxieties out in the open here – and maybe my precious credibility – because in considering 'craft' in storytelling I do feel rather uneasy. I have a constantly recurring nagging feeling that I am not a writer. It's a feeling that wells up when I'm at academic conferences and the sea of professional, novice, ageing and renowned researchers in the conference auditorium makes me question where I see my own standing. It's also a feeling I get when I reread *Catcher in the Rye* (okay, I never left adolescence) and think: 'I could never write like this – so funky and seductive.' I feel better when I remember that researching life stories is about embracing a gamut of narrative styles and that, just as with music, the many forms of storytelling give it its richness and depth. Anyone – I mean anyone – can tell a story. The question is – is it a good one? In the final analysis, perhaps, the qualities of a story will depend on audiences (which we look at in detail in the next chapter) and their expectations. When I see Gerry and his peers now, I feel happy with the story because I feel it has done some justice to their achievements. I also think that Gerry has a cracking story to tell.

Lessons from Colleen – *Rebecca Lawthom*

Considering emancipatory approaches and the voice relational method, a key issue is collaboration. The participants in this approach are not passive, disinterested, absent individuals, but have a key role to play in the design, analysis and shaping of the story. Working with informants, and gaining their confidence, is an important feature. Listening to women's voices is one of the broad research traditions in feminist psychology (Wilkinson, 1999). Gilligan (one of the founders of VRM) noted,

> I picked up what you're not supposed to pick up in psychology – that there was a voice, and I asked 'who's speaking?', 'whose voice is this?', 'whose body and where's it coming from?' If you listen to the imagery of sexuality and separation . . . you realise this is a man's body. This is a man's voice speaking as if from nowhere.
>
> (Kitzinger and Gilligan, 1994, p. 413)

The different voice (with which women speak) prompted the emergence of the voice relational method and its radical potential:

> we begin to see the outlines of new pathways in women's development and also to see new possibilities for women's involvement in the process of political change.
>
> (Brown and Gilligan, 1993, p. 32)

One of the strengths of this approach is its accessibility for informants and co-researchers. Working within an emancipatory framework, and involving storytellers in the analysis, allow full inclusion in the research process and the possibility for emancipatory understanding. Working closely with co-researchers upon the text, allows positive storytelling and/or alternative narratives (as in narrative therapy). Storytellers can be shown the significance of their tales and their emancipatory stance. The fourth reading of the VRM allows storytellers to see the structural (often determined) nature of agency, within which they may contexualise their own story. Moreover, the social nature of subjectivity suggests that the 'person is connected socially and culturally to others' (Nicholson, 1996).

Research production is often portrayed as an individualised identity project – gathering data for this purpose will enable particular publications and dissemination activities, which more often than not contribute more to the researcher's life than the informant's. Working inclusively with informants may potentially allow change on the part of the storyteller, as reflection, alternatives and ambiguity are discussed and analysed. Moreover, the VRM sets data in a wider context, which potentially removes blame from the storyteller (the idea of discourse framing action). The personal is political and VRM shifts analysis between these two spheres and connects them.

An important idea in allowing stories to emerge is a belief (on the part of the researcher) that a 'good' story will emerge. A research focus deemed appropriate by the researcher will not necessarily fit into the narrative told by the informant. All people have stories to tell, but research formats with implicit demand characteristics often do not allow data to emerge. Rather, we presume that a format will yield interesting data, but who defines 'interesting'? Seeing narratives as central to meaning-making is an important part of the voice relational method. The acceptance of the story, and the clarity of the researcher's stance, allow informants to feel that what they have to offer is appropriate. After interviews have been conducted and the tape recorder is switched off, informants often ask 'Was that alright?' or 'Did you get what you wanted?', as if they need to expose some deep and meaningful psychological truth. Here we are arguing that, by getting to know informants and their stories, data will emerge. Respecting the stories people have to offer involves both transparency on the part of the researcher and a consideration of ethics.

Ethical considerations

Relatedness is key to this approach, but whose voice dominates? More equal research relationships might shift the balance of power, but ultimately the openness of the process may still position the researched as knowing less (and thus vulnerable). Larson (1997) notes that when working with narrative, conversation is important:

> This monological method of storytelling and taping felt far more akin to poor therapy than to a collaborative effort to make meaning of life experience.
>
> (Larson, 1997, p. 457)

Using VRM in an emancipatory fashion, the presentation of the narrative (polished and edited by the analysis) at least allows a hidden voice to be presented as a 'self' rather than as a collection of selves distributed and fragmented across themes or discourses. Ethically, the storyteller retains editorship of the narrative and thus can present divergent and contrasting selves within the narrative. The researcher (always cognisant of final outputs) needs to be flexible in the process and to allow ambivalence and ambiguity to emerge.

Colleen's story is a great example of a story that has element of ordinariness about it (leading her to think that this would be a boring story) and elements of utter individuality. The mosaic of experiences, once pieced together, gives a rich and varied picture of one woman's life. Colleen is now probably closer to you as well, and yet you already have a Colleen figure near you, who has a story to tell.

What are the key points here?

- VRM allows us to gaze on the emotional world (relatedness) and material world.

- Working with informants in this way can be political and inclusive.
- The relationship between the researcher and the researched is key to the process.
- The researcher should share his or her theoretical stance and acknowledge this as a relativist position (i.e. it is simply one position and not *the* position).

Lessons from David – *Michele Moore*

In the regular world of 'good research practice', a decision to set about researching life stories would involve strategic planning of the work. There should be negotiation with whoever is to be the focus of the research over the terms of their – and the researcher's own – engagement. Judicious consultation should take place throughout the course of the project over ongoing processes of collecting and making sense of data to ensure that the analysis being produced is not manipulated by the researcher in ways that go against the interests of the person whose story is being researched. What I have found, however, is that life story research often originates in situations where complications abound and the usual principles of well-organised research design fly out of the window. This was the case in the project with David. I didn't go to meet David thinking I was about to embark on life story research; rather I found myself having stumbled into his life, affected by it and affecting it and only later, once the life had ended, did I come to think 'maybe there was some life story research in that'.

Originally I had conventional research notions about perhaps interviewing David and other 'key stakeholders'. I toyed with the idea of trying to collate observations of his interactions with his parents and various caregivers and at one stage I even wondered about trying out some personal construct techniques (Bannister, 1977), which not only promised insight into how he saw the world but also, having respectable roots in psychology, might have provided the kind of data that could be afforded a modicum of recognition by the armies of providers looking at David's situation from a medical perspective. All of these activities seemed to me to be legitimate 'research' activities. But I was frustrated by the lack of openings for 'proper' research in my dealings with David: he just did not want to know. I felt very strongly from the minute I met him that what was happening to him was important, that other people needed to know and that collusion with the silencing of David's story was not an option, but 'just telling his story' seemed whimsical, insubstantial and likely to be inconsequential.

Looking back now, my concerns about the value of storytelling were very wide of the mark. The stated reservations seem incredible, not least because my chief coping mechanism at the time was to immerse trusted others in the story. Hours went by on the phone, going over the latest instalment, and many more were spent trying to make sense of the story with colleagues who had first-hand experience of disability or disability in the family. David's story was one that people wanted to know and comment on and contest, but it still didn't occur to me at the time that the first thing to be done as a researcher agitating for change was to 'get his story out there'. What I have learned is that the power of the story – told even as it is in the style of awkward and amateur first fictions – is immeasurably greater than scraps of interpreted transcript, appraisals of interactions witnessed through the lens of an outsider, or the polarised manipulations of a lay construct analyst. So the first lesson I would pass on is to encourage confidence in the value of life story research, and the second is to be aware of what is happening around you because you can be embroiled in life story research without knowing it at the time.

Often in situations where research seems prohibitive, the potential, and imperative, for life storytelling is there. For example, last year I assisted in the delivery of a friend's baby that had died. During and after the delivery, every researcher instinct I possess told me I should record and interrogate many harmful and traumatising aspects of professional practices observed. Disabling assumptions about the presumed quality of the baby's life were used to negate the tragedy of her death in brutal and unthinking ways. The situation unfolded too quickly, emotions were too raw and the stakes were too high to elaborate careful research practices. In the end we are left with 'only' the story to tell.

But the simplest story of what went on, combined with analysis grounded in the social model of disability, would generate clear and immediate practical recommendations for nurses and other practitioners involved in the delivery of babies who have died, with transforming consequences for parents. I couldn't research the story *in situ*. I can't do it yet, but practising life story research provides a possible strategy for not losing such critical witnessings. The story can be picked up when the individuals concerned, including the participant researcher in this case, become able. The necessity for 'research' to be done soon can be obviated. The power of the story will not diminish. With the benefit of hindsight and having learned much from the failings of my work on David's story, I hope it would be possible to protect against diminution of the analysis by more effectively thinking ahead on proposed dissemination mechanisms this time. However, this piece of life story research, if it does ever materialise, can be based firmly upon a premise of consultation and many of the ethical contortions that have characterised the researching and telling of David's story might not surface. The pointer here for other researchers would be to understand the scope for life story research that emerges through your own life experiences. Our own experiences are often the source of our deepest and most intimately informed understandings. In the context of supervision of research students and researchers in the field, I have seen the potential of life story research in sensitive situations being realised many times.

Telling stories provides an accessible and familiar starting point for both researchers and those who are 'the researched'. Life story research is invaluable when conventional research options are closed down. It is also invaluable in all those situations where, looking back, you feel you may have missed the moment or where, looking forward, you know that the situation precludes the possibility of systematic enquiry. For whatever reason, telling the story will have to suffice. What I understand, having come through the journey of telling David's story, is that life story research is not a methodological strategy of last resort but frequently the methodological strategy of choice.

I have learned that 'the devil really is in the detail'. Details can carry a story and a missing detail can render the essence of something indescribable. Note-making (not necessarily the same as note-taking) is immensely important for getting the story to work in the way you intend, particularly if you want to achieve a sense of realism. I have unending regret that I made notes about what happened to David with a view to detailing the sequence of main events but recorded little else. I didn't note the sights and sounds of his exclusion or the signs of his pain, and there would be lessons to learn – as well as audiences to capture through those details. Above all, I remember the smells of David's skin as being unexpectedly expressive but I cannot recall the associations that would evoke understanding of this for a reader. Write down – or talk onto tape – as much as you can about what you notice. Even fleeting details can be precious. But the most important thing I know now is that life story researchers must open up the processes of consultation as early as we possibly can, because, as David's story shows, events may overtake you.

Lessons from Frank – *Peter Clough*

The stories in this book (and it must be remembered that they *are* stories) can offer up this bit and that bit in ways which make the reader the analyst. *Frank*, for example, is a story that requires at least two levels of analysis. The first has been done by the author – sorting and sifting the various themes of the data – deciding on the order in which they appear, deciding how much to tell about 'Frank'. The second has to be done by the reader; reading *Frank* is difficult because it becomes a story only when the reader takes on the role of researcher and is prepared, in some way, to ask questions of the story as it is presented. Lessons from *Frank* are learned only as the reader is prepared to select important themes for her/himself. Importantly, readers of *Frank* must not only take from the data but also *add* data which help them to make sense of the story in terms of their own lives and their own experiences. So – there will be many 'readings' of *Frank*; the data and their meanings will take many forms. The seven themes that I have selected in the discussion of the 'contexts' of Frank (see Chapter 9) are effectively categories for analysis – but there could be many more.

For example, I asked a woman colleague to read *Frank* and tell me about the lessons she derived from it. For her the forceful lessons were not those of religion, sexuality, or her father; the most powerful connection she made was with the notion of 'roots' and of belongingness. She talked at length with me about how she never felt she belonged anywhere because her family were forever on the move – moving out of the area, out of difficulty, away from debt, away from trouble and, eventually, she and her mother moved 'one more time' (so she was told) away from the abuse of her mother's lover. For her, *Frank* opened up her own story of 'moving' – she's still on the move 'First scent of trouble – I'm off,' she said, 'no roots – no history – no relationships – no debts to anyone'.

The lessons from *Frank* are intensely personal. My lessons are not yours – no one will 'read' the same story.

Conclusion

Researching Life Stories leads us into a complex arena of ethical debate. While the usual criteria of assessment such as informed consent, anonymity and potential withdrawal contain much social scientific research, life story research throws up a host of difficult considerations. Perhaps, what all of our musings have in common is a not uneventful engagement with the lives in life story research. We are concerned that narrative does not disserve the very people it is meant to represent and address. This leads to a more qualitative and interactional view of the ethics of research – to critically embrace a deontological view of research: to have a sense of duty to support others' rights. With such views in mind we are forced to think about significant others – including our audience, to which we now turn.

Chapter 12

A/Effecting

Audience and effects in researching life stories

Introduction

Who are our stories for? When we wrote our 'target audience' section of the book proposal we not only included under/postgraduates and other researchers in the social sciences but also non-academics with an interest in stories. These might include practitioners – from psychotherapy and counselling, social workers, nurses, doctors, teachers and other educational professionals. Moreover, we hope/d that the mention of stories might whet the appetite of the reader searching Internet bookshops for a cracking good yarn, but we doubt it. We expect that readers will be academic, researcher or practitioner by trade, with an interest in qualitative research and, perhaps, in some of the epistemological and theoretical debates hinted at in the title of the book. But of course, we did not just think of audience groupings. When we came to write this book we were also thinking of the possible dispositions and expectations of our audience. We suspect some readers have – or maybe had – some doubts about the doing of life story research. We also suspect that readers from our disciplines of psychology, education, sociology, feminist studies and disability studies might have stumbled across this text. We have heard many times the argument that researchers cannot hope to alter the things that audiences do with the research they disseminate. We would share such a view. We do not expect to radically alter the mindsets of the readers we have in mind (though we secretly hope that we have influenced at least a few). However, we do know that our perceived potential engagement with an audience has affected the stories we have written and the exposition of methodology and analysis produced in this book. This chapter aims to explicitly consider how life story researchers conceive of their audience and how such conceptions impact upon researching life stories.

'Is it really like that?' Towards enlightening stories – *Dan Goodley*

A Design for Life exists as a story with the potential to illuminate the readers' understandings of what life is like – or can be like – for a group of people disempowered by society and its institutions. The story fits the mould of a lot of ethnographic and biographical writing in the learning difficulties field which has drawn attention to what Dexter (1956) called the social problem of learning difficulties. I have described elsewhere how a number of accounts of people with learning difficulties have clarified the socially constructed nature of disability (Goodley, 2000). These include *The World of Nigel Hunt* (Hunt, 1967), Ed Murphy's story by Bogdan and Taylor (1976, see also 1982), *Tongue Tied* by Joey Deacon (1974), Kaufman's (1988) account of a mother and disabled daughter and Atkinson and Williams's (1990) anthology of prose, artwork and poetry. In addition, Korbin (1986) presents the life course of *Sarah – a Down's syndrome child* to show the impact of social factors on development, and Lea (1988) refutes pathologising clinical definitions via the poetry of people defined by such criteria. Potts and Fido (1991, see also Fido and Potts, 1989) collected the oral histories of a number of long-term residents in an English mental hospital, and Oswin (1991) uncovered people with learning difficulties' experiences of bereavement. Cheston (1994) provides the accounts of 'special education leavers', while Angrosino (1994) talks of how he collected life stories in *On the Bus with Vonny Lee*, and Booth and Booth's (1994) *Parenting under Pressure* explores the personal stories of parents with learning difficulties. All of these narratives – to which perhaps we could add *A Design for Life* – can be considered to be enlightening stories. These accounts aim to move the reader into feeling the lifeworlds of people whom they may not (want to) know in a number of ways.

Possibilities

In writing *A Design for Life* and its subsequent analyses, I wanted to present to the reader the possibility of life not being lost even when one is at the margins of society. With practitioners in mind, I was reminded of Means and Smith's (1994) argument that in the context of community care, those involved often tend to become so caught up in the change elements of the system that they ignore the very real conditions of oppression that still exist for some of society's most marginalised people (including people with learning difficulties). The Disability Discrimination Act (1995) and the White Paper *Valuing People* (2002) are examples of legislation that have only just started to take seriously the potential for victimhood that can afflict people with learning difficulties (and we return to them in Chapter 13). *A Design for Life* was written at a time when these policy debates were very much ongoing. Hence the stories of David, Katy, Kevin and Ricky demonstrate the impacts of being objectified, assessed and governed every moment of every day of one's life. The aim here is to draw the reader into the full horrors of 'disablement':

an experience of exclusion of people with impairments (Oliver, 1996).
But this is not only about eliciting sympathy. It should also be about
empathy and camaraderie – to relate with our characters, to feel their
pains and, also, to celebrate their successes. This latter point links in with
another possibility: the stories of Gerry and Maddie suggest better lives.
Gerry O'Toole is a person with the label of learning difficulties who has
done much. Not only has he managed to find a fruitful place in society
– he has done so against the odds. Also, though he perhaps doesn't know
it, he has lived a life that says much about disabling society – which has
failed to keep him down. All good heroic tales engage with the audience's
optimistic side: by sharing tales of winning against the odds. The story
aims to enlighten the readers about the submerged dangers and hidden
treasures of life (Corbett, 1998).

Exaggeration

We have tried to demonstrate in this book that researching life stories is
very much a challenge to taken-for-granted orthodoxies of social scientific research. In telling stories we want to suggest that researchers may
have to leave their well-used methodological and analytical tools behind.
Plummer (1983) suggests that narrative research means turning to the
tools of the poet, the artisan and the dramatist. Often, such a call is seen
only to refer to the stages of narrative construction – what we might call
method/ology. In addition, I would suggest, life story research – stories
plus analyses – must provide twists in the tale: to present scenarios that
the reader might not be expecting. To turn back to the discourse analysis
in Chapter 9, Gerry is depicted as a theoretical doer in the greatest possible
sense – he deconstructs and disrupts the social conditions around him,
as he moves in and out of welfare-dependent contexts, in an almost
cavalier fashion. His narrative is theoretically imbued. His actions are
praxis in the classic Marxist sense – action and meaning-making intertwined. He goes into the day centre to sit passively before the staff member
baking the cake. He excuses it as an opportunity to see his mates, moving
on to the market or the pub football team: a wealth of experiences ahead
of him. His deconstruction, so often just a wordy, cognitive phenomenon,
is active and real. Gerry, the great poststructuralist (O'Toole, G. (2004)
Poststructuralism in Practice, Somewhere in Britain: The Realworld
Publishing House – anyone?). Nisbet (1976) argues that when sociology
embraces the arts, we want to garner readers' support for our ideas about
the world through appealing to their affective as well as cognitive sides.
The beauty of emotion is that it so often works its way through a tide
of repressive rational thought. What may seem exaggerative to the rational
may seem plausible to the emotive. An exaggerated point of analysis may
well seem viable in the hands of an authentic character. Presenting a

'handicapped person' as the purveyor of elegant theories seems so much more at home in a story than it does in the rational context of the social *sciences*.

Dealings with reality and relativism in researching life stories

For all this talk of art, my storytelling was driven by a clear resolve: to insist to the reader that people with learning difficulties, in terms of cultural and economic capital, live in poverty; but the news of their demise is premature. Analysis driven by poststructuralism will necessarily aim to challenge *radical relativism*, the philosophy that accepts a zillion interpretations. Instead, the conquest may be seen as one of the *critical realist*; accepting that there are many interpretations out there but they are always underpinned with ideological (and discursive) foundations which we need to allude to. Gerry's story says a lot about living with the label of learning difficulties, especially the way in which this object/subject position permits professionals an intrusive role. The accompanying analyses aimed to tackle the construction of the very real phenomenon of 'learning difficulties'. Here, perhaps, we have the transition state of poststructuralism. Following Harding (1992), in deconstructing 'learning difficulties' we are in danger of leaving it as a phantom entity – far from real in a discursive no man's land – now firmly held in the fist of the poststructuralist writer. This is the contradiction of postmodernity, where any deconstruction is transitional – neither real nor fiction. A way forward, following Parker (1998), is offered by a critical realist position which recognises that the end point of deconstruction involves recourse to society. So, learning difficulties is understood as a real phenomenon, that people are defined in relation to (having it or not having it), bringing with it a host of ideological baggage. It does not disappear with deconstruction, it is reborn but as a socially created thing that needs to be viewed with a critical eye. Here is another argument for analysing life stories: to persuade the reader of the real and not so real things of the timbres of a narrative. They are real, Captain, but not as we know them.

'So it could be like that'. Emancipatory stories – Rebecca Lawthom

Reconceptualising participants, reconceptualising the audience

Working within an emancipatory project is a very different way of doing research. Working with people rather than on people allows the emergence of a liberated psychology (e.g. Kagan, 2002). In contrast to other ways of measuring and monitoring human experience, community psychology takes social change and social action seriously.

> A liberated academic psychology must position itself in solidarity with those who are marginalized and have hitherto been without a voice in the discipline, or indeed in society.
>
> (Kagan, 2002, p. 10)

Community psychologists work within an emancipatory paradigm, sharing information, collaborating with people who are experts about their lives, working with people often marginalised by the social system and working towards empowerment. This is a distinctly different agenda. Indeed, Rapaport asks us to

> consider how differently we would speak, what different priorities we might have, and how differently we might relate to our own (and mainstream psychology's) rhetoric if we spoke with 'the people' and 'oppressed communities' rather than to ourselves and other psychologists ... We might begin to see that our own practices and promises are often naïve, elitist, romantic, reifying and/or obfuscating ... our struggle for legitimacy and impact would be different if instead of being aimed at journal editors, departmental heads, and colleagues, it were directed at those people and communities we profess to champion.
>
> (Rapaport, 1977, p. 313)

Whilst we are not professing to be doing community psychology, we are trying to work in emancipatory ways. By presenting narratives of difference that have been co-collected, co-authored and co-analysed, we can hopefully present an array of possibilities for readers. These possibilities may be experienced as recognition of experience, celebration of women, personal change and ultimately social action. We are not claiming that reading narratives incites people to join social movements, but that there are undeniable impacts upon the audience.

The audience operates on a number of levels. There are similarities with Augusto Boal's (1979, 1992, 1995) notion of the 'spect-actor', who, upon watching a performance, can stop the action and transform from a passive spectator into an actor, who enacts an alternative course of action. In the same way, our audiences may well draw parallels with our characters' lives or envision alternatives. In this way, we may reach audiences who, previously disempowered by or dislocated from research, can make sense of stories, as research.

By inviting Colleen into the collaborative venture of this research, I aimed to make clear the links between actuality and academia. Following the tenets of a liberating view of community psychology, the aim here is to invite people into research who are so often the distant audiences of our research. Historically, psychology, for example, has created a body of knowledge on people, about people, with the aim of restoring normality or betterment to people's lives. Potentially and in contrast, researching life stories demonstrates an approach to emancipatory research, which locates research paradigms – such as psychology – back in the community. Now located, our traditional passive recipients of psychological theory become co-researchers and theoreticians, challenging the distinction between expert and client, psychologist and participant and researcher and researched. One key intended audience of such an approach to research will be other similar co-researchers. Hence, the aim here is reconsider our participants and by doing so we rethink the audiences that we hope to pass our stories onto.

Transformative research, transforming audiences

With narrative, as with many research processes, there are immediate (proximal) audiences and wider (distal) audiences. We talked of the way in which narrative may be constructed as linear (with intended audience in mind) in Part 2 of this book. Colleen wanting to present an orderly tale, which made sense. However, the authorial shaping was jointly undertaken and thus a declared feminist lens was added. In Colleen's audience design her desire is to make sense of her own life. In my intended academic community, I want to present (implicitly and explicitly) a feminist reading. Moreover, the emancipatory element inspires us to present positive change. So, who might read and be a/effected by Colleen's story?

The wider feminist community is a sector of the audience. Millennium feminism (in its various theoretical perspectives) should still be energised by politics. Social activism is 'the project within which we conduct our work' (Fine, 1992, p. viii). Moreover, women and men who read Colleen's narratives (as non-feminists) may see the possibility of change and the gendered practices that constrain the 'doing' of masculinity and femininity. It becomes possible when reading Colleen's story to see how patriarchal discourses shape lives, impacting upon agency. Colleen directly addresses the audience when she talks of gender relations and work–family–life balance:

> whether ever anyone will ever think it is a really wonderful job that women do I don't know. Whereas when men stay at home to look after the children as a househusband permanently or whatever, everyone thinks that is absolutely wonderful and will talk about it . . .

The very fact that Colleen herself (despite not wanting to talk about her present relationship in detail) talks about leaving her husband for a woman partner is indicative of a number of points. First, Ochs and Capps (2001) note that sometimes narratives remain untold if perceived to be inappropriate or politically unfeasible. However, Colleen situates the leaving episode within her narrative and it remains there following the editing process. Second, the leaving episode is not presented as unproblematic or positioned as a high moral stance. Colleen skilfully articulates the new relationship (with a woman) without 'coming out' forcefully. The story also has much to say about the development of self (whether that is labelled as confidence, esteem, or character) in the modern world. Rather like the children who 'grow like flowers' in Colleen's story, Colleen herself through social relationships transforms into a confident woman (able to leave a non-functioning relationship). This new position is further highlighted by her marginalised lesbian status in a dominant heterosexual society.

Such slices of life taken from Colleen's narrative demonstrate, I hope, the storying of emancipation, so much so that some readers may say 'So it could be like that?' The story is viewed as potentially transformative. Rather than viewing knowledge production as knowledge for knowledge's sake, I would suggest that Colleen's narrative can be seen as an emancipatory narrative that may well stimulate and inspire or, at the very least, allow others to rethink their own views of, say, gender differences and the expectations of women. Stories are peculiar cultural artefacts that have the potential to stir minds and promote action. We have only to look at the impact of song, film and drama to see how our very opinions and perhaps actions can be thrown into sharp relief by a (moral or political) tale. The same view of narrative research can be taken – that we aim to inspire audiences rather than lay them dormant by academically grounded research endeavours.

'It shouldn't be like that'. Didactic stories – Michele Moore

What are these stories for? What are they designed to do?

David's story was written to prompt critical insight into the dominance of medical and individualised discourses in a disabled person's life and to raise questions about the ways in which these discourses shape other people's lives. It has been written to encourage an appreciation of different approaches to disability and impairment and to provide a vehicle for critical evaluation of values and problems which continue to be of immediate contemporary concern. It tries to provide some affirmation of David's life following spinal cord injury. It is a story written to make a writer feel less guilty about her own role in the silencing of oppression. It is a story born out of anger and disillusion intended to make explicit that David's experience 'shouldn't have been like that', to provoke resistance and to persuade a reader to confront abusive support practices.

One of the most important things to get across through David's story was the uneven distribution of power between him and his allies and the professionals involved in his life. Regrettably this imbalance is also a feature of the way in which his story has been produced. At this point in the book it will be very clear to the reader that potential for misuses and abuses of power in life story writing is large – especially when the person whose life being written about is dead. Telling David's story may raise his issues, but neither the process of constructing the story nor its final production or dissemination will benefit him. Arguably, placing the story in this academic and relatively erudite book on research method-ology, distances knowledge of what happened to David from the bigger arena of debate about personal assistance and disabled people's entitle-ments, which was at the heart of his own concern. All of this reminds us that there are obvious and challenging questions to be posed regarding the purposes of life story research. To add to the list, the relationship between the written language of the story and the actuality of events is treacherously ambiguous. There is no one 'true' narrative for a reader to get hold of, but many possible interpretations of what went on. Because all stories, in their writing, reading or telling, are cultural products, embedded in the specific personal, political and social contexts occupied by the author, the characters and the readers, the impact of any story on prospective readers is difficult to envisage.

What effect do the stories have on whom?

The effect David's story can have will depend on who gets to read it. This offers a dispiriting prospect. For example, in Hampshire, where local authorities have decided that disabled people should lose 100 per cent of their disposable income to pay for charges for non-residential services, policy officials need to read it (NCIL, 2003). Campaigners who treat uncritically the assumption that personal and intimate care for men with spinal injuries should be provided by their mothers, need to read it. Disabled people seeking the right to 'mercy killing' because they find the pain of starvation unbearable, 'with cramps and headaches and general body pain' (Such, 2003), might find that the story presents new challenges to exclusionary systems, values and practices. It is unlikely that the story will fall naturally under the gaze of such audiences, but it will put any reader in mind of how we each need to do something about recognising and challenging disabling policies and practices wherever we find them.

The hard work of responding to David's story to bring about change in organisations, or processes to advance an inclusive society, falls to the reader. Living with impairment in a disabling world is no joke, and delivery on the right to an ordinary life produces a terrifying amount of anxiety for the vast majority of service providers. To work to advance David's right to an ordinary life, in the target-driven and commissioning culture that characterises service provision in the UK, requires readers to have high expectations of themselves and those with whom they work. The story won't achieve anything on its own; it requires readers:

> to 'see' that things can be better and to trust that those around them – despite much evidence to the contrary – with a bit of help from the social model, with its emphasis on breaking down the barriers which create exclusion, can and will change their practice and improve their game.
>
> (Dunn, 2004)

The telling of David's story and its analysis attempt to achieve just this. It identifies prospects for more enabling responses to the experience of impairment, and urges readers to listen to and act on what disabled people are saying about the support that they want. It may reveal something of the actuality of David's life, illustrate the processes by which he was disabled, and go some way towards demystifying the problematic relationship between community care and disability politics. It might open up questions about everyday understandings of the 'able' body, it might inspire a willing practitioner to reconceptualise the way in which they link impairment to social roles and behaviour, it might encourage critical reflection on the extent to which ideas about how people with impairments continue to be controlled by non-disabled people in the twenty-first century. Whether it can do any of this ultimately depends on the reader.

The only thing to say with certainty is that engaging in life story projects makes a massive impact on the researcher. Researching and writing this small part of David's life has left me with a sense of deep gratitude to him for helping to make the world a more enabling place to be. It has allowed me to 'give sorrow words' (William Shakespeare, *Macbeth*, Act IV) and taught me that storytelling has an important role to play in dismantling the myths that turn impairment into personal tragedy.

'It is like that.' Resonating stories – *Peter Clough*

What are these stories for? What are they designed to do? In the case of *Frank* each reader is a unique 'audience' – who takes his/her own lessons from the story. *Frank* is a story for any reader who chooses to seek to learn lessons. It is a story designed to provoke something of the self in the reader. Many people keep a notebook, save old letters, have some-thing to say about a family photograph or two, are intrigued about that 'gap' in family history which remains unmentioned but which – in some way – exists in the collective consciousness. 'Something happened' but we don't really know what. *Frank* is that kind of story.

If we are arguing for the use of narrative in research reports there has to be a critical questioning of the purpose of such accounts. We must ask: Who are these stories for? What effect do the stories have on whom?

The use of narratives and fictions in social science research makes it possible to render the lives of others in such a way that others might access something of the raw truths of their lives. Conventional research reports (often) effectively render out the personal. Their genre (usually) requires a sort of sanitisation. Lives and difficulties are disinfected and presented 'steam-cleaned', and – though creased and worn – they are offered up to the reader in a relatively painless way. These are lives served up with the appropriate dosage of painkiller to make things easier on the reader. Such reports render data analysed and dosed with the morphine of refereed publication.

There is an important place for such writing and for such accounts, but narrative and fictional accounts of lives lived are, arguably, best presented as stories such that others can 'read into' and 'read off' them. In such situations the audience does the greater work – and they can succeed in that work only if the author has created a work that confronts the reader with the difficulties of lives laid bare, a work which challenges, confronts and provokes. At their best, narrative research reports in the form of life stories – stripped from the structure and protections of the traditional genre of research report – demonstrate the actualities of life.

Conclusions

Audiences often occupy a silent – perhaps sinister – place in social scien-tific research. They are often patronisingly viewed as unknowing (the 'lay audience'), equals (read 'academic audience') and so often passive recipi-ents of the knowledge that researchers promulgate. Yet, *Researching Life Stories* displays a host of philosophical, political, personal and theoretical preoccupations of the writer – and the anticipated baggage of the audi-ence – that will necessarily impact on the telling of a tale. Furthermore, as we aim to embrace some key literary strategies and techniques in turning to story, so the audience becomes paramount. Our view is that audiences – readers – are never naive, passive recipients of ideas. Good stories stir minds and souls. We should be mindful of these potential stirrings.

Applying

Policy, practice and theory in life story research

Introduction

We end this book with considerations that are so often at the start of books. By now, you will have at least some idea as to how and why the stories in Part 1 were written. In this final chapter, we present a number of applications of the stories to our chosen fields and audiences of enquiry. Each of us will demonstrate how our narratives contribute to thinking in terms of theory, practice and policy. We know that researching life stories is not writing stories for writing's sake – though perhaps we should be celebrating this in itself. To the reader who is left asking, 'Okay, but what does all this life story stuff tell us about the world?' we hope that this chapter at least partly answers your question. Our research preoccupations involve sociology, disability studies, feminist psychology, inclusive education, educational policy analysis. We feel that our stories have many things to say that are of use to these disciplines, their related practitioners and policy makers and – crucially – those people who have allowed their stories to be told.

Applying Gerry O'Toole's story – *Dan Goodley*

Gerry says much about the contemporary policy, professional and theoretical contexts in relation to the phenomenon of learning difficulties. For this chapter, I develop some analyses that I made in a seminar paper that drew directly on Gerry's story (Goodley, 2003). The focus of the seminar was on disability studies, education and work. I turn now to what Gerry's story tells us about the educational and training experiences of people with the label 'learning difficulties', as one example of the application of his story, with a focus on policy, professionals, politics and theory.

Policy

Many people with 'learning difficulties' remain in some form of educational or training provision throughout their lives. The nature of lifelong learning and the learning society is exclusively one of segregation (Riddell *et al.*, 2001). From special schools, to learning support units, to involvement with one-to-one support in mainstream schools, to adult training centres (now, interestingly, termed social education centres), to group homes and sheltered workshops, people with 'learning difficulties' are subjected to educational interventions from a gamut of specialist professionals. Social and life skills classes dominate (Sutcliffe and Simons, 1993); users of centres are invited to partake in training for user consultation meetings (Simons, 1992); sheltered employment opportunities are provided with crude learning skills identified (Nourozi, 2003). Conformity to these institutions is paramount. Challenging behaviour is tackled through therapy, psychotropic drugs such as Ritalin (Breggin, 1993) or, more recently, anger management classes (Goodley, 2000). Education as specialist instruction reigns, and few real work opportunities exist (Baron *et al.*, 1998). Recent policy initiatives develop further the case for people with 'learning difficulties' to be educated. The White Paper *Valuing People* (2001) sets out plans for the constitution of consultation arenas such as partnership boards, people's parliaments across services and nationwide training in self-advocacy skills (see the website www.viaorg.uk). These recommendations are steeped in the rhetoric of 'training up' unknowing people with 'learning difficulties'. This sets a worrying policy climate for people with 'learning difficulties'. Yet again, they are the recipients of well-meaning interventions, which aim to school them in a host of life skills, consultation methods and, now, user-representative experiences. Unlike disability legislation which has arguably been ground out through consultation with representative organisations of disabled people, *Valuing People* appears to keep the existing self-advocacy movement at arm's length: away from the real stuff of policy development. Education in its broadest sense is presented as a top-down practice to be formally maintained in service settings. In contrast, Gerry's story alerts us to the ways in which education, self-knowledge and work opportunities often exist despite policy interventions. While many of Gerry's peers live in closely controlled and managed educational experiences, he boasts a rich life. Some of this richness is down to his involvement with a self-advocacy group, where comrades such as Maddie Harrison and Gerry work together to forge identities away from the policy-led contexts of group home and day centre. In this sense, life stories can illuminate the private experiences of forging educational and work opportunities often outside or against the public policy context.

Professionals

There is intensive professional involvement in the lives of people with 'learning difficulties'. In schools, children hit a wall of assessment bureaucracy and narrow definitions of intelligence (Ryan and Thomas,

1980/1987). Such standards are made even harder to achieve by the deficit thinking held by a host of professionals (Goodley, 1997). Moreover, as Booth and Booth (1994, 1998) observe, there is a double standard of professionalism. First, professional assessment is never-ending, so that children and adults have their every move observed by one professional or another. Second, and in contrast, even in this high-pressure situation, professionals often set superhuman criteria for children and parents to pass: whether it be demonstrating that one displays appropriate behaviour in class (Clough, 2002), displaying a hyper-work ethic in an employment context (Nourozi, 2003), or showing that one is, incredibly, able enough to parent a child (Booth and Booth, 1994). Failure to meet these criteria often means separation: from classmates, from work colleagues, from one's own children. For many disabled people, professionalisation threatens identity. In terms of lifelong learning, steeped in the rhetoric of the 'learning society', *Valuing People* (2001) provides initiatives that will further develop the role of professionals in the lives of people with 'learning difficulties'. The move towards nationally recognised accredited qualifications or the Learning Disability Awards Framework (LDAF) may seem from the outside to at last be taking seriously the professionalism of working with clients with 'learning difficulties'. Another view might be that such a move will further professionalise services to the detriment of service users' ownership of service provision. Page and Aspis (1997) note how self-advocacy is often framed in terms of what professionals can offer to people with 'learning difficulties', rather than as processes owned and developed by people with 'learning difficulties'. Bhavnani (1990) criticises this view of empowerment: the powerful giving some power back to the powerless. The problem with this, she notes, is that often only some power is given back (if any at all). Professional power brings with it a number of dilemmas. Indeed, key concerns of the disability movement are troubled by these recent developments in professional practice. The issue of direct payments is somewhat complicated for people with 'learning difficulties' due to the ways in which professionals are consistently embedded in their daily life experiences. Choosing professional support is anathema to many people with 'learning difficulties'. Professionalisation is an inevitable consequence of being labelled as having 'learning difficulties'. Not choosing professional involvement might be a more radical departure for many people with 'learning difficulties'. Questions remain about the role of professionals. Against this policy backdrop, Gerry's story makes one significant point – that empowerment for people with learning difficulties may often mean escape from professional gaze and surveillance. Too often, policy making is based upon long-held beliefs – such as the caring nature of the welfare state. Gerry reminds us that for all these policy developments, the promotion of professional practice can actually hamper rather than enable self-empowerment.

Politics

The self-advocacy movement challenges professional dominance and top-down policy making. The maxim of this movement is speaking up for oneself: demonstrating one's competence in a culture that assumes incompetence (Dybwad and Bersani, 1996; Goodley, 2000). A culture of self-help, self-empowerment and consciousness-raising is promoted by the self-advocacy movement. Unlike policy making and professionalisation, the onus is on the self-organisation of people with 'learning difficulties' to challenge devaluing labels, promote positive images and reject incompetent service provision. However, questions have been raised about the political potency of self-advocacy. It has been criticised for being professionally led (Page and Aspis, 1997), individually rather than collectively focused and a creation of well-meaning professionals (Simpson, 1999). As Page and Aspis (1997) point out, the danger for self-advocacy is that it becomes yet another focus of an adult training centre's curriculum: it is depoliticised and recuperated back into traditional educational and training initiatives. Gerry's story reminds us, however, that the self-organisation of oppressed groups can lead to the development of new social movements. While it is only right to remain critical of developments in 'self-empowerment' – particularly when well-meaning others are calling the shots – we must keep in mind the significant impact that such groups can have on identities. Perhaps Gerry's story is a testimony to the power of self-organisation on the part of people with learning difficulties.

Theory

Gerry's story says a lot about the construction of versions of humanity. His tale could be seen as a social constructionist one (Burr, 1995): where identity, personhood and psychology are constructed through the relationships he has with other people (particularly professionals), institutions, knowledge systems and socio-cultural structures. His story contributes to recent work on the social construction of learning difficulties (e.g. Ferguson et al., 1992; Whittemore et al., 1986) and the social construction of impairment in disability studies (Hughes and Paterson, 1997; Goodley, 2001). Rather than viewing people so labelled as having some biological, individualised and tragic condition, Gerry alerts us to the ways in which social theory should illuminate the construction of 'learning difficulties'. His story, then, is a resource contributing to general constructionist and constructivist writing in the social sciences. Furthermore, Gerry demonstrates the resilience that exists in the face of such constructions: structuralism is not the dominant understanding – resistance is.

Applying Colleen's story – *Rebecca Lawthom*

Colleen's story (perhaps because it is 'real') has a plethora of potential links to theory and practice. Historically, it tells us much about gender, career and expectations. Childcare and caring generally feature in the plot. From a contemporary perspective, lifelong learning, lesbian identity and feminism feature. Here we explore Colleen's story and its contribution to theory and links with policy.

Theory

Rich links are present in Colleen's telling of the story. A key contributory arena is that of feminist theory. Feminism has had much to say and offer to a debate about gender but it is questionable how much of the theory reaches everyday women (outside of academia). Reay (1998) talks of the paucity of work that considers working-class women and their experiences within feminist literature, and Colleen's story sheds light on this rather typical life history. Gender cannot be a homogenous category and Colleen's story is fractured by both class (Ussher, 1997) and sexuality. A diverse literature now focuses on and gives voice to 'other' sexualities – 'queer', bisexual, lesbian and gay identities. Colleen's upbringing sees alternative and non-dominant sexualities as necessarily 'other'; thus her coming out of the dominant heterosexual marriage into a lesbian relationship is atypical and 'strange' to those around her. Exploring people *in situ*, within contexts, seems important if we are to advance theory about non-dominant groups.

The work and career history of Colleen is also a story about self-esteem, expectations, confidence and, of course, gender. The intersection of work and family is rarely viewed through a gendered lens (Lawthom, 2000). The expectations for women and career were historically limited and Colleen's story writes this large. However, while the gender wagon rolls on and girls now outperform boys at almost every compulsory level of education (in the UK), what are the implications? Salary differentials and glass ceilings are still in place within workplace settings. Patterns of employment are still feminised, with women located in particular sectors. Girls may well be achieving potential within schools, but the politics of organisations, set against a wider societal context of patriarchy, make career equality impossible (Nicholson, 1996). Women, like Colleen, work in paid arenas and still continue to do most of the domestic chores. Theoretically, the psychology of workplaces (organisational/occupational/ work psychology) has little to say about this domain. Feminists have written widely about promotion and difference in organisations and cultures (e.g. Alimo-Metcalf, 1994). The issue of discrimination is now rarely heard in these 'post-feminist' times, but difference still exists. A more insidious practice, that of covert discrimination, makes it difficult for women to manage home and work interfaces successfully, without 'giving the game away'. Colleen's story tells us much about ways in which women manage childcare, work and family commitments. Historically, working women were less visible and less vilified (the 'bad mother' discourse). In contemporary society, the provision for childcare has clearly increased and improved, but have the gender relations? Women perhaps now work on top of domestic work, blurring the boundaries between paid and unpaid work. Brannen (2000) has talked of the need for an informed discussion on defining care and relationships.

In the work–family–life balance literature, the metaphor of a scales is useful to show how one manages work and family pressures. More recent literature has erased balance and instead talks of work–life integration, a seamless integration between public and private arenas providing maximum benefit for all. Colleen's complex mosaic of gender, work, relationship and identity issues means that theories proposed in one arena (for example, occupational psychology) need to be more inclusive in their understanding. Boundaries between home and work, public and private, are less evident and theory needs to mirror this successfully.

Policy

Colleen's upbringing, educational experience and subsequent career change provide rich fodder for policy makers. Stories need to be understood in the context of time, and thus contemporary policies take up many of these issues. Educationally, the removal of the tiered educational access around the 'eleven-plus' should mean more equal access for all. Sadly, in certain areas, the selection has been maintained and education becomes a commodity to be seized upon alongside 'good housing' in 'nice areas'. Even in areas where selection at age eleven does not happen, other initiatives have raised public consciousness about 'good schools'. The publication of league tables, alongside labels such as 'beacon' schools, continues to create a tiered system. Competition now happens between parents fighting for access to quality education. For Colleen, some of the initiatives occurring now such as Excellence/Challenge and the widening participation agenda may well benefit children from socially disadvantaged areas. Expectations and self-esteem are now firmly on the educational agenda to widen access.

There is also much implied change regarding class status. What constitutes work and how career provision happens are important themes. Colleen is an advocate for lifelong learning – age is unimportant and you can learn things in later life (or build/develop skills already utilised in life experience). Women's participation in the labour force has grown hugely and Colleen's story highlights the way in which training can be a formalised routine or concretised ability:

Having come from the background I have come from, it is almost like you don't have to go to the North Pole to know it is cold, but I think, as a mature student, and now working, I think, I feel I have got a lot more to offer than someone straight out of school. Because when you are dealing with families you just need to be so aware of what is going on other than what you can see, you know, that it is not always visible, is it?

The idea of learning being for all and a lifelong process emphasises the opportunity to learn across the life span. Colleen's experience supports this as a useful policy, as she successfully retrained, graduated and is now in employment. The timing of this for Colleen (when children were adolescent) suggests that childcare is still an issue. Many of the schemes which should give incentives to work are failing. The recent working family tax credit difficulty (and administrative problems) has left many women with no money in the short term to support childcare. Moreover, few tax benefits and expensive childcare make working life difficult. Whilst maternity benefits have changed slightly, by standards in other countries in the European Community, the UK is a poor provider (Brannen *et al.*, 2002). This policy backdrop will not enable women to flexibly work and contribute to the economy – despite the fact that more women (in the UK) now work than ever before. Women's intermittent participation in the workforce (due to having and caring for children) also problematises career and promotion opportunities.

Joined-up policies that knit together caring provision (for all) with work flexibility would do much for gender politics. Unpaid and invisible caring within the economy is mainly done by women. If girls are performing so well in the educational sector, why not provide more flexibility around employment and parenthood?

Applying David's story – *Michele Moore*

What is clear to me now, having told David's story and attempted various explanations of what it says and why it was written, is that it *can* contribute to thinking about theory, practice and policy relating to support offered to disabled people and their families. 'Material circumstances produce prose' (Steedman, 1992) and any attempt to describe these material circumstances, however inept, renders experience more tangible. Challenges relating to independent living and personal assistance for young men with high-level spinal cord injury are clear from David's story, not unquestionable but quickly recognisable, and they can be related to the experience of disabled people more generally. Applying David's story to disability theory and research, and to policy and practice issues, *could* alter some of the relations that produce and reproduce disablement.

The story functions to make clear the extent to which we are operating within a theoretical framework of struggle – a theme which has resonance in previous chapters. Characteristic struggles, between aspirations of disabled people, academics and practitioners can be identified in the story. The struggle between advocates of the social model of disability and those committed to a medical perspective is self-evident. The medical model is overtly challenged and further shamed, but theoretical questions might also be raised about the adequacy of the social model of disability for explaining David's experience, and about the relative importance of psychological determinants of his response to social pressures. The complexity of 'social' and 'psychological' interactions remains a shadowy and undertheorised area of debate and consequently the boundaries between appropriate resistance and pathologisation can easily be manipulated. Removing the barriers to an ordinary life would only in part have lessened the pain and anger David felt at his exclusion. Veck (2002) discusses the place of psychological responses to exclusion; it is possible that many of the tensions which built up in David's life could be explored further by engaging with a disability research paradigm that expands the orthodox features of the social model of disability to incorporate the contingent nature of social relations (see Scott-Hill, 2002).

At the levels of policy and practice, the story shows that power and control over one's own life is key to positive outcomes following spinal injury. This finding is far from new, but David's story adds further to the evidence base that seeks to advance a policy agenda for independent living. His story exposes the destructive power of discourses which limit the amount of control disabled people have over their own lives and suggests that the beneficiaries of this limiting of control are service providers who have a less arduous role if attention can be shifted away from what disabled people want and confined to the realms of what services can offer with least possible effort and resources. There is currently scope to feed these messages into relevant policy-making fora such as the Disability Rights Commission, collecting evidence to support a campaign for a right to independent living.

Things have moved on. National policy development relating to independent living is coming into place but still needs to be backed up by a direct payments scheme that will ensure options for independent living are available on the basis of equality. These objectives are embedded in the aims of the newly established National Centre for Independent Living (NCIL), and progress in respect of these commitments could mean that the belittling and undignified pleading that characterised the depressing events of June recounted in David's story might be avoided in similar discussions today. On the basis of stories currently being collected about the lives of people with spinal injuries, however, I doubt it. What is becoming clear through Cowe's (ongoing) work is that for many spinal injured people, the 'seven core areas of need' – information, counselling, housing, technical aids, personal assistance, transport and access – identified over twenty years ago as an agenda for disabled people wishing to live independent lives remain unmet (Davis, 1981). There have been policy and political changes for the better since David's time. Under new regulations that came into effect in April 2003 councils are now obliged by law to offer direct payments to every eligible user. An Independent Living Association in the region of England in which David lived and died is now actively exploring ways of making independent living a reality for disabled people living in the county, but the National Centre for Independent Living still advises disabled people that 'lots of different people might block your progress' (www.ncil.org.uk). There are more stories to be told.

And so in developing and advocating life story research we are faced with hard questions about when a piece of life story research can be drawn towards conclusion. From David I have learned that a story does not end when it is finished. Presenting his story might effect some small change. But it leaves unnecessary suffering uppermost in my mind.

Applying Frank – *Peter Clough*

'Frank' was desperate to have his story told. And some of his experiences in working in social/educational difficulty must have held in them something worth telling. But 'Frank' was more interested in himself, his identity and his inheritance which – I think – he sought as justification for his exit from teaching at 48.

> he had worked for some years as an auxiliary in a mental hospital – this was the early seventies – then teaching part-time in a borstal before joining a school for 'maladjusted' boys as a houseparent. By thirty-one he was deputy headteacher, and got his own school – one of the largest residential places in the country for what were now emotionally and behaviourally disturbed boys – at thirty-four. At forty-eight he tore it all up, and at fifty-one he phoned me to ask: would I write his story?

What lies behind *Frank* is a series of questions about teacher identity. 'Frank' wants to find an identity in a publication which features something of him. He's over – at least in terms of his professional life in educational difficulty. But he is desperate to reclaim some of the 'glory' of his days as a headteacher. He was one of those heads in one of those schools that everyone knew about. Teachers (and other heads) visited to find out 'how they did it'. 'Frank' was a regular 'turn' on the platforms of LEA and regional conferences. But he lost it. Much of this story revolves around him contemplating his own self, his roots, religion, sexuality, his relationship with his father.

His story is yet another story 'behind the headlines'. It takes off from a previous story of *Rob* whose assault on a pupil resulted in dismissal and newspaper headlines:

> When Rob Joynson was forty-three he came into school on a Tuesday morning much as usual; and passing at 10.40 by a Maths class taken by Michelle G. – a probationer of twenty-three – and hearing terrible noise; and seeing through the window a boy at the back fetch a fat gob on Michelle's back as she walked down the aisle smiling smiling too, too nervously, her hands doing 'down, please: down, down' at the noise; seeing this marbled yellow gob on Michelle's ordinary blouse on her decent body, Rob Joynson rushed into the room and to the back and took the boy – Mark something – by the ears, both ears, and pulled him up out of – through almost – his desk and repeatedly smashed his head against a chart of tessellations on the wall. And Michelle pulled at him from behind and screamed, and he twisted the boy down by his ears and pushed at him with his foot, kicking until he was quite under the desk. Then Rob started to cry and there was terrible silence – where there had been terrible noise – but for Rob searching for breath to fuel the small fearful wails which broke from him. When – thank God – someone laughed finally, unable to stay with the pain a moment longer, Rob fled the room.
>
> (Clough, 2002, p. 37)

These two stories emanate from the policy context of the late 1990s where (some) teachers' lives were being wrecked by the policy and practices of inspection, league tables, achievement targets, diminishing resources and lack of professional development. The point at which the story can be applied to our understanding of policy, education, professionalism and teacher identity is that 'Frank' burnt out – in some way – or simply gave up because he had not yet understood himself. There was no 'main event' for 'Frank' – nothing as dramatic as what he had read in the story of *Rob*, but 'Frank' still 'tore it up'. Something here reaches into the newspaper report of a headteacher, 'Mr Harries', who was reported to have suffered a breakdown due to his Ofsted experience, which the TES reported thus:

> Mr Harries' life now lies in tatters. He has contemplated suicide; he has received psychiatric counselling; he is still taking antidepressants for the nervous breakdown ... Mr Harries, 47, a father of two, is unable to work again. His doctor diagnosed reactive depression and post-traumatic stress disorder. He was forced to take early retirement due to ill health from his job as headteacher.
>
> (Mendick, 1998)

'Frank' was one of the many professionals who crept away quietly. Just simply gave up. And the story of *Frank* is a story of him trying to justify his opt-out. It digs behind the event or the action and seeks to find the aspects of self which are at work and which may be responsible for more public aspects of lives.

Conclusion

We are often asked as life story researchers, 'But what is the point of storytelling?' When asked what we do with our lives, we would probably dredge up more respectable titles of researcher, psychologist, policy analyst or academic. Storyteller still smacks of the last period of primary school, still lacks seriousness in the adult world. But we hope that *Researching Life Stories* has contributed in some small way to make telling stories a respectable venture. Stories are more than individual tales. They are the products of complicated research relationships. They are imbued with theory, with practice and policy implications and with humanity. They say so much about society that the preoccupation with scientific methods and quantitative analysis of much human and social science seems ever more redundant and archaic. Having said these things, perhaps our only hope is that this book has made the case for the use of life stories and illuminated some of the fascinating research journeys that can occur along the way. What is the point of storytelling? The points are in the telling of stories.

References

Abberley, P. (1987) The concept of oppression and the development of a social theory of disability, *Disability, Handicap & Society*, **2** (1), 5–19.

Alimo-Metcalf, B. (1994) Waiting for fish to grow feet! In M. Tanton (ed.), *Women in Management: A Developing Presence*. London: Routledge.

Angrosino, M. V. (1994) On the bus with Vonnie Lee: Explorations in life history and metaphor, *Journal of Contemporary Ethnography*, **23** (April), 14–28.

Armstrong, F. and Moore, M. (eds) (2004) *Action Research for Inclusive Education: Changing places, changing practices, changing minds*. London: RoutledgeFalmer.

Assiter, A. (1996) *Enlightened Women: Modernist Feminism in a Feminist Age*. London: Routledge.

Atkinson, D. and Williams, F. (eds) (1990) *'Know me as I am': An Anthology of Prose, Poetry and Art by People with Learning Difficulties*. Sevenoaks, Kent: Hodder & Stoughton in association with the Open University and MENCAP.

Atkinson, R. (1998) *The Life Story Interview*. London: Sage, 1998.

Baker, R. (1995) Life with mother. In W. Zinsser (ed.), *Inventing the Truth: The art and craft of memoir*. Boston: Houghton Mifflin.

Bannister, D. (1977) *New Perspectives in Personal Construct Theory*. London: Academic Press.

Bannister, P., Burman, E., Parker, I., Taylor, M. and Tindall, C. (1994) *Qualitative Research Methods in Psychology: A Research Guide*. Buckingham: Open University Press.

Barnes, C. (1997) Disability and the myth of the independent researcher. In L. Barton and M. Oliver (eds), *Disability Studies: Past, Present and Future*. Leeds: Disability Press.

Barnes, C. (2003) What a difference a decade makes: Reflections on doing 'emancipatory' disability research, *Disability & Society*, **18** (1): 3–18.

Baron, S., Riddell, S. and Wilkinson, H. (1998) Best burgers? The person with learning difficulties as worker. In T. Shakespeare (ed.), *The Disability Reader*. London: Cassell.

Belenky, M. F., Clinchy, B. M., Goldberger, N. R. and Tarule, J. M. (1986) *Women's Ways of Knowing: The development of self, voice and mind*. New York: Basic Books.

Bertaux, D. (ed.) (1981) *Biography and Society: The Life History Approach in the Social Sciences*. Beverly Hills, CA: Sage.

Billig, M. (1996) *Arguing and Thinking: A rhetorical approach to social psychology* (2nd edn). Cambridge: Cambridge University Press.

Bhavnani, K. (1990) What's power got to do with it? Empowerment and social research. In I. Parker and J. Shotter (eds), *Deconstructing Social Psychology*. London: Routledge.

Bird, L. (1999) Towards a more critical educational psychology, *Annual Review of Critical Psychology*, 1: 9–23.

Boal, A. (1979) *The Theatre of the Oppressed*. London: Pluto Press.

Boal, A. (1992) *Games for Actors and Non-Actors*. London: Routledge.

Boal, A. (1995) *The Rainbow of Desire*. London: Routledge.

Bogdan, R. and Taylor, S. (1976) The judged not the judges: An insider's view of mental retardation, *American Psychologist*, 31: 47–52.

Bogdan, R. and Taylor, S. (1982) *Inside Out: The Social Meaning of Mental Retardation*. Toronto: University of Toronto Press.

Booth, T. and Booth, W. (1994) *Parenting under Pressure: Mothers and Fathers with Learning Difficulties*. Buckingham: Open University Press.

Booth, T. and Booth, W. (1998). *Growing Up With Parents Who Have Learning Difficulties*. London: Routledge.

Borland, K. (1991) "That's not what I said": interpretive conflict in oral narrative research. In S. B. Cluck and D. Patai (eds), *Women's Words: The feminist practice of oral history*. New York: Routledge.

Bowker, G. (1993) The age of biography is upon us, *Times Higher Education Supplement*, 9, 8 January.

Bradbury, M. (1975) *The Novel Today*. Harmondsworth: Penguin.

Braginsky, D. and Braginsky, B. (1971) *Hansels and Gretels: Studies of Children in Institutions for the Mentally Retarded*. New York: Holt, Rinehart and Winston.

Brannen, J. (2000) Mothers and fathers in the workplace: The UK debate. In L. Haas, P. Hwang and G. Russell (eds), *Organizational Change and Gender Equity*. London: Sage.

Brannen, J., Nilsen, A., Lewis, S. and Smithson, J. (eds) (2002) *Young Europeans, Work and Family Life: Futures in transition*. London: Routledge.

Breggin, P. (1993) *Toxic Psychiatry*. New York: St Martin's Press.

Brown, L. M. and Gilligan, C. (1992) *Meeting at the Crossroads: Women's Psychology and Girls' Development*. Cambridge, MA: Harvard University Press.

Brown, L. M. and Gilligan, C. (1993). Meeting at the crossroads: Women's psychology and girls' development, *Feminism and Psychology*, 3: 11–35.

Brown, L. M., Debold, E., Tappan, M. and Gilligan, C. (1991) Reading narratives of conflict and choice for self and moral voices: A relational method. In M. William and J. Gewirtz (eds), *Moral Behaviour and Development, Volume 2, Research*. Hilldale, NJ: Lawrence Erlbaum.

Brown, L. M., Tappan, M. B., Gilligan, C., Miller, B. A. and Argyris, D. E. (1989) Reading for self and moral voice: A method for interpreting narratives of real-life moral conflict and choice. In M. Packer and R. Addison (eds), *Entering the Circle: Hermeneutic investigation in psychology*. Albany: SUNY Press.

Brown, T. and Jones, L. (2002) *Action Research and Postmodernism: Congruence and Critique (Conducting Educational Research)*. Buckingham: Open University Press.

Burman, E. and Parker, I. (eds) (1993) *Discourse Analytic Research: Repertoires and Readings of Texts in Action*. London: Routledge.

Burman, E. (ed.), Alldred, P., Bewley, C., Goldberg, B., Heenan, C., Marks, D., Marshall, J., Taylor, K., Ullah, R. and Warner, S. (1996) *Challenging Women: Psychology's Exclusions, Feminist Possibilities*. Buckingham: Open University Press.

Burr, V. (1995) *An Introduction to Social Constructionism*. London: Routledge.

Butler, J. (1990) *Gender Trouble: Feminism and the Subversion of Identity*. New York: Routledge.

Butler, J. (1993) *Bodies that Matter: On the Discursive Limits of 'Sex'*. New York and London: Routledge.

Chamberlayne, P., Bornat, J. and Wengraf, T. (eds) (2000) *The Turn to Biographical Methods in Social Science: Comparative Issues and Examples*. London: Routledge.

Charmaz, K. (1995) Grounded theory. In J. A. Smith, R. Harré and L. V. Langenhove (eds), *Rethinking Methods in Psychology*. London: Sage.

Cheston, R. (1994) The accounts of special education leavers, *Disability & Society*, **9** (1): 58–69.

Cicourel, A. V. (1980) Three models of discourse analysis: The role of social structure, *Discourse Processes*, **3** (2): 101–131.

Clough, P. (1995) Problems of identity and method in the investigation of special educational needs. In P. Clough and L. Barton (eds), *Making Difficulties: Research and the Construction of Special Educational Needs*. London: Paul Chapman.

Clough, P. (1998) Differently articulate? Some indices of disturbed/disturbing voices. In P. Clough and L. Barton (eds), *Articulating with Difficulty: Research Voices in Inclusive Education*. London: Paul Chapman.

Clough, P. (2002) *Narratives and Fictions in Educational Research*. Buckingham: Open University Press.

Clough P. and Corbett, J. (2000) *Theories of Inclusive Education*. London: PCP/Sage.

Clough, P. and Nutbrown, C. (2002) *A Students' Guide to Methodology: Justifying enquiry*. London: Sage

Corbett, J. (1998). *Promoting an Inclusive Culture in a Climate of Fear and Stress*. Paper presented at the Policy, Failure and Difference Seminar, Ranmoor Hall, Sheffield.

Corker, M. (1997) *Deaf and Disabled, or Deafness Disabled?: Towards a Human Rights Perspective*. Buckingham: Open University Press.

Corker, M. and Shakespeare, T. (2002) *Disability/Postmodernity: Embodying Disability Theory*. London: Cassell.

Cowe, H. (ongoing) Living with personal assistance. PhD research University of Sheffield.

Davies, J. and Watson, N. (2002) Countering stereotypes of disability: Disabled children and resistance. In M. Corker and T. Shakespeare (eds), *Disability/ Postmodernity: Embodied Disability Theory*. London: Continuum.

Davis, K. (1981) 28–38 Grove Road: Accommodation and care in a community setting. In A. Brechin, P. Liddiard and J. Swain (eds) (1981) *Handicap in a Social World*. London: Hodder & Stoughton.

Deacon, J. (1974) *Tongue Tied*. London: MENCAP.

Denzin, N. and Lincoln, Y. (eds) (1994) *Handbook of Qualitative Research*. Thousand Oaks, CA: Sage.

Denzin, N. and Lincoln, Y. (eds) (1998) *The Landscape of Qualitative Research*. Thousand Oaks, CA: Sage.

Derrida, M. (1994) *Spectres de Marx*. Paris: Galilée.

Dexter, L. A. (1956) Towards a sociology of the mentally defective, *American Journal of Mental Deficiency*, **61**: 10–16.

DHS, Disability Handicap & Society (1992) Special Issue: Researching Disability, *Disability, Handicap and Society*, 7 (2). (Renamed *Disability & Society* in 1993.)

Dick, R. (1990) *Convergent Interviewing*, version 3. Brisbane: Interchange.

Dick, R. (2002) Grounded theory: a thumbnail sketch. Online at http://www. scu.edu.au/schools/gcm/ar/arp/grounded.html.

Didion, J. (1968) *Slouching Towards Bethlehem* (2001 edn). London: HarperCollins.

Dingham, H. F. (1968) A plea for social research in mental retardation, *Journal of Mental Deficiency*, **73** (1): 2–4.

Doerr, H. (2002) *(Un)Collected Short Stories*. London: Faber.

Du Bois, B. (1983) Passionate scholarship: Towards more creative methods for collecting data on gender and household labour. In L. Morris and S. Lyon (eds), *Gender Relations in the Public and the Private*. London: Macmillan.

Duffy, K. G. and Wong, F. Y. (1996) *Community Psychology*. Boston: Allyn and Bacon.

Dunn, K. (2004) Challenging behaviour: Ours not theirs. In F. Armstrong and M. Moore (eds), *Action Research for Inclusive Education: Changing places, changing practices, changing minds*. London: RoutledgeFalmer.

Dybwad, G. and Bersani, H. (eds) (1996) *New Voices: Self-advocacy by People with Disabilities*. Cambridge, MA: Brookline.

Eagleton, T. (1983) *Literary Theory*. London: Macmillan.

Edgerton, R. (1976) *Deviance: A Cross-cultural Perspective*. London: Benjamin/ Cummings.

Edgerton, R. and Bercovici, S. (1976) The cloak of competence: Years later, *American Journal of Mental Deficiency*, **80** (5): 485–497.

Edgerton, R. B. (1967) *The Cloak of Competence: Stigma in the Lives of the Mentally Retarded*. Berkeley, CA: University of California Press.

Edgerton, R. B. (1984a) Introduction. In R. B. Edgerton (ed.), *Lives in Process: Mentally Retarded Adults in a Large City*. Washington, DC: Monograph #6, American Association on Mental Deficiency.

Edgerton, R. B. (1984b). The participant-observer approach to research in mental retardation, *American Journal of Mental Deficiency*, **88** (5): 498–505.

Erben, M. (ed.) (1998) *Biography and Education*. London: Falmer.

Erlandson, D. A., Harris, E. L., Skipper, B. L. and Allen, S. D. (1993) *Doing Naturalistic Inquiry*. Newbury Park, CA: Sage.

Fairclough, N. (1989) *Language & Power*. London: Longman.

Ferguson, P. M., Ferguson, D. L. and Taylor, S. J. (eds) (1992) *Interpreting Disability: A Qualitative Reader*. New York: Teachers College Press.

Feyerabend, P. (1975) *Against Method*. London: Verso.

Feyerabend, P. (1978) *Science in a Free Society*. London: Verso/NLB.

Fido, R. and Potts, M. (1989) 'It's not true what was written down!' Experiences of life in a mental handicap institution, *Oral History*, (Autumn): 31–35.

Finch, J. (1984) It's great to have someone to talk to: The ethics and politics of interviewing women. In C. Bell and H. Roberts (eds), *Social Researching: Politics, problems, practice*. London: Routledge & Kegan Paul.

Fine, M. (1992) *Disruptive Voices: The possibilities of feminist research*. Ann Arbor: MI: University of Michigan Press.

Foucault, M. (1973a) *The Birth of the Clinic: An Archaeology of Medical Perception*, trans. A. M. Sheridan. New York: Pantheon Books.

Foucault, M. (1973b) *Madness and Civilisation: A History of Insanity in the Age of Reason*, trans. R. Howard. New York: Vintage/Random House.

Foucault, M. (1977) *Discipline and Punish: The Birth of the Prison*, trans. R. Howard. New York: Pantheon Books.

Foucault, M. (1980) *Power/Knowledge*. Brighton: Harvester Press.

Foucault, M. (1983) The subject and power. In H. L. Dreyfus and P. Rabinov (eds), *Michael Foucault: Beyond Structuralism and Hermeneutics*. Chicago: University of Chicago Press.

Glaser, Barney G. (ed.) (1995) *Grounded Theory 1984–1994*, Volume 2. Mill Valley, CA: Sociology Press.

Glaser, Barney G. (1998) *Doing Grounded Theory: Issues and discussions*. Mill Valley, CA: Sociology Press.

Glaser, Barney G. and Strauss, Anselm L. (1967) *The Discovery of Grounded Theory: Strategies for qualitative research*. Chicago: Aldine.

Goffman, E. (1959) *Presentation of Self in Everyday Life*. Garden City, New York: Doubleday.

Goffman, E. (1963) *Stigma: Some Notes on the Management of Spoiled Identity*. Harmondsworth: Penguin.

Goodley, D. (1997) Locating self-advocacy in models of disability: Understanding disability in the support of self-advocates with learning difficulties, *Disability & Society*, 12 (3): 367–379.

Goodley, D. (1998) Stories about writing stories. In P. Clough and L. Barton (eds), *Articulating with Difficulty: Research Voices in Special Education*. London: Paul Chapman.

Goodley, D. (2000) *Self-advocacy in the Lives of People with Learning Difficulties: The Politics of Resilience*. Buckingham: Open University Press.

Goodley, D. (2001) 'Learning difficulties', the social model of disability and impairment: Challenging epistemologies, *Disability & Society*, 16 (2): 207–231.

Goodley, D. (2003) De/constructing learning difficulties: The Life Story of Gerry O'Toole. In C. Barnes (ed.), *Exploring the Social Model: education and work*. Leeds: Disability Press.

Goodley, D., Lawthom, R., Tindall, C., Tobbell, J. and Wetherell, M. (2002) *Understanding People: Qualitative Methods*. Oxford: Alden Press.

Goodson, I. (1992) *Studying Teachers' Lives*. New York: Teachers College Press and Routledge.

Goodson, I. and Sikes, P. (2001) *Life History in Educational Settings: Learning From Lives*. Buckingham: Open University Press.

Gordon, T., Holland, J. and Lahelma, E. (2001) Ethnographic research in educational settings. In P. Atkinson, A. Coffey, S. Delamont, J. Lofland and L. Lofland (eds), *Handbook of Ethnography*. London: Sage.

Griffin, C. (1989) I'm not a women's libber but . . .: Feminism, consciousness and identity. In S. Skevington and D. Baker (eds), *The Social Identity of Women*. London: Sage.

Haraway, D. (1991) *Simians, Cyborgs, and Women: The Reinventions of Nature*. New York: Routledge.

Harding, S. (1986) *The Science Question in Feminism*. London: Routledge.

Harding, S. (1992) Is there a feminist method? In S. Harding (ed.), *Feminism and Methodology*. Bloomington, IN: Indiana University Press.

Hedges, W. (2000) Using Deconstruction to Astonish Friends & Confound Enemies (In Two Easy Steps!). Online at http://www.sou.edu/English/Hedges/Sodashop/RCenter/Theory/Howto/decon.htm.

Heidegger, M. (1971) *On the Way to Language*, trans. P. Hertz. New York: Harper & Row.

Heller, K., Price, R., Reinharz, S., Riger, S. and Wandersman, A. (1984) *Psychology and Community Change*, 2nd edn. Homewood, IL: Dorsey Press.

Henriques, J., Hollway, W., Unwin, C., Couze, V. and Walkerdine, V. (1984) *Changing the Subject: Psychology, Social Regulation, and Subjectivity*. London: Routledge.

Henwood, K. L. and Pidgeon, N. F. (1992) Qualitative research and psychological theorising, *British Journal of Psychology*, **83**: 97–111.

Hofstadter, A. (1965) *Truth and Art*. New York: Columbia University Press.

Hollway, W. and Jefferson, T. (2000) *Doing Qualitative Research Differently*. London: Sage.

Homan, R. (1991) *The Ethics of Social Research*. Essex: Longman.

Hughes, B. and Paterson, K. (1997) The social model of disability and the disappearing body: Toward a sociology of impairment, *Disability & Society*, **12** (2): 325–340.

Humm, M. (1992) *Feminisms: A reader*. London: Prentice-Hall Europe.

Hunt, L. (1998) Women to women support: Lessons from an Australian case story, *Patient Education and Counselling*, **33** (3): 257–265.

Hunt, N. (1967) *The World of Nigel Hunt*. Beaconsfield: Darwen Finlayson.

Inglis, F. (1969) *The Englishness of English Teaching*. London: Longman.

Iser, W. (1971) The reading process: A phenomenological approach, *New Literary History*, **3**: 279–299.

Kagan, C. (2002) Making the road by walking it. Inaugural professorial lecture, Manchester Metropolitan University, 30 January.

Kagan, C. and Lewis, S. (1989) Where's your sense of humour? Swimming against the tide in higher education. In E. Burman (ed.), *Feminists and Psychological Practice*. London: Sage.

Kaufman, S. Z. (1988) *Retarded ISN'T Stupid, Mom!* Baltimore: Paul. H. Brookes.

Kitzinger, C. and Gilligan, C. (1994). Listening to a different voice: Celia Kitzinger interviews Carol Gilligan, *Feminism and Psychology*, **4** (3): 408–419.

Klages, M. (2001) *Poststructuralist Feminist theory*. Online at http://www.colorado.edu/English/engl2010mk/cixous.lec.html.

Korbin, J. E. (1986) Sarah: The life course of a Down's syndrome child. In L. L. Langness and H. G. Levine (eds), *Culture and Retardation*. Kluwer: D. Reidel Publishing Company.

Kundera, M. (1984) *The Unbearable Lightness of Being*. London: Faber.

Kurtz, R. A. (1981) The sociological approach to mental retardation. In A. Brechin, P. Liddiard and J. Swain (eds), *Handicap in a Social World*. Sevenoaks, Kent: Hodder & Stoughton in association with the Open University Press.

Langness, L. and Levine, H. (eds) (1986) *Culture and Retardation*. Kluwer: D. Reidel Publishing Company.

Lapsley, H., Nikora, L. and Black, R. (2002) *'Kia Mauri Tau!' Narratives of recovery from disabling mental health problems*. New Zealand: Mental Health Commission. Online at www.mhc.govt.nz/publications/2002/Kia_Mauri_Tau. pdf.

Larson, C. (1997) Representing the subject: Problems in personal narrative inquiry. *Qualitative Studies in Education*, **10** (4): 455–470.

Lawthom, R. (1997) What do I do? A feminist in non-feminist research, *Feminism and Psychology*, **7** (4): 533–538.

Lawthom, R. (2000) Women, stress and work; exploring the boundaries. In J. Ussher (ed.), *Women's Health: Contemporary International Perspectives*. Leicester: BPS.

Lea, S. L. (1988) Mental retardation: Social construction or clinical reality?, *Disability, Handicap & Society*, **3** (1): 63–69.

Lofland, J. and Lofland, L. H. (1984) *Analyzing Social Settings: A Guide, Qualitative Observation and Analysis*, 2nd edn. Canada : Wordsworth.

Lubbock, P. (1963) *The Craft of Fiction*. New York: Viking Press. Orig. pub. 1921.

Lyotard, J. (1979) *The Postmodern Condition*. Paris: Minuit.

Malinowski, B. (1922) *Argonauts of the Western Specific*. London: Routledge.

Mama, A. (1995) *Beyond the Masks: Race, gender and subjectivity*. New York: Routledge.

Marx, K. (1845) Theses on Feuerbach. In K. Marx and F. Engels (eds), *Selected Works*. London: Lawrence & Wishart.

Mauthner, N. (2002) *The Darkest Days of My Life: Stories of Postpartum Depression*. Cambridge, MA: Harvard University Press.

Mauthner, N. S. and Doucet, A. (1997) Reflections on a voice-centred relational method: Analysis of maternal and domestic voices. In J. Ribbens and R. Edwards (eds), *Feminist Dilemmas in Qualitative Research: Public knowledge and private lives*. London: Routledge.

McNay, L. (1992) *Foucault and Feminism: Power, gender and the self*. Cambridge: Polity.

Means, R. and Smith, R. (1994) *Community Care: Policy and Practice*. Basingstoke: Macmillan.

Mendick, J. (1988) A life destroyed, *Times Educational Supplement*, 13 May.

Mercer, J. R. (1973) *Labeling the Mentally Retarded: Clinical and Social System Perspectives on Mental Retardation*. Los Angeles: University of California Press.

Milbourne, L. (2002) Life at the margin: Education of young people, social policy and the meanings of social exclusion, *International Journal of Inclusive Education*, **6** (2): 325–343.

Miller, R. L. (2000) *Researching Life Stories and Family Histories*, London: Sage.

Mischler, E. (1986) *Researching Interviewing: Context and narrative*. Cambridge, MA: Harvard University Press.

Mitchell, J. (1974) *Feminism and Psychoanalysis*. London: Penguin.

Mitroff, I. and Killman, R. (1978) *Methodological Approaches to Social Science: Integrating Divergent Concepts and Theories*. San Francisco: Jossey-Bass.

Moore, M. (ed.) (2000) *Insider Perspectives on Inclusion: Raising voices, raising issues*. Sheffield: Philip Armstrong Publications.

Moore, M. and Dunn, K. (1999) Disability, human rights and education in Romania. In F. Armstrong and L. Barton (eds), *Disability, Human Rights and Education: Cross-Cultural Perspectives*. Buckingham: Open University Press.

Moore, M. and Skelton, J. (2000) *Enabling Future Care*. Birmingham: Venture Press.

Moore, M., Beazley, S. and Maelzer, J. (1998) *Researching Disability Issues*. Buckingham: Open University Press.

Morris, J. (1997) *Community Care: Working in Partnership with Service Users*. Birmingham: Venture Press.

Namenwirth, M. (1989) Science seen through a feminist prism. In R. Bleier (ed.), *Feminist Approaches to Science*. New York: Pergamon Press.

NCIL (2003) National Centre for Independent Living, www.ncil.org.uk.

Nicholson, P. (1996) *Gender, Power and Organisations: a psychological perspective*. London: Routledge.

Nisbet, R. (1976) *Sociology as an Art Form*. London: Heinemann.

Nourozi, G. (2003) The employment experiences of people with learning difficulties. Paper presented at the Disability Studies Conference, Lancaster, September.

Oakeshott, M. (1933) *Experience and its Modes*. Cambridge: Cambridge University Press.

Oakley, A. (1981) Interviewing women: A contradiction in terms. In H. Roberts (ed.), *Doing Feminist Research*. London: Routledge.

Ochs, E. and Capps, L. (2001) *Living Narrative: Creating lives in everyday storytelling*. Cambridge, MA: Harvard University Press.

Ochs, E. and Jacoby, S. (1997) Down to the wire: The cultural clock of physicists and the discourse of consensus, *Language and Society*, pp. 479–506.

Oliver, M. (1987) Re-defining disability: Some implications for research, *Research, Policy and Planning*, 5: 9–13.

Oliver, M. (1990) *The Politics of Disablement*. Basingstoke: Macmillan.

Oliver, M. (1996) *Understanding Disability: From Theory to Practice*. London: Macmillan.

Oliver, M., Zarb, G., Silver, J., Moore. M. and Salisbury, V. (1988) *Walking into Darkness: The Experience of Spinal Cord Injury*. London: Macmillan.

Oppenheim, C. (1998) An overview of poverty and social exclusion. In. C. Oppenheim (ed.), *An Inclusive Society*. London: IPPR.

Orne, M. T. (1962) The nature of hypnosis: Artefact & essence, *Journal of Abnormal & Social Psychology*, 58: 277–299.

Oswin, M. (1991) *Am I Allowed to Cry? A Study of Bereavement amongst People Who Have Learning Difficulties*. London: Souvenir Press.

Page, L. and Aspis, S. (1997 [Dec. 1996/Jan. 1997]) Special feature, *Viewpoint*, pp. 6–7.

Parker, T. (1963) *The Unknown Citizen*. London: Hutchinson.

Parker, T. (1990) *Life After Life: Interviews with Twelve Murderers*. London: Secker & Warburg.

Parker, I. (ed.) (1998) *Social Constructionism, Discourse and Realism*. London: Sage.

Plato (1963) The Republic. In E. Hamilton and H. Cairus (eds), *Plato: The Collected Dialogues*. Princeton, NJ: Princeton University Press.

Plummer, K. (1983) *Documents of Life: An Introduction to the Problems and Literature of a Humanistic Method*. London: George Allen & Unwin.

Postman, N. (1992) *Technopoly: The surrender of culture to technology*. New York: Knopf.

Potter, J. and Wetherell, M. (1987) *Discourse and Social Psychology: Beyond attitudes and behaviour*. London: Sage.

Potts, M. and Fido, R. (1991) *A Fit Person to be Removed: Personal Accounts of Life in a Mental Deficiency Institution*. Plymouth: Northcote House.

Priestley, P. (1999) *Disability Politics and Community Care*. London: Jessica Kingsley.

Ramazanoglu, C. (1987) Sex and violence in academic life or you can keep a good woman down. In J. Hannermar and M. Maynard (eds), *Women, Violence and Social Control*. Basingstoke, Hants: Macmillan.

Rappaport, J. (1977) *Community Psychology: Values, research, and action*. New York: Holt, Rinehart, & Winston.

Reason, P. (ed.) (1988) *Human Inquiry in Action: Developments in New Paradigm Research*. London: Sage.

Reason, P. (ed.) (1994) *Participation in Human Inquiry*. London: Sage.

Reason, P. and Hawkins, P. (1988) Inquiry through storytelling. In P. Reason (ed.), *Human Inquiry in Action*. London: Sage.

Reay, D. (1998) *Class Work: Mothers' Involvement in their Children's Schooling*. London: UCL Press.

Rennie, D. L. (2000) Grounded theory methodology as methodological hermeneutics, *Theory and Psychology*, 10: 481–502.

Richardson, L. (1994). Writing: A method of enquiry. In N. K. Denzin and Y. S. Lincoln (eds), *Handbook of Qualitative Research*. Thousand Oaks, CA: Sage.

Riddell, S., Baron, S. and Wilson, A. (2001) *The Learning Society and People with Learning Difficulties*. Bristol: Polity Press.

Riessman, C. K (1993) *Narrative Analysis*, London: Sage.

Rimmon-Kenan, S. (2002) *Narrative Fiction: Contemporary Poetics*, 2nd edn. London: Routledge. (Orig. pub. 1983.)

Robbe-Grillet, A. (1955) *From Realism to Reality*. Oxford: Oxford University Press.

Robinson, D. N. (2000) Paradigms and 'the myth of the framework': How science progresses, *Theory and Psychology*, 10: 39–47.

Rose, N. (1999) *Governing the Soul: The Shaping of the Private Self*, 2nd edn with new Preface and Afterword. London: Free Association Books.

Ruddick, S. (1989) *Maternal Thinking: Towards a politics of peace*. Boston, MA: Beacon.

Russell, L. M. (ed.) (1996) *Dictionary of Feminist Theologies*. London: John Knox Press.

Ryan, J. and Thomas, F. (1980/1987) *The Politics of Mental Handicap*, rev. edn 1987. London: Free Association Press.

Salmon, P. (2003) How do we recognise good research?, *Psychologist*, **16** (1): 24–27.

Sandelkowski, M. (1994) The proof is in the pottery: Towards a poetic for qualitative enquiry. In J. Morse (ed.), *Critical Issues in Qualitative Research Methods*. London: Sage.

Scholes, R. (1974) *Structuralism in Literature*. New Haven, CN, and London: Yale University Press.

Schatzman, L. and Strauss, A. L. (1973) *Field Research: Strategies for a Natural Sociology*. Englewood Cliffs, NJ: Prentice-Hall.

Schwandt, T. (1997) *Qualitative Inquiry*. Thousand Oaks, CA: Sage.

Schwandt, T. A. (2000) Three epistemological stances for qualitative inquiry: Interpretivism, hermeneutics and social constructionism. In N. Denzin and Y. Lincoln (eds), *Handbook of Qualitative Research*. Thousand Oaks, CA: Sage.

Scott-Hill, M. (2002) Policy, politics and the silencing of 'voice', *Policy & Politics*, **30** (3): 397–409.

Sidell, M. (1989) How do we know what we think we know? In A. Brechin and J. Walmsley (eds), *Making Connections: Reflecting on the Lives and Experiences of People with Learning Difficulties*. London: Hodder & Stoughton in Association with the Open University Press.

Simons, K. (1992) *'Sticking Up For Yourself': Self Advocacy and People with Learning Difficulties*. Community Care Publication in Association with the Joseph Rowntree Foundation.

Simpson, M. (1999) Bodies, brains and behaviour: The return of the Three Stooges in learning disability. In M. Corker and S. French (eds), *Disability Discourse*. Buckingham: Open University Press.

Smith, J., Harré, R. and Langenhove, L. (eds) (1995) *Rethinking Methods in Psychology*. London: Sage.

Sparkes, A. C. (1994) Life histories and the issue of voice: Reflections on an emerging relationship, *Qualitative Studies in Education*, **7** (2): 165–183.

Spradley, J. P. (1979) *The Ethnographic Interview*. New York: Holt, Rinehart & Winston.

Stanley, L. and Wise, S. (1993) *Breaking Out Again: Feminist Ontology and Epistemology*. London: Routledge.

Steedman, C. (1992) *Past Tenses: Essays on writing autobiography and history*. London: Rivers Oram Press.

Sterne, L., cited in Johnson, B. S. (1977) Aren't you rather young to be writing your memoirs?. In Bradbury, M. (1977) *The Novel Today*. London: Fontana.

Strauss, A. and Corbin, J. (1990) *Basics of Qualitative Research: Grounded theory procedures and techniques*. Newbury Park, CA: Sage.

Strauss, A. and Corbin, J. (eds) (1997) *Grounded Theory in Practice*. Thousand Oaks, CA: Sage.

Stronach, I. and MacLure, M. (1997) *Educational Research Undone: The Postmodern Embrace*. Buckingham: Open University Press.

Stronach, I. and MacLure, M. (1998) *Educational Research Undone*. London: Routledge.

Such, P. (2003) Dying man abandons hunger strike, *Health*, 6 February.

Sutcliffe, J. and Simons, K. (1993) *Self-advocacy and Adults with Learning Difficulties: Contexts & Debates*. Leicester: The National Institute of Adult Continuing Education in Association with the Open University Press.

Tedlock, B. (2001) Ethnography and ethnographic representation. In N. Denzin and Y. Lincoln (eds), *Handbook of Qualitative Research*. Thousand Oaks, CA: Sage.

Thomas, W. I. and Znaniecki, F. (1958) *The Polish peasant in Europe and America*. New York: Dover Publications. (Originally published in 5 volumes, 1918–1921.)

Titchkovsky, T. (2002) Cultural maps: Which way to disability? In M. Corker and T. Shakespeare (eds), *Disability/Postmodernity: Embodied Disability Theory*. London: Continuum.

Toone, I. (1997) Discourse analysis. Unpublished MA thesis, University of Nottingham.

Tremain, S. (2002) On the subject of impairment. In M. Corker and T. Shakespeare (eds), *Disability/Postmodernity*. London: Continuum.

Turner, M. (1991) Literature and social work: An exploration of how literature informs social work in a way social sciences cannot, *British Journal of Social Work*, **21**: 229–243.

UPIAS (1976) *Fundamental Principles of Disability*. London: Union of the Physically Impaired Against Segregation.

Ussher, J. M. (ed.) (1997) *Body Talk: The material and discursive regulation of sexuality, madness and reproduction*. London, Routledge.

Valuing People: A New Strategy for Learning Disability for the 21st Century (2001). White Paper, HMSO. Online at http://www.archive.official-documents. co.uk/document/cm50/5086/5086.htm.

Veck, W. (2002) Relational and psychological processes of exclusion, *Disability and Society*, **17** (5): 529–540.

Vidich, A. and Lyman, S. (2000) Qualitative methods: Their history in sociology and anthropology. In N. Denzin and Y. Lincoln (eds), *Handbook of Qualitative Research*. Thousand Oaks, CA: Sage.

Walmsley, J. (1993) Explaining. In P. Shakespeare, D. Atkinson and S. French (eds), *Reflecting on Research Practice: Issues in Health and Social Welfare*. Buckingham: Open University Press.

Wareing, D. and Newell, C. (2002) Responsible choice: The choice between no choice, *Disability & Society*, **17**: 419–434.

Weedon, C. (1987) *Feminist Practice and Poststructuralist Theory*. Oxford: Basil Blackwell.

Whittemore, R., Langness, L. and Koegel, P. (1986) The life history approach to mental retardation. In L. Langness and H. Levine (eds), *Culture and Retardation*. Kluwer: D. Reidel Publishing Company.

Wilkinson, S. and Kitzinger, C. (1995) Introduction. In C. Kitzinger and S. Wilkinson (eds), *Feminism and Discourse*. London: Sage.

Wilkinson, S. (1999) Feminist psychology: Values and visions, *Psychology of Women Section Review*, **1** (1): 20–32.

Wilkinson, S. and Kitzinger, C. (1996) *Representing the Other: A feminism and psychology reader*. London: Sage.

Witherell, C. and Noddings, N. (1991) *Stories Lives Tell: Narrative and dialogue in education*. New York: Teachers College Press.

Yalom, D. (1991) *Love's Executioner: And other tales of psychotherapy.* Harmondsworth: Penguin.

Young, K (1987) *Taleworlds and Storyrealms: The phenomenology of narrative.* Dordrecht: Martinus Nijho Publishers.

Yuval-Davis, N. (1993) Beyond difference: Women and coalition politics. In M. Kennedy, C. Lubelska and V. Walsh (eds), *Making Connections: Women's studies, women's movements, women's lives.* London: Taylor & Francis.

Zarb, G. (1992) On the road to Damascus: First steps towards changing the relations of research production, *Disability, Handicap and Society,* 7 (2): 125–38

Zhang, L. (1999) How women's experiences introduced me to the psychology of women, *Psychology of Women Section Review,* 1 (1): 41–42.

Index

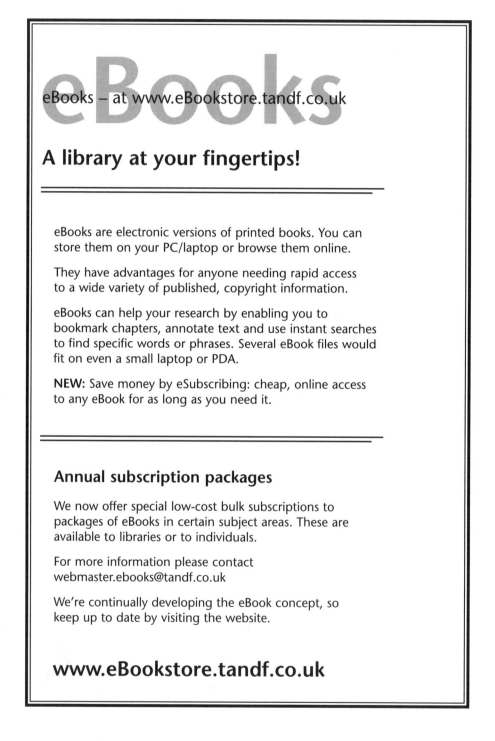